IN THE BELLY OF THE DRAGON

Taisen Deshimaru

Rei Ryu Philippe Coupey

IN THE BELLY OF THE DRAGON

A ZEN MONK'S COMMENTARY ON THE *SHINJINMEI* BY MASTER SOSAN (D. 606)

SECOND EDITION

REI RYU PHILIPPE
COUPEY

FOREWORD BY
RICHARD REISHIN COLLINS

HOHM PRESS
CHINO VALLEY, AZ

Cover Design: Hohm Press
Interior Design and Layout: Kubera Book Design, Prescott, Arizona

Library of Congress Control Number: 2020936641

ISBN: 978-1-942493-53-2
e-book: 978-1-942493-56-3

Hohm Press
P.O. Box 4410
Chino Valley, AZ 86323
800-381-2700
http://www.hohmpress.com

This book was printed in the U.S.A. on recycled, acid-free paper using soy ink.

The first Part (strophes 1-31) of this book was published by the American Zen Association, 2005.

Previous ISBN: 978-0972804912

I dedicate this book to my master,
the sitting dragon.

ACKNOWLEDGEMENTS

I would like to thank Blanche Heugel, Jim Newkirk and Jonas Endres for their help on this book. I would like to thank in particular my editor of longstanding Regina Sara Ryan, without whom this book would not have been possible.

CONTENTS

FOREWORD TO THE TWO-VOLUME EDITION

S'en sortir sans sortir

This phrase, seen scrawled on a Paris wall during the 2020 coronavirus pandemic, can be roughly translated as "getting away without getting away." Used to great effect in another but certainly no more surreal century by Max Ernst and Gherasim Luca, it could serve as a catchphrase for the Sangha sans demeure of Philippe Rei Ryu Coupey. Not only does it encapsulate the freedom to be found in confinement and the slippery ambiguity of language, it also captures the sly spirit of Zen play and the profound activity in the stillness of just sitting.

The phrase is less an aporia than a koan (if indeed there can be any real distinction drawn between the two—isn't every koan an aporia; isn't every aporia a potential koan?). Today, though, we are less concerned with a philosophical contradiction than with an existential impasse. It is an impasse confronted—if not always overcome—by the expansive heart of Coupey's teaching, so faithfully represented in the pages of *In the Belly of the Dragon*, and summed up in a word as "generosity." Not the generosity of giving to charity and claiming it on your taxes, but the cosmic generosity of the Way.

Fifteen years ago, with the publication of volume one, Coupey left us with a cliffhanger of sorts, concluding the first half of his commentary on the *Shinjinmei* with a discussion of Strophe 31:

The substance of the great Way is generous.
It is neither hard nor easy.

> The thirty-first strophe of the *Shinjinmei*, which is almost the center of the poem, is one of its most famous and most poetic verses.
>
> *The great Way* is wide, vast, generous—generous meaning "cosmic," "unlimited."
>
> We often hear that zazen is the door to the Way. But I don't think that's a very good image. The Way is big—so big, so wide, that it has no door. And there's no place where you could put one. Can there be a door to the cosmos? How could the Way have a door when it has no way in and no way out? What good would a door be, knowing that no one enters and no one leaves?
>
> *The great Way* is the normal, original condition of the mind. How can you enter or leave the normal, original condition? (p. 147)

With "no door" to the Way, there is no simple way of getting away. No entrance and no exit, no beginning and no end. So, in that sense, there is no now and no then, no Part I and no Part II.

And, despite the disclaimer that appears on page 153 between Part I and Part II, citing the different methods of composition (Part I via the spoken word through *kusen* transcribed and edited, and Part II via the written word directly), I detect little contrast between the two parts. For me, the "spontaneity" of the two volumes are consistent, perhaps with a slight increase in authorial independence and confidence. With the appearance of the second volume, we take up the conversation where we left off, as we do with certain old friends "over coffee," as if without interruption, as though we were really returning to "the normal, original condition of the mind." In both volumes, the "tone can fluctuate from satirical to serious, from impertinent to benevolent," because Coupey's "cosmic" generosity in the grasp of the Way is all-inclusive, embracing "anger, disappointment and frustration," as well as "the magnitude of the practice as shown in this ancient Zen text" (p. 153).

I like to think of the fifteen-year gap between the publication of the first and second parts of this commentary less in terms of time and more in terms of an abyss of experience. (For us in New Orleans, it is the fifteen years spanning two disasters: Hurricane Katrina and the coronavirus pandemic.) The two parts of this commentary on a poem all about non-dualistic thinking forms a bridge, or a ferry, if you like, taking us to the other side. In his comments on the two strophes that end Part I and begin Part II (strophes 31 and 32), Coupey coincidentally takes on the subject of Zen time in the story of the eager samurai in search of perfecting his swordsmanship: the time of too much intentional effort that bears no result, or the time of the spontaneous, natural, automatic effort that Deshimaru encouraged in the here and now. The time in which past and future disappear in the universal present, the time being. Satori is not to be rushed.

The gateless gate is pitiless—and playful. Without a door to get away through, there is no dwelling to escape or enter. Coupey's Paris-based *Sangha sans demeure* ("sangha without fixed abode") announces itself as being in the lineage of "Homeless" Kodo Sawaki. But I can't help hearing in the name a whisper of the English homonym (demure). Indeed, we can hear in Coupey's at times wise-cracking tone an American straightforwardness, a lack of "demureness," that gives a New York edge to his European erudition and experience. There is a Huck Finn element to Coupey's Zen teaching in the tradition of the poets Ikkyu and Ryokan, so that *s'en sortir sans sortir* might also mean getting away *with* something without getting away with it. That is, one pushes the boundaries without relinquishing responsibility for one's actions. Discipline is not the opposite of freedom; it is the natural condition under which freedom flowers.

The playful-serious spirit of *s'en sortir sans sortir* in both senses—as penetrating the gateless gate as well as getting away with what can't be gotten away with—may be Philippe Coupey's greatest contribution to the ever-increasing library of books devoted to Zen.

Richard Reishin Collins
New Orleans Zen Temple
April 2020

PREFACE TO THE FIRST EDITION

***In the Belly of the Dragon*, Vol. I (2004)**

From the moment we pick up any English version of the *Shinjinmei* of Sosan (Seng Ts'an, d. 606), we are already entangled in the nets of translation. Neither of the two favored translations in the title, "Faith in Mind" or "Trust in Mind," is adequate; each has its strengths, each its weaknesses; and even both together do not do the trick. First there is the problem of the Chinese conflation of Mind and Heart (*hsin*). But let's assume that the Western estrangement of the two halves of this "not-two" spiritual organ, its decay or falling away into specialized parts, can be overcome in a leap of the poetic imagination à la William Blake, so that feeling and thinking are one, automatic, natural, spontaneous. There remain in the title the separate connotations of Faith versus Trust. To choose "Trust" over "Faith" is a bow to the secular mind of America ("In God We Trust" is on the money: God as reliable business partner or benevolent banker). "Faith," though, labors under an unavoidable load of piety, a suggestion of theism (faith with an object, anathema to Zen practice). So neither term satisfies. Yet combining the two into a title something like "Faith/Trust in Heart/Mind" would be just a barbaric coupling and multiplication of dualities; like the gender-avoiding pronoun creations "he/she" of "s/he," such slashing recreates and reifies more of the very duality it attempts to overcome.

How, then, do we solve this Faith/Trust dichotomy? If we grasp the poem, we should not *solve* this dichotomy, nor *resolve* it, but *dissolve* it. For as soon as we begin to sort out the semantic subtleties, we are entangled—in cultural assumptions, political constructions, religious implications, linguistic contortions, logical reductions. The entire thrust of the *Shinjinmei* is to go beyond these structures of dualistic thinking so that there be no petty squabble between Trust and Faith, just as in Zen practice there be no bickering between Heart and Mind.

Such dualities are resolved only experientially—in zazen.

A similar argument can be made when we begin to look at the origin of the text of the *Shinjinmei*, asking, as we should of all such texts, about its attributions and its authenticity. These are interesting textual questions and should be explored by religious and literary scholars (for the complexity of the background of these issues, see Mu Soeng, *Trust in Mind: The Rebellion of Chinese Zen*. Boston: Wisdom, 2004). But Taezen Maezumi made an excellent point, entirely in the spirit of the *Shinjinmei* itself, when he dissolved these textual questions with the fact of its favorable reception—and citation—over the centuries: "The masters' frequent references to the poem have authenticated it as a genuine expression of the spirit of Zen" (quoted by Dennis Genpo Merzel, *The Eye Never Sleeps: Striking to the Heart of Zen. Boston: Shambhala*, 1991, xvii).

The true test of a Zen text, it seems, is not its origin or authenticity but its serviceability. It helps if the style is succinct and suggestive, the better to be passed down orally, like koans, but it must in the end go beyond the beautiful, the entertaining, the instructive; it must above all be useful in the everyday practice of Zen training. Whoever actually wrote the *Shinjinmei*—and there is some question whether it is from the brush of Sosan—this relatively brief poem set the standard for all Zen texts to come in terms of the sheer ordinary usefulness of its pronouncements.

Each strophe restates the first in a bravura performance of 73 permutations. It doesn't matter: any part of an authentic Zen text will, in the manner of DNA, identify the whole. Lift a speck of dust and you lift the world. Grasp the first bodhisattva vow—*shujo muhen seigan do*: "however innumerable sentient beings, I vow to save them all"—and you grasp them all. Grasp the opening strophe—"Entering the Way is not difficult, / But you must not love, or hate, or choose, or reject"—and you grasp the essence of the *Shinjinmei*. The net than entangles also lifts up.

What, then, is the test of a text like Philippe Coupey's *In the Belly of the Dragon*, a comparatively voluble commentary by a contemporary Zen monk on the most ancient Zen text? By its nature, a commentary will be less succinct and more expansive, more explanatory, and perhaps more serviceable by showing its relevance for today. Coupey shows the *Shinjinmei's* relevance again and again, as he emphasizes the principle of "not-two." In an interview published in *ZenBulletin*, Coupey explained the relevance of the poem this way:

> I, for example, cannot call myself a detached man. Maybe Sensei [Deshimaru] took this position, or maybe Sosan would have taken it. But who are we kidding? Of course I'm attached: I fall in love, I have money problems, I'm always running for something—a train, a play.... I'm always in the tumult of daily life. And I think that's a good thing: from there, true, deep and authentic satori can appear. Because we're not protected. We're in the wind, like a tree on the edge of a cliff that could fall at any moment. We always have this impression that we're going to go completely crazy because of the life around us, the attachments...the suffering... And if we can find satori in such a situation, for me it's a very strong satori.

To find satori in the tumult of daily life is one of the hallmarks of the Deshimaru lineage, which avoids many of the monastic constraints of Zen practice and encourages lay practice in the dojo next door. For Coupey, this accessibility is also the essence of the *Shinjinmei*:

> The strength of this poem, its direct quality, is particularly well suited to practice in this lineage. In other practices—and even in other Zen schools, including Soto Zen—there is a lot of talk about progress and degrees. We hear this all the time—but not in the teaching of Kodo Sawaki and Taisen Deshimaru. Our practice is

> to achieve satori here and now. Only here and now, and that way there is no more wrong, no more right in the mind. (p. 29)

When asked in the *ZenBulletin* interview "Who is in the belly of the dragon?" Coupey answered: "WE are! The person reading the book is in the dragon's belly." Some people will mistakenly call the book by the title that inspired it, *In the Belly of the Beast*, by Jack Henry Abbott. But in the East the Dragon is, traditionally, symbolic of the vigorous cosmic energy that comes from deep within. So the Dragon of the title is both inside and outside—inner power (*joriki*) and outer power (*tariki*)—because, again, these are *funi* ("not-two").

Newcomers to the New Orleans Zen Temple (founded by Coupey's brother monk, and fellow Deshimaru disciple, Robert Livingston Roshi) are often surprised to find that we are not teetotalers or vegetarians. They bring their preconceptions about Buddhism, their misconceptions about Zen. If life's complexities sometimes appear to be simplified by Zen, it is not by exclusion or reduction. Zen, says Coupey, uses everything: words, shouts, meat, alcohol, slaps, everything. Just don't cling to your veggies, your smokes, your meat, your ideas, your words, your non-words.

This message has come down to us in ten thousand ways, yet it is still misunderstood. How many koans restate the same idea? In the Soto tradition, koans are used on an ad hoc basis, without having coalesced into a curriculum; koans are, we might say, the literary heritage of Soto Zen, its lore. Many Soto *kojos* use lectures (*teisho*) as their primary mode of teaching; the edited and reworked lectures of Shunryu Suzuki in *Zen Mind, Beginner's Mind* are a famous example.

Instead of koans or *teisho*, the Deshimaru lineage uses *kusen* as the primary way of verbally transmitting the teachings. More or less spontaneous oral teachings during zazen, *kusen* are, we might say, this lineage's calligraphy, written on air, sometimes recorded, sometimes transcribed, but originally and naturally composed in the medium of breath. (A frank discussion of the controversy surrounding the use of *kusen* was published as "Dossier: Kusen—maintaining and protecting it" in two parts, in *Lettre de la sangha sans demeure*, number 19, May 2017.)

How then should one read the transcription of an oral record like the first volume of *In the Belly of the Dragon?* It is helpful to know that these *kusen* were delivered over a period of some eight years, during many sittings, at many sesshin, to many different students, in many different dojos in France and Germany. The book should probably be read—as it was "composed"—not at a single sitting but over time, in fragments to be digested piecemeal and not as a snake swallows its prey, whole.

Also, the chapters of Part I should be considered "talks" rather than writings, to be "received" rather than read, to be "absorbed" rather than thought about. To hear *kusen* while sitting in zazen is very different than hearing a lecture or reading a book. During zazen one's concentration is focused not on the words or voice of the speaker of the *kusen*, but on the *kusen's* subject, which is ultimately always zazen itself. In the case of these *kusen*, the subject of the focus of zazen is identical to the subject of the *Shinjinmei*; the subject is not the *Shinjinmei* itself, which is only the finger pointing at the moon. To hear *kusen* during zazen is, in this sense, nothing more than an encouragement to focus on concentration itself: it is, perhaps, a little like hearing a lecture on your experience of the Grand Canyon while you are actually *in* the Grand Canyon, rather than hearing a lecture delivered before or after your hike, while on the impressive but still peripheral rim. Zazen itself shows us all we need to know about zazen, but we can always use the assistance of a geologist who can identify the ancient strata of the canyon wall we're gazing at, or a park ranger who can tell us a good story or two about the early explorers of that old, natural abyss.

Kusen are the calligraphy of the Deshimaru lineage. *Kusen* are not sermons; they do not offer discourses of spiritual use to the listener. It would be more accurate to compare *kusen* to *zuihitsu*, the indigenous Japanese literary form that plays on a theme by "following the brush." But the *zuihitsu*, for example, of the fourteenth-century monk Kenko in his *Essays in Idleness* are just that, "essays." *Kusen* are not essays, not "attempts" like Montaigne's or "meditations" like Loyola's. *Kusen* are spontaneous oral teachings that illuminate the dojo, like an ember of dojo (incense) drawn on the semi-darkness. They can take the form of exhortation as a single word ("Concentrate!") or a phrase ("Head presses the sky!"); or they can become a poetic essay as deep and firmly structured as the posture of zazen itself.

Reading Rei Ryu Philippe Coupey's commentaries, I am, oddly reminded of the apparently very different *kusen* styles of my own master, Robert Livingston Roshi, who was also nurtured on the *kusen* of Master Deshimaru in the dojos of Paris and La Gendronniere. My teacher's *kusen* became increasingly pared down over the years, revealing the bare bones of the practice, the essential germ of the practice, featuring fewer explanations and more silence punctuated by shouts of "Don't move!." Philippe Coupey's approach, on the other hand, is voluble and literary in the French tradition, allusive, full of explanations and asides, theories, quotes, Zen stories, and anecdotes. I am reminded of Ihab Hassan's book *The Literature of Silence*, which contrasts the volubility of Henry Miller with the reticence of Samuel Beckett, two postmodern voices with the same effect, a tendency toward getting at the truth of what is offered in the ambiguity of silence, which is another Way of talking about the Way that cannot be talked about. (More recently, Lawrence Shainberg has explored a similar comparison between Beckett and Mailer in his memoir, *Four Men Shaking: Searching for Sanity with Samuel Beckett, Norman Mailer, and My Perfect Zen Teacher*. Boston: Shambhala, 2019). Whereas Miller sets out to exhaust language, Beckett pares it down to ellipsis and mime.

The *kusen* voices of Philippe Coupey and Robert Livingston, too, are strong, distinct, different yet essentially the same, and contained in the deep belly-chant of the Dragon himself. For if we listen carefully, in each case, we hear the voice of Master Deshimaru coming through.

Richard Collins
New Orleans Zen Temple
December 2004/April 2020

SHINJINMEI VERSES ON FAITH IN MIND

by Master Sosan

1
Entering the Way is not difficult,
But you must not love, or hate, or choose, or reject.

2
If you feel neither love nor hate,
Your understanding of the Way will be clear and penetrating.

3
If a distinction as minute as a particle is created in the mind,
An infinite distance immediately separates sky and earth.

4
If you achieve satori here and now,
The idea of right and wrong will no longer enter your mind.

5
The struggle between right and wrong in our conscience
Leads to a sick mind.

6
If you cannot penetrate the source of things,
Your mind will exhaust itself in vain.

7
The Way is round, at peace and perfect, wide as the vast cosmos,
Without the slightest notion of rest or rupture.

8
In truth, because we want to seize or reject,
We are not free.

9
Do not run after *shiki*
And do not dwell on *ku*

10
If your mind remains tranquil,
It vanishes like a dream.

11
If you stop all movement, your mind becomes tranquil,
And afterwards, this tranquility will provoke movement again.

12
If you dwell on extremes,
How can you understand One?

13
If you do not concentrate on the original,
The merits of both extremes will be lost.

14
If you accept only one existence, you will fall into that single existence.
If you become attached to *Ku*, you will turn yourself against it.

15
Even if your words are correct, even if your thoughts are exact,
It is not in accordance with the truth.

16
Abandoning language and thought
Will lead you beyond all places.

17
If you return to the original root, you touch the essence.
If you follow enlightenment, you lose the original source.

18
If you are enlightened in all directions, even for an instant,
It is superior to ordinary *ku*

19
Change in ordinary *ku*
Requires the birth of illusions.

20
Do not seek the truth;
Simply be free from prejudice.

21
Do not dwell on opposites.
Do not seek out dualism.

22
If you still have the slightest notion of right or wrong,
Your mind will sink into confusion.

23
Two depends on One;
But do not be attached, even to One.

24
If no mind appears,
Phenomena will be free from error.

25
No error, no Dharma;
No Dharma, no mind.

26
Following the object, the subject vanishes;
Following the subject, the object collapses.

27
The object can be fulfilled as a true object through its dependence
on the subject.
The subject can be fulfilled as a true subject through its dependence
on the object.

28
If you wish to understand subject and object,
In the end you must realize that both are
ku.

29
A *ku* identical to both
Includes all phenomena.

30
Make no distinction between subtle and gross.
There are no sides to take.

31
The substance of the great Way is generous.
It is neither hard nor easy.

32
People with narrow minds will sink into doubt.
The faster they want to go, the slower they will be.

33
If you adhere to a petty mind, losing all measure,
You will veer onto an erroneous path.

34
If you express it freely, you are natural.
In your body, there is no place to go and stay.

35
If you trust nature,
You can be in harmony with the Way.

36
Sanran opposes the truth;
Kontin escapes from it.

37
The mind that escapes from the truth is troubled.
So what is the point of being partial?

38
If you wish to go by the sole and supreme vehicle,
You must not hate the six impurities.

39
If you do not hate the six impurities,
You can attain true buddhahood.

40
The sage is inactive;
The fool loves and attaches himself.

41
There is no differentiation in the Dharma;
But the fool attaches himself.

42
Using mind with mind:
Great confusion, or harmony?

43
In the state of doubt, *sanran* and *kontin* arise.
In the state of satori, love and hate do not exist.

44
You want to think too much
About the two aspects of all elements.

45
Your life is like a dream, a ghost, a flower of emptiness.
Why should you suffer to grasp this illusion?

46
Gain, loss, true, false:
Please, abandon them.

47
If the eye never sleeps,
All your dreams will vanish.

48
If the mind makes no discriminations,
All beings in the cosmos become one.

49
If your body profoundly realizes One,
You can instantly cut all relationships.

50
If you consider all existences with equanimity,
You will return to your original nature.

51
Once you examine this,
You cannot compare it to anything.

52
If you stop movement, there is no more movement.
If you set stillness in motion, there is no more stillness.

53
Since two is impossible,
One is as well.

54
Finally, in the end,
There is neither rule nor regulation.

55
If mind coincides with mind,
The seeds and traces of actions vanish.

56
Since the fox's doubt does not exist,
Passions completely disappear, and suddenly true faith appears.

57
All elements being impermanent,
They leave no trace in the memory.

58
Illuminating your inner self with the light of emptiness
Does not require the power of the mind.

59
As far as *hishiryo* is concerned,
It is very difficult to consider.

60
In the cosmic world of reality as it is,
There is neither ego-entity nor differences.

61
If you want to realize One,
It is only possible in Not-Two.

62
In Not-Two,
All things are alike, beyond contradictions.

63
Sages and all of humanity
Go towards the teaching of the original source.

64
The original source being beyond time and space,
One instant becomes ten thousand years.

65
Neither existence nor non-existence,
Everywhere before your eyes.

66
The minimum is identical to the maximum;
The borders between places must be erased.

67
The largest is identical to the smallest;
Boundaries are invisible.

68
Existence is non-existence.
Non-existence is existence.

69
If this is not so,
You must not protect it.

70
One is all things,
All things are One.

71
If this is so,
Why is it necessary to think about the not-finished?

72
Faith in mind is Not-Two.
Not-Two is faith in mind.

73
Finally, the path of language will be cut off,
And past, present and future will not be limited.

THE COMMENTARIES

PART I: 1-31

The Commentaries in this Part (Strophes 1-31) were transcribed and translated from talks given by Rei Ryu Philippe Coupey during sesshins and teaching sessions.

NOTE TO THE READER

In keeping with current editorial policy adopted in many publication houses, in the U.S. and elsewhere, I have agreed to have the gender-specific pronouns and references that I used in my original talks, as well as in my written commentaries, changed to make them non-gender specific for purposes of this publication. The reader will therefore take note that, in many cases, the use of "he and she" or "they" or "a person" for example, were not my original renditions. For purposes of communicating the dharma contained in the *Shinjinmei,* the words of which were not altered in any way, I sense that these changes to my commentaries will not essentially affect the meaning of the text and teachings being transmitted.

For an expanded explanation of my view of this issue, however, the reader is asked to consult the Appendix at the end of the book.

Thank you, Ph. Rei Ryu Coupey
Paris 20/2/2020

1

Entering the Way is not difficult,
But you must not love, or hate, or choose, or reject.

If you want to know what Zen teaches, there it is, summarized in two lines. In the first line, Sosan is referring to Buddhahood, our Buddha-nature; in the second, he explains what makes us able to see it—or not. Buddha-nature is the nature we all have, even before birth, even after death. Buddha-mind. The mind of rocks. The mind of the Way.

Following the great Way is not at all difficult: trees grow in it, fish swim in it. We all follow it—even when we make mistakes. The Way is right in front of our eyes, right under our noses and under our zafus. And this has not changed since ancient times, since Bodhidharma, since Buddha, since before Buddha.

"From ancient times down to today," writes Master Jiun, himself an ancient, "the great Way has not changed. It is." Then he adds, "The head on top, the legs below to either side." It's a little like when Master Dogen returned from China and was asked, "What have you discovered about Buddhism?" He replied simply, "Eyes horizontal, nose vertical."

This is not difficult at all. But understanding and practicing it is not so easy. *Entering the Way is not difficult.* Sure. But we could also say, "Entering the Way is not easy."

Trees follow the Way; rivers, rocks, birds and fish follow it. For them, it's not hard. But for human beings, it's not always easy, because of "small mind," the mind of selection and choice. With your personal mind, your personal consciousness, your preferences, your desire to stay in bed when everybody's getting up, you can become complicated. You're looking for love, you want to be spoiled: "I like the zazen posture, but not the ceremonies, or *samu*—why should I do *samu*? I want to relax."

There are people who have been practicing for twenty years with this attitude. They're wasting their time. They'd be better off going bowling. Other people see the dojo for the first time, get into zazen posture, hear the bell, and their lives are changed forever. But for people who don't even know that the Way exists, it's very difficult. Very difficult also for those who know that the Way exists but have no idea of how to go about it. So they turn towards Tibetan Buddhism, Hinduism, the Church, Zen, Sufism, macrobiotics, New Age practices. There are many roads one can follow, but going from one to another makes the practice of the Way very difficult.

∽

But you must not love, or hate, or choose, or reject.

The second line explains what blocks us on the path, what hinders us. It means don't select, don't take this and reject that, don't love this and detest that. That's the essence of this strophe: no egotistical love or egotistical hate; no blind love or blind hate.

Love is very quickly transformed into its opposite. People kill each other every day because of love which has turned into hate. There's also admiring love: you love someone but don't dare approach him; you think he's out of your reach. Society functions a lot along these lines—with celebrities, for example. The same goes for love based on understanding: "I understand, therefore I love." "I understand the benefits of zazen, so I practice it." All of this is relative love, just one side.

In *mondos*, there are always questions concerning love. But which love are we talking about? It's rarely the love that transcends the you/me duality, the love that is called compassion. We could also call it wisdom. It's the love beyond man and woman, beyond human and buddha.

One shouldn't confuse the two: small love and cosmic love; narrow love, based on you and me, and love that does not rely on you or me—a love that can blossom even within the couple. This love or compassion takes place when there is no difference between man and woman, before the thought "he's a man, she's a woman" appears. Before any thought. Before small mind arises.

But that's not what Master Sosan is talking about in the first strophe of the *Shinjinmei*; he's talking about small, everyday love: love for my girlfriend, for my wife, for myself; love based on attachment to the six senses—sight, smell, hearing, touch, taste and consciousness. That love is not at all necessary; it makes life complicated. It can even make you crazy. We've all experienced it, and if not, we dream of encountering it. Of course, you can still live in a couple, beyond egoism. *You must not love* doesn't mean don't love; it means study the right way to love. Ask yourself, "How should I be with someone? How should I love?"

No choice or rejection means not choosing with your personal consciousness, and also not choosing your thoughts. We're always busy picking and choosing. Even in classical meditation, we choose our thoughts—we choose to meditate on good thoughts rather than bad ones. Before I encountered zazen, I practiced a little Hindu meditation; we meditated on the beauty of the sunset, or on universal love. This has nothing to do with Zen practice. During zazen, we don't pick our thoughts; we don't assign them a value; we don't say, "This thought is better than that one." Whether we're thinking about sex or Buddha, it's the same thing: they're thoughts, *bonnos*, illusions.

In everyday life—at work, for example—you obviously have to choose your thoughts. But this happens automatically. If you're cooking in the kitchen, you're not making scientific calculations, and vice-versa. In daily life, people follow the Way unconsciously, even if they don't know about zazen. Otherwise, life becomes very difficult, and you find yourself endlessly confronted with choices: "Should I go to sesshin or not?" "Should I stay or should I leave?" Practiced this way, the Way becomes difficult.

On the other hand, as Sosan writes, if you don't fall into this dilemma of choosing and rejecting, the Way is not difficult. When you do a sesshin, you follow the sesshin without thinking too much. You get up with everybody else, you do zazen, you eat *genmai*. That's following the Way.

Master Sosan is saying that practicing the Way is not difficult if you are *mushotoku*—not trying to get anything. Of course, in the beginning, it's normal to want to obtain something. You come to the dojo for years, you go to sesshin, you set aside time and money for the practice, you put aside your personal affairs, you put aside your family. And why? To get nothing? It may seem absurd. So inevitably you want to get something in exchange, or at least come home happy and deep. But that doesn't always work. Sometimes you want to show you're serene and wise. You come home after three days of zazen . . . and right away there's a fight!

It's hard to see if one is progressing. Often, you might even have the impression that you're regressing. When on top of the wave, you see the horizon; you feel like you're advancing. But later, when you find yourself in the crook of the wave, and can't see anything, you think you're regressing: all there is, is the wave. It's a matter of perspective—the view from above, the view from below.

If you practice for ten or twenty years, you have some perspective on those ten or twenty years and you see a progression. If your ego is making the choices, you see only the superficial side: you earned money, now you have the car and the house, you're better off than you were before. But if it's not your ego making the choices, you see something else. That's why the master's reply to the disciple is often, "No, there is no progress." The master is talking to the person's ego.

It's obvious that something changes in our lives thanks to an authentic practice. But it's impossible to grab hold of this fact, to focus on it, to say, "That's it!"

Practicing with a goal is like trying to catch a feather with an electric fan. Wanting to get something—wisdom, or satori, for example—is making a separation between *samsara* (a life of transmigration) and nirvana (satori). And in the beginning, it's true, you think there's a difference between the ordinary person and Buddha, between *bonnos* and satori. Everybody thinks that way. But these are ideas that block our perception and understanding. Because satori lies beyond the choices of the conscious mind. In the final analysis, choosing and rejecting are only ideas, distinctions that you make. And in the end, it is this life of selection that is difficult: being obliged to choose, always feeling that you have to choose.

But if you practice Zen—zazen—then the Way is not difficult. Zazen is the perfect illustration of not-difficult, of not choosing. For example, try understanding zazen through books. You have to start by choosing the books. And this booklearning very quickly becomes complicated and hard; whereas the study of Buddhism and Zen through zazen is very simple. When zazen becomes simple, you stop comparing yourself with other people, or even with yourself, to see whether or not you're making any progress. Life inside the dojo, and also daily life outside of it, becomes simple, and you easily manage to harmonize with all things. You're no longer led by your emotions, by love, hate, choice or rejection.

Finally, this Way, this splendid and wonderful Way, is perhaps neither easy nor hard, neither internal nor external. Don't empty out your head; don't fill it up, either. Don't create an inside; don't create an outside.

Nose vertical, eyes horizontal: this is the practice of the Way.

2

If you feel neither love nor hate,
Your understanding of the Way will be clear and penetrating.

The second strophe of the Shinjinmei is a confirmation of the first: if you do what is said in the first strophe—in other words, not choose, not to always be putting your own preferences first—then the understanding of the Way will be clear and penetrating.

The Chinese *kanji* (ideogram) for "clear and penetrating" is the image of daylight when it enters a cave. A literal translation gives us the following:

> *Do not have either good or bad thoughts. You will have spontaneous understanding, clear as the light which enters a cave.*

Here is my own version:

> *If you feel neither love nor hate, the understanding of the Way will blind you with its obviousness.*

Obvious, like the moon reflected by the water.

But the image of the cave has more nuance than this. There is a metaphorical sense: nothing provokes the light that enters a cave. It's the same for understanding and the mind. Master Deshimaru said, "'Cave' also means entering the cave or entering the mountain, in other words, becoming the mountain." He translated the second line more literally: "Your understanding of the Way will be as clear as daylight entering a cave."

∽

Neither love nor hate. "Love" in the sense of chasing after, of attraction; "hate" in the sense of running away from, of repulsion.

Many people do not understand *Neither love nor hate.*

When Master Deshimaru came to Europe, this teaching raised a lot of questions. People found Zen quite severe, and not very compassionate. Sensei did not realize the extent to which we Westerners cared about our loves—girlfriends, boyfriends, friends, etc. He didn't understand that love is an everpresent criterion for us. In this respect, it's a good thing that some masters today are Westerners: they're in a position to respond to this type of question.

We shouldn't retreat into ourselves, into our personal loves, our personal hates. This only creates subjective complications. The self should be empty of its own self. Yet some people do just the opposite. They're so caught up in their own world that even zazen practice can't help them. Masters often deal with people who are imprisoned by endless personal problems. It's because they're always going from thought to thought, and have been doing so for a very long time.

Neither love nor hate means freeing yourself from stupid attachments. If you're attached, you're not free, and your mind loses its purity. You notice this all the time, especially if you practice zazen.

Not being attached certainly seems difficult, and yet it simply means: be free, and available, everywhere. That way, you can be attached to everything freely—to human beings, birds, insects—without complicating your life.

For me, this means "no attachments," or rather, "don't be handcuffed by attachments." One master said, "You must be detached, always detached, and even more detached." In other words, detach yourself from the sense organs. Don't be attached to what you see or hear. You must feel and understand with your body, not just with your eyes and your head. Don't be taken in by the senses, don't be attracted to beauty, don't be repulsed by ugliness.

If you look at an object or a person and feel attachment at that moment, then you fall into the devil's snare. In Zen teaching, it is always said that we should not let ourselves be abused by the demons of sight, smell, touch, etc., and that we should not become prisoners of sex, food or the environment. Don't be attached to lovely metaphysical Buddhist sayings, either. Don't be attached to words: "The master said it, so that's how it is." To avoid this, things are often phrased negatively in Buddhism, so that you don't fall into the word trap. You must not run after the masters' words, or follow them to the letter, but follow what the masters followed instead. They're two very different things.

It's like the image of the monk Hotei pointing to the moon with his finger. You shouldn't look at the finger (the word), but at the moon. This may seem obvious, but it's not.

> There was once a hermit named Senrin. One day, a friend came to visit him and slept in his hut. The next day, Senrin wanted to give him a gift. He took a block of stone and transformed it into pure gold. Naturally, the friend in question was very impressed. A block of gold! But he quickly grimaced. So Senrin figured maybe he wanted a second one. He pointed his finger at another rock, which immediately changed into gold. But the friend was not any happier.
>
> "I give you two blocks of gold and you're still not happy. What do you want?" asked Senrin.
>
> "I want your finger!" screamed the friend.

∽

Love, in the sense of attachment and dependence, distances us from the Way. Love is very beautiful: love for your wife, for your husband. But it makes life complicated.

The love that Sosan is talking about is personal, subjective love, which shuts you up in yourself and creates major complications. It's not about compassion, but something exclusive that is just for you. You mustn't be too attached to this love, nor to the happiness or unhappiness it brings—because happiness always goes hand-in-hand with its opposite. Some people are attached to happiness, others to unhappiness. It's a reflection of the ignorance which afflicts all of us to some degree.

I think we can love without falling into the trap of attachment. But to do this, we must understand what attachment is. This understanding is essential. Attachment is thinking that the object of your attachment—a woman or a man, for example—is a real object with substantial existence. This is an illusion: we are continuously changing. We are not what we were yesterday, nor what we will be tomorrow. Everything is transient. We are change itself. But because of attachment, we grab hold and we can't let go anymore, we can't forget. We're always thinking, "She's not the same person anymore. She doesn't respect me the way she used to." Well, of course—she's not the same person anymore. Neither are you. Neither am I. We change all the time. So what do we attach ourselves to in the end? To the past.

Yet, it is possible to love without being attached, or at least not blindly. So be careful not to get caught up in yourself, with your personal feelings, always subjective. No one is above this, and it's an occasion to look at yourself: "She loves me—she loves *me*—but who am I?"

∽

When you receive the ordination, you don't reject your family; you cut your attachment to them and go towards something higher. This doesn't mean that you refuse the love of your wife or husband or children. It's the exclusivity that you're cutting: "I want to protect my wife and children. But that one over there isn't my child, so I'm not interested; he can do what he wants. I only have one child, not ten thousand." But that's exactly the point: why not have ten thousand?

To think that our children belong to us is rather simplistic. Your children have come from the sky, from heaven, for a moment. Your house and furniture too. Every thing and every human being has a life of its own. Nobody belongs to anybody. Everything, absolutely everything, is a gift. Everything is received from the sky and returns to the sky. And everything that comes to you comes only for a moment.

Even the painting an artist creates, or the book she writes, no longer belongs to her once the work is finished. She may have the copyright, but the work is no longer hers. Anyone who creates has the almost physical feeling that they're not doing the creating: they are simply a channel through which creative energy passes. But for this energy to circulate freely, you must not have personal ideas because they only block the way. With this mind, you can paint or write masterpieces, because it is no longer the small self that is producing.

Everything has its own life: the person you love, the child that supposedly belongs to you, the painting, the book, the objects. It is important to understand this profoundly. And if you can understand it in your bones, in your *hara*, then you can live in peace and have compassion for everything: other people, animals, objects, and even the air you breathe.

∽

In the end, neither love nor hate brings us to *funi*, not-two. Neither this nor that is not-two. But not-two is not beyond the interdependence of things. Sosan is talking about the love and hate that go together.

> In 676, Master Eno left his retreat with fishermen in southern China and went to Canton, where he walked by the temple of the Nirvana School, which is not very different from Zen. A few monks were talking about a flag waving above their heads. One said, "The flag is moving." Another, "No, the wind is moving." And Eno said, "Mind is moving." The monks were very impressed.

That's the classic version of the flag story, the one found in Paul Reps's book[1] and other collections of Zen stories. But according to another source of Master Deshimaru's, the first monk said, "The flag is moving," the second monk said, "No, it's the wind," and the third monk, Eno, replied, "No, it's consciousness that's moving." At that

---

1 Reps, Paul and Nyogen Senzaki, ed., *Zen Flesh, Zen Bones: A Collection of Zen and Pre-Zen Writings* (Boston: Tuttle, 1989).

moment a nun who was passing by overheard the discussion and said to the other three, "No. You are all mistaken. Everything is moving: flag, wind and mind."[2]

Neither love nor hate. That means, don't fall into contradictions and duality. (Is it the flag or is it the wind? Unless it's the mind?) It's another way of saying that we have to stop discriminating between good and evil. Not-good-or-evil. No need to choose, no need to reject. Not-good-or-evil and immediately the Way appears before you.

"When you think of neither good nor evil," said Eno to Domyo, "what is your true face, your true self?" Eno's question has become a famous koan.

> Eno worked in the kitchen of Konin's temple, in charge of the mortar used to crush the rice. He practiced zazen on the *gaitan*, since he was forbidden to enter the dojo on the grounds that he was uneducated and could neither read nor write. Eno received the transmission from Master Konin, even though everyone thought it would go to Jinshu, the most cerebral, best educated and most scholarly of all the disciples. The other monks were furious, especially General Domyo, who set out in pursuit of Eno. Following the advice of Konin, who feared the other monks' jealousy, Eno had fled in the night, as soon as he had received the transmission. Domyo, who was traveling on horseback, caught up with Eno in two days. Eno placed the bowl and the kesa—the emblems of the transmission—on a rock and hid behind a bush. He thought the general would content himself with these objects and give up the idea of killing him. But when Domyo went to take the bowl and the kesa, he couldn't lift them, because they had suddenly become very heavy. The general was furious. Eno came out from

2 Taisen Deshimaru, *Za-Zen* (Paris: Editions Seighers, 1974, 102).

> behind his bush and asked, "Why have you come? For the Dharma, or for the bowl and the kesa?"
>
> "For the Dharma, of course," replied Domyo. "I have come for the Way! Please, transmit it to me."
>
> And it was then that Eno pronounced the words: "Think of neither good nor evil. At this moment, what is your true face?"

There are other interpretations of this question; for example, "Without thinking about what is true or false, seek your face before the birth of your parents." One version by Master Deshimaru says, "You, Joza! Without thinking of good or evil: who are you?"

All the masters have expressed themselves on this matter. Ikkyu, a fifteenth-century Japanese monk, wrote this poem:

My old self, which never originally existed,
Has nowhere to go after death, absolutely nowhere.

The Not good-or-evil. Be beyond. This practice is the Way.

3

If a distinction as minute as a particle is created in the mind,
an infinite distance immediately separates sky and earth.

Since Sosan composed the *Shinjinmei*, many other masters through the centuries have referred to it in their own writing: Sekito in the *Sandokai*, Yoka Daishi in the *Shodoka* and Tozan in the *Hokyozanmai*, as well as other Soto masters such as Fuyodokai, Wanshi, Dogen, Keizan, Daichi, Menzan and Kodo Sawaki; Taisen Deshimaru; and in the Rinzai School, Mumon Ekai in the *Mumonkan* and Engo Kokugon in the *Hekiganroku*.

For example, here is what we find in the second paragraph of Master Dogen's *Fukanzazengi*: "If the slightest gap exists, the Way remains as distant as the sky from the earth."

Master Deshimaru's comments on this strophe come down to this: "If a gap of a hair's breadth is created in our minds, the Self no longer coincides with the ego, nor the mountain with the mountain." Even though the master talked a lot about the ego, he never said that we should get rid of it. He was even known to criticize religions that tried to crush the ego, to always make it smaller: "My ego's smaller than yours!" And the master, by way of reply, said: "My ego is bigger. I have a super ego—it is as vast as the cosmos."

∽

Don't make distinctions. That's what the first three strophes of the *Shinjinmei* are talking about. By separating the sky and the earth, we create a division in our own minds. So don't have any seeds inside you. Let nothing grow! Neither for nor against. As soon as you show the slightest preference or the slightest antipathy, your mind is divided and lost in confusion.

> One day Master Maezumi asked his disciple Genpo, "Are you a vegetarian?"
>
> Genpo replied, "I never eat meat."
>
> "Do not be attached to any philosophy or any thought," said Maezumi.
>
> The same question was asked of Master Dainin Katagiri.
>
> "Are you a vegetarian?"
>
> "A tiny little bit," he replied.

No separation, no distinction. But this doesn't mean that we raze the mountains and fill up the valleys. It is simply about mind, big mind, and how this mind quickly becomes very small. Running after the *shiho* (Dharma transmission), running away from the *shiho*—that's small mind, the mind that makes distinctions.

We shouldn't try to attain anything. The result isn't important. It's not like a contest, where the arrow has to hit the middle of the target. The arrow is shot exactly, and that's all that matters.

The practice is what's important, exact practice. It is said that we must cultivate the Way. I don't like the term "cultivate"; I prefer "take care of." In order for a tree to grow, it has to be able to drink through its roots, so water must be able to penetrate the ground. That's why you loosen the soil around a tree. That's taking care of it. And it's identical to the attention you give to the practice of the Way.

One must always take care. Today, one makes a small distinction; tomorrow, that distinction will take on larger proportions. A particle in the mind, a speck of dust, an atom . . . and the error becomes infinite.

One night I was sailing my father's boat, which was going to Corsica. I was navigating by compass. In the morning, we found ourselves just off the coast of the island of Elba, fifty or so miles to the east. A mistake is a mistake; there's no "almost." A drop of ink in a glass and the water isn't clear anymore. Just one particle and the sky and earth are separated. Missing the target by an inch is the same as missing it by a mile. Anyway, there is no target.

What's important is climbing the mountain, not the view from the peak. Sometimes, people climb to the top of a mountain and once they're up there they can't see anything because of the clouds. Then, they think they've missed something.

Wanting to get something is entering into the dualistic world. But that world exists, and sometimes it's necessary to want to obtain. So how do you know when, where and how to go about it?

Wisdom, which is not separate from compassion, can show us what is or is not necessary to do. Not ordinary wisdom, but *maka hannya* (*maka*, "great"; *hannya*, "wisdom"). A wisdom that is neither particularly human nor particularly inhuman, but which comes from *ku*, which comes, quite simply, from nothing.

∽

In this strophe, Sosan talks about *a distinction as minute as a particle*. This concerns the thinker, the person who discriminates. Just a tiny notion of right or wrong, and you become confused, or, as Sosan puts it, you "separate sky and earth." The sky and the earth cannot be separated; and what's more, one cannot exist without the other. Sosan is saying that thinking complicates everything. "This lovely flower is blooming for me. This fly is annoying me." Separation.

Don't create the particle that will put an infinite distance between the sky and the earth; don't wind up in hell. Hell is not a place: it's a state of mind. Making distinctions means creating hell and heaven, because separation creates heaven just as surely as it creates hell. As soon as you start making choices, you're adopting the perspective of the ordinary person who thinks there's an awakened human being on one side and an ignoramus on the other.

Some religions don't seem at all bothered by this cleavage between heaven and earth, with one above and one below. On the contrary, they like it. It has the advantage of simplifying. I mean, it simplifies things: if you're good, you go to heaven; if you're bad, you go to hell. And never imagine that it's all in the head and nowhere else.

Of course, everything also depends on your point of view. If your point of view is high and your perspective wide, then at that time there is no creation of distinctions. "The master, the Buddha, speaks to me directly." That's the religious mind *par excellence*, as when Buddha said, "I alone am awakened." Here, no more distinctions, no more separation between sky and earth. From the point of view of an awakened person, everyone has Buddha-nature. Originally, fundamentally, everyone is awakened. Our true natures are in perfect harmony with the cosmos. Our true nature is calm and peaceful, and we should all discover what we've always had, and what it is all about.

But where does the master place himself when he declares that an awakened person sees everyone as awakened, whereas the non-awakened person makes the distinction between the man of satori and the man of *samsara*? Does the master consider himself awakened or not?

I think the awakened person simply does not see himself in these terms. Words are a form of communication that we should leave behind us, like a raft once we have crossed the river.

4

If you achieve satori here and now,
The idea of right and wrong will no longer enter your mind.

We can see every strophe of the *Shinjinmei* as an explanation of what satori is, or what it isn't. Such is the case for the fourth strophe. The translation by Richard B. Clarke reads:

If you wish to see the truth, Then hold no opinions
for or against anything.[3]

But "to see the truth" is not as concrete as to *achieve satori here and now.*

We might also say, "If we achieve the Way here and now, everything appears before us and our conscience is pacified."

The strength of this poem, its direct quality, is particularly well suited to practice in this lineage. In other practices—and even in other Zen schools, including Soto Zen—there is a lot of talk about progress and degrees. We hear this all the time—but not in the teaching of Kodo Sawaki and Taisen Deshimaru. Our practice is to achieve satori here and now. Only here and now, and that way there is no more wrong, no more right in the mind.

According to Sosan, we are not walking on the Way as long as we are driven by judgments such as right or wrong, for or against. It is said that suffering results from the clash of opposites. And that, if we manage to abandon such ideas of right and wrong, everything appears before us and our conscience is pacified.

So if you want to see the truth, do not take a stand for or against anything. Anyway, "for" becomes "against" and "against" becomes "for."

---

3 Cited in: Merzel, Dennis Genpo. *The Eye Never Sleeps: Striking to the Heart of Zen* (Boston: Shambhala, 1991, 127).

We've all experienced this: wanting something but being unable to obtain it, we change our attitude, we stop loving and we start hating.

Of course, sometimes you must take a stand. But you can do it naturally: take a stand without taking a stand. If one puts water in a round container, it takes the shape of a round container; if one puts water in a square container, it takes the shape of a square container. And yet, water is always water. This means, don't force things in one direction or another this way, that way, to the north, to the south. Do not choose.

∽

One master explained it this way: "If our mind and our conscience are at peace, always tranquil here and now, we can preserve this state of tranquility. Without it, we cannot be happy."

"If our mind is tranquil here and now..." But how does this happen?

Zen is finding your original nature, which is completely different for each of us, yet at the same time similar for everyone. This original nature is absolute tranquility. And what is absolute tranquility? I think it is faith, faith with no objective.

Tranquility lies within faith; it is something that slips in and becomes ingrained in everything, in all the nooks and crannies of our daily life. It is said that if our mind is in a state of true tranquility, neither failure nor misfortune can cause suffering.

Naturally, everyone has moments of tranquility. In fact, everyone struggles in his own way to obtain just that. You work hard to be able to go home and finally have some peace. But I'm not talking about that tranquility, which disappears as soon as you find yourself in a difficult situation. I'm talking about the tranquility of the person who is aware of his original nature in any situation.

"Unconscious" is a word that Master Deshimaru used often; but this does not mean "unaware." An awakened master is "unconscious" as a tree is unconscious, or a mountain. And he is something more as well. He is awakened.

Wanshi was a great practitioner of zazen, and one day he said something to this effect: "When there is nothing in our mind, nothing special, we know there is nothing. And if we do not know, it is Zen-disease and not true Zen." Wanshi talks about "transparent mind." It's not correct to say there's nothing there, he points out, because transparent mind is there.

When you walk, you know you're walking, even if you're totally concentrated on the walking itself. When you sleep, there are several ways to sleep: there's the person who falls into bed like a sack of potatoes; others fall asleep but somewhere remain awake—not exactly conscious but not unconscious either. They are really asleep, but they also have a mind that stays out of sleep, a light mind, which doesn't fall asleep for or against, and doesn't wake up for or against either.

∞

So, best not to think in such terms. Don't complicate your mind. Don't complicate things. Because all of it is just personal thoughts; and that's what weighs the most, that's our heaviest baggage.

Master Dogen said in the *Shobogenzo* that our possessions, our thoughts and our opinions are not real. They are dependent on karma. So, put down your baggage. Be light, don't carry anything unnecessary; don't carry anything at all. The higher you want to go, the more you have to leave everything behind and go naked.

Be profoundly tranquil, natural in every situation. Be yourself. And that doesn't mean having a personal point of view. Here and now, simply find your original nature.

Be like the tiger entering the forest, or the dragon penetrating the sea. For the tiger, the forest is home; he is protected there, he cannot be shot at as on the plains. He is no longer hunting; he is entering the forest. It can be the same when you enter your own home and are naturally yourself. And it's the same for the dragon. And the monk getting into the posture is also the same thing.

5

The struggle between right and wrong in our conscience leads to a sick mind.

The fifth strophe is fairly simple to understand; it is completely connected to the fourth and responds to it.

Just, unjust: most religions pit one against the other, and "just" becomes "justice," which becomes punishment. But in Buddhism, this duality does not exist. This is why Sosan says *the struggle between right and wrong in our conscience leads to a sick mind.*

Right, wrong, for or against: from this inner struggle between desire and rejection, from this for-or-against which permeates the mind, sickness is born. For example, the person we love doesn't love us—immediately, we start hating them. This is one of the symptoms of a diseased mind, at an advanced stage. We've all experienced it. Master Deshimaru said, "Do not create differences, do not follow anything, do not fight, do not look for God or Buddha, do not run after the Dharma. All of this causes sickness in the mind. We must cut off all things. We must cut the ten thousand relations; we must not imagine anything, but not destroy anything either. The fruits of feelings of love and attachment are desire and hate." All masters of the transmission speak this way.

Don't create differences between yourself and others, don't make yourself sick by looking at them with a judgmental eye, which establishes categories or follows a line of conduct. It's not necessary to analyze, to see if a certain person or thing is good or bad; we're all both good and bad. Sometimes the master criticizes his disciples, but it's never a judgment—you can immediately recognize someone who doesn't judge. It was always to awaken our true nature, our original nature, the Buddha-nature we can see if we look at ourselves. And with the practice, we wind up seeing this original nature in others as well. Then we begin to see them differently; there is no more for, against, good or bad . . . no more sick mind.

∽

What we suffer from the most is too much thinking. Following a particular behavior or system of thought creates inner conflicts. And this disease, this purely mental suffering, creates neurosis.

Sometimes people who are beginning zazen practice suffer quite a bit physically. In zazen, the muscles (which are in fact in their normal state) work in a way that is different from how they work in ordinary life. They hurt due to lack of practice. And the best cure for the physical pain of zazen is obviously to practice more zazen. But when you stop hurting physically, sometimes an even greater suffering appears—that of the mind. Your mind hurts, you stagnate in your thoughts, you get sick.[4]

Almost a thousand years ago, Master Fuyodokai said, "Monks should hate the dirty work of the mind, be beyond life and death, stop the activity of the mind and reject all complicated relationships." "Complicated relationships" refers to human relationships, but also to the activities of our conscience.

The problems which existed in Fuyodokai's time were not so different from ours, except that today they're much worse. Why? Because things become more pronounced with time. You shoot at a target placed a yard away and you miss by an inch. Put the target ten-thousand yards away and you miss by a mile. Today, mental suffering is far greater than physical suffering.

Masters today talk a lot about our civilization, pointing out that we human beings have become weak, weaker than ever, and that we find ourselves defenseless. In the subway in Paris, the advertising billboards target weaker-minded types and those afflicted by personal and emotional problems, daily agitation, noise, professional concerns, the need to earn a living. This leads to a sick mind. That's why zazen is so important.

---

4 "After a while," writes Kennett Roshi, "the newness wears off, and then the hard work begins [...], then, when 'interesting things' stop happening, they're at a loss. They think they're doing it wrong or there's no point; it 'isn't working'." *Roar of the Tigress* (Mt. Shasta, Calif.: Shasta Abbey Press, 2000).

∽

Zazen is observing your thoughts. But this does not mean observing the chain of thoughts. In fact, when you observe thoughts, their connection is broken. Observing means observing the birth and death of a thought, and in so doing, freeing yourself from it. You observe a thought; it dies and leaves room for another thought, which is, in its turn, transformed into non-thought and dies.

And so, zazen is observing life and death. Observing *mujo*, impermanence, change—the cause of which is often mental illness. In Zen, it is said that everything is change, that there is nothing but change; but we could also say that there is no real change, that change is only apparent, that it is limited to form. Someone who is completely detached, who is not driven by his ego, can easily understand this. It's true. What changes, really? The packaging. The essence does not change.

Letting your thoughts pass, without stopping them: that's all you have to do, today and tomorrow, for one year, five years, ten years. Because, if you practice observation this way, all inner conflicts, all mental sickness, disappear. The mind returns to its normal condition and your original Buddha-nature appears. Then you achieve the Way in the here and now.

"Do this for ten years," said Master Joshu, "and I promise you, you will find the Way. Otherwise, you can cut off my head and use it as a washbasin."

6

If you cannot penetrate the source of things,
Your mind will exhaust itself in vain.

The fifth strophe explains that if your brain works too hard, it becomes sick. The sixth tells us that if you don't penetrate the depth of things, beyond dualistic categories like good and evil, your mind also becomes sick.

This strophe contains the *kanji* "gen," which means "the origin," "the source of things," "the source of existence." This means that if we don't know the deep meaning of things, we are needlessly disturbing our original mind.

The original principle, deep nature, is not a product of our six senses—six including consciousness—and that is what the sixth strophe is talking about a world beyond consciousness. In deep nature, said Fyodokai, there is neither dualism nor monism. As he said, not the left head or the right head (dualism), or the head in the middle (monism). Like the man who is surprised by his shadow (we could also say image). Sometimes people run after their shadow, sometimes they want to escape it. The shadow is only a phenomenon. Yet, many people think it is true happiness.

Another translation of strophe six, by Master Sheng-yen, says that we should recognize "the mysterious principle."[5] Mysterious, because deep nature has nothing to do with our eyes and what we see, with our ears and what we hear, with our mind and what we think. It is, in fact, a world beyond consciousness: the invisible world.

Through the practice of zazen, we become sensitive to the invisible world, we come into contact with it: the half-dead, the half-alive, the *pretas* and *devas*. And we come into contact with the original source: non-desire, or *ku*.

---

5 Master Sheng-yen, *Faith in Mind: A Guide to Ch'an Practice* (Elmhurst, NY: Dharma Drum Publications, 1987).

In China, under the T'ang Dynasty in the 800s, Raisan (nicknamed "the farting master") lived in the plains where he grew sweet potatoes. He was a great Zen master, and famous in his time, even if only one anecdote is known about him. We don't even know if he had any disciples—apparently you don't always need disciples to be a master, even a famous one.

The emperor, who had heard about Raisan, wanted him to come pay a visit, because he wanted to get some information about Zen. So he sent a messenger to Raisan with the mission to bring him back. An entire retinue of noblemen from the palace accompanied him. They arrived at the monk's hut, in the middle of a field, at lunchtime. The messenger knocked on the door, saying "Open up! I am the emperor's envoy! He is waiting for you and my mission is to bring you back with me to the court."

Raisan was eating a sweet potato. When you eat sweet potatoes, you fart a lot, and so he was doing exactly that. He didn't answer the emperor's messenger. It wasn't the right time. Now he was eating. The messenger said, "If you do not come, I will take back your head without your body." This did not disturb Raisan in the least.

The messenger finally decided not to bring Raisan's head back to the emperor, but to return to the palace and tell him the story. When he heard it, the emperor, furious, cried, "Bring him here this instant! I want to hear him speak about Zen!"

So the messenger went off again to Raisan's hut. It happened to be lunchtime again. He knocked at the door and shouted, "Open up! This time I will bring back your head if you refuse to come with me!" But Raisan ignored him and continued to eat his sweet potato. The messenger walked around the outside of the hut and

> looked through an opening that served as a window. From there he saw Raisan eating a sweet potato.
>
> "Open up. The emperor wants to see you right away." No answer. The messenger was dumbfounded. He could have killed Raisan. That was when he noticed that the monk's nose was running. The snot was dripping down his mouth and onto the sweet potato. "Hey, Master, your nose is running," he said.
>
> "So what?" answered Raisan. "I'm eating."
>
> The messenger once again gave up on cutting off his head. Perhaps he had understood something. Anyway he accepted this answer and set off homeward. When he arrived at the palace, he told the emperor how Raisan had not wiped his nose because he was eating. The emperor burst out laughing and said, "All over the world, people think it a great honor to meet me. But not this master."
>
> And so the emperor issued a decree which protected Raisan's sweet potato fields. He had the neighboring field purchased without the monk's knowledge, so that he could continue to farm his potatoes in utter tranquility for the rest of his days.

This is a true story. It's about non-desire, about *ku*, the great void, the origin of all things.

∽

If you cannot penetrate the source of things,
Your mind will exhaust itself in vain.

If you can understand what is original, *ku*, then complications will cease to arise in your consciousness and in your life. If not, things become complicated in your head. Some people practice for years and become more and more complicated. You ask yourself, "Why is this person, who has practiced for twenty years, even more asinine than before?" You tell yourself, "Maybe it's because he doesn't have deep karmic roots. Maybe he doesn't have faith." Well in that case, what can you do? You can *pretend* to have deep karmic roots, you can *pretend* to have faith—because, in any event, you have to start somewhere. You put on a black robe, for example; you do zazen; and then, during the ceremony, you concentrate on *gassho* and think about Buddha; during *sampai*, you drop to your knees and hit your head hard on the ground, thinking all the while that you are dropping everything. This will bring you more wisdom, and more faith in due time.

No need to be strong or profound to practice zazen. Maybe we become so. But when the ego's functioning stops, a human being becomes a human being, a tree becomes a tree, a mountain becomes a mountain.

What do you become when you practice zazen? You become normal. You just come back to the normal condition. And then what? And then you enter the stream, or as it is said in the sutras, you enter the true path of Liberation.

7

The Way is round, at peace and perfect, wide as the vast cosmos, without the slightest notion of rest or rupture. The Way is round.

Round like the cosmos, round like the universe, round like the earth, round like the moon, round like the sun, round like the eye that sees. Not long or short. Round.

In *La Rondeur des jours* (*The Roundness of Days*), Jean Giono writes, "Days do not have a long shape, the shape of things which move towards goals, an arrow, a road, the human race; they have a round shape, like the sun, the world, God."[6]

The Way does not have the shape of things that move towards a goal either, like an arrow shot into the target, like a road going somewhere, like the human race.

The Way is round; it has no beginning or end. It is always said that things begin now and finish later. The day begins . . . But when does day begin? At what point in time? And when exactly does it end, please?

There are many translations of this strophe. They only say, "The Way is perfect." This one, however, says *The Way is round.* Round like Buddha, round like God. Round like *ku*. Not big or small, but round like a pea, round like the earth and the universe.

The Way is round, at peace and perfect, wide as the vast cosmos

The vast cosmos does not mean "nothing," or "emptiness," but rather "everything," which is *ku*. However, although the vast cosmos includes everything, it is in no way a matter of everything individual, everything personal. It is not metaphysics, it is not psychology, and as Sosan always says, it has nothing to do with what we like or don't like.

---

6 Giono, Jean, *Rondeur des jours* (Paris: Gallimard, 1970).

∽

Without the slightest notion of rest or rupture.

One day, a young woman told me that she was very troubled because she thought her zazen practice was not exact. But even that's just a lingering thought. Even if you can't breathe well, it's the Way; even if your posture is twisted, it's the Way. We never think or say, "That tree is imperfect," or "That tree is not manifesting its original nature." In a dojo or in the street, who is not manifesting his or her original nature?

Without the slightest notion of rest or rupture means that there is nothing missing and nothing extra.

When he received the transmission from Bodhidharma, Eka, the second patriarch, understood that wanting to get something leads to nowhere. (You get it and you're happy, then you want something else, because you finally see that you didn't get anything the first time, and so maybe the next time . . .)

And when Sosan received the transmission from Eka, he understood that it is futile to reject anything at all. (Even if you succeed in rejecting something—a great desire for someone or something, for example—the desire doesn't necessarily disappear from your head.)

The practice of the Way is not that of the social world—getting, getting—and it does not consist in rejecting the world, either. We don't even reject our thoughts, not even "bad" ones. We all have thoughts; that's okay, as long as they go away—in other words, as long as we don't try to hold onto them or reject them.

The Zen monk is called *shukke*, "out of the house," one who has left home. But that doesn't mean he ends up at a street corner. He will always live somewhere. What has he left, then? He has left the thought of home—no set thoughts, no set home. This means that every place is your home. No need to live outdoors, in a ditch, in a hole, or even in a monastery. No need to go to Eiheiji in Japan to look for the Way. (Of course everybody knows that by now, but they go there anyway.) The Way is not something outside yourself, something outside your mind. The Way is round. It is everywhere.

8

In truth, because we want to seize or reject, we are not free.

Here again, Master Sosan is talking about dualism, about duality and non-duality. It's a recurring subject that Sosan develops throughout the *Shinjinmei.*

Because we're always wanting to seize or reject, we don't perceive the true nature of things, so much so that we're not free, and of course once again we suffer.

In Buddhism, this suffering is expressed by the image of the wheel of life, whose movement hurls people by turns into the six states: *gaki*, the world of insatiable desire; *asura*, the world of violence and aggression; *chikuso*, the animal world; *naraka*, hell; *shomon*, the human world of personal satisfaction; *deva*, the world of the gods.

For example, if you are greedy, you may become obsessed with money, or sex, or power. You can't get enough. You become like a *gaki*, always wanting more, and it's impossible to find peace. From this state of desire and greed, you fall into violence, the world of the *asura*. You're angry with people who have more than you, aggressive with people who come between you and your desires. Then, you become like an animal, *chikuso*; you're suffering so much from your desires that you maybe even kill someone. So, you fall into *naraka*, you go to prison. There, you're filled with regret and you promise yourself you'll change. This returns you to *shomon,* the human state. You reflect on your experience. You write a book about it. It's a bestseller. It's picked up by a Hollywood producer and gets made into a movie. You're on top of the world, feeling very satisfied with yourself. You're like a *deva*, everything's great.

But soon desires arise again.[7]

---

7 And the desires themselves change as well. When, for instance, the celestial world no longer holds the devas' interest, their clothes become torn and the

Each state can span a lifetime or a few years. Some people experience all of them in a single day. Whatever the case may be, in general the cycle continues until death.

In most Buddhist texts and schools, what I've just explained is taught in dualistic terms, in terms of the negative-positive opposition associated with the law of causality: "Because I do this, I become that." The action of this law of causality can be observed everywhere; after the cold comes the heat, and, eventually, the cold again. There's no end. It's the same for people: pleasure/pain, love/hate, *mushotoku/ushotoku* . . .

∽

Buddhism, especially Zen, teaches us the importance of the present moment. Here and now, who are you?

This is how we can become free from moment to moment. And this true freedom is *inmo*, "like this." Dogen said, "*Inmo* is body and mind in the eternal present." The body and mind of the eternal present.

This strophe has nothing to do with philosophy, and the comments I am making on it are not at all abstract. It has to do with our lives here and now, our relationship to others—our relationship to our supervisors at our jobs, the relationship between leaders and those who follow them, and finally, our relationship to ourselves.

Sosan's words apply to all of us: we are not free, we are not *inmo*—hence our agitation. Why? Because most of our thoughts are thoughts of desire and selection—"I like, I don't like." Almost everyone functions this way without even realizing it. Always thinking about the past, for example, is not *inmo*. Neither is thinking about the future. And yet, we devote a lot of time to this kind of rumination.

A person who is not free functions as if in a sort of dream. When you're sleeping, you don't know you're asleep.

---

flowers in their hair, quite disheveled by now, become faded, and decay is everywhere; the devas have come to smell bad, and it's time they became something else.

∽

It is said that, through our choices and preferences, we limit our awareness. The small mind wants things for itself; what it doesn't want, it discards. It's the same with everything. We cultivate the pretty flowers and destroy the ugly ones. This is small mind. Great mind is something else, for it desires *both* the pretty and the ugly. Indeed, great mind doesn't mean we don't desire anything, but the contrary; it's not a matter of wanting or not wanting, nor is it a matter of what we ourselves want, rather it's wanting what the universe wants.

But how do we know what the universe wants?

> One day Joshu asked his master Nansen, "What is the Way?"
>
> Nansen answered, "Everyday mind is the Way."
>
> "Should I steer myself towards it or not?"
>
> "If you go towards it, you will distance yourself from it," replied the master.
>
> "But if I do not go towards it, how can I know what the true Way is?" asked the disciple.
>
> "The true Way is beyond knowing or not knowing."

In the end, we must abandon this question of wanting or not wanting, liking or not liking, because, from the point of view of the universe or the Way, there is no separation. We are not separate from each other. What we like and what we dislike are not separate. Nor are the pretty flowers and the ugly: they're "like this," *inmo*.

Master Dogen explains that *inmo* means grass, trees, tiles, stones, the four elements, the five *skandha*; he says that this is all just mind, a single mind, in other words, true form—*inmo*.

Diversity becomes One. One is diversity. Essence is One, not two. Love is two, compassion is One. And the greatest compassion is to love the weeds too, with no separation.

∽

Master Tokusan is famous for his motto, "Thirty blows if you speak, thirty blows if you're silent." Yet, ironically, his disciples were often angry with him because they thought he had become too gentle and kind.

> There was, in Tokusan's sangha, an ordained monk who was also a bit of a scoundrel. Some of the monks came to Tokusan and complained about their fellow monk: "Do you realize that this guy stole money from his father and spent it all on alcohol? What's more, he was disinherited by his family and spent a long time in prison."
>
> "Oh really?"
>
> "Every chance he gets, he's plotting something he steals our own things behind our backs!"
>
> In Tokusan's temple, there was a room reserved for sick people. One night, when they were all asleep, the monk in question sneaked into the infirmary and stole their money as well.
>
> "There, you see, Master? Helping this guy is throwing pearls before swine! He'll eat your pearls and defecate them, and that's all."

Tokusan didn't agree, "He is not a bad man. Sin and sainthood are *ku*. The snake swallows the frog, the toad swallows the worm, the falcon eats the sparrow, the pheasant eats the snake, the cat catches the rat, the big fish devours the little fish and everything is fine. The monk who has offended the precepts does not fall into hell."

9

Do not run after shiki and do not dwell on ku.

It's a shame that materialistic people aren't spiritual as well. It's a shame that spiritual people aren't materialistic, too.

Do not run after shiki means don't run after phenomena, don't run after conditioned existence, don't be attached. Don't be attached to your thoughts, to your body, to the environment. The country is nice; so is the city.

It's the same for *ku*. Do not dwell on emptiness.

Some Zen practitioners think that everything is an illusion and therefore nothing is important. They practice for years with this perspective and then one fine day they leave. Why do they leave? Because they wind up thinking that even the practice is not important.

On the other hand, other people come to practice to get something: *shiki*, tangible benefits. They immediately get themselves a zafu, a kimono or a kolomo, and get ordained as monks, nuns, with rakusu and kesa. Thus equipped, they stay another few years. Then, they leave. Why? Because, in the end, they realize that they haven't gotten anything at all from the practice of the Way. Sometimes, they've actually lost something: their boyfriend, their wife, their job.[8]

These two types are very common, and elder disciples see them come and go all the time. In the main reception room at La Gendronnière Temple in France, there's a large photograph which was taken in 1981. One of our favorite pastimes is to look at it and say, "Hey, remember him? Remember her? We never hear from them anymore." At least three-quarters of the people in the photo have completely disappeared. Andwhen you look at a 1973 photo, four-fifths of the people are gone.

And yet, we are as numerous as we were in the 70s. What we're practicing here is not a kind of training to attain something. It's not

8 As in my own case, but anyhow I continued.

like a university, where you get a diploma and you leave. It's not like some Rinzai practices either, where once you've succeeded in solving a hundred or so koans, the master says, "Okay, you can go now, goodbye." He gives you a certificate of recognition and you leave at once, never to return.

Here's a quote from Master Hakuin, a great Rinzai master who died in 1769. In this passage, he uses a somewhat point-blank vocabulary, but never mind:

> The masters of our school, said he one day, have never transmitted the smallest scrap of Dharma to their disciples. Not because the masters were concerned with protecting the Dharma, but because they were concerned with protecting themselves. Today, the disciples who arrive are generally ignorant, stupid and unmotivated. The masters in question instruct these people and treat them with tender care. They might just as well take a heap of cows' heads, line them up, and try to get them to eat. In the end, it's actually a heap of [sic] that they're stuffing them with, after which they send them back out into the world equipped with duly stamped *shiho* certificates. The difference between them and Isan or Kyogen [two great masters in the lineage] is like the difference between mud and clouds.
>
> What we are doing when we are going to the dojo is an eternal continuation with others. This is important. To stay together and to practice. Naturally one can change temples or dojos. One can go wherever one wants. But wherever you go, as the master would say, don't forget that the practice is for life—for two lives, even. For all lives.

∞

Don't run after *shiki*; don't dwell on phenomena. Don't dwell on *ku* either: emptiness, truth. Don't even have any ideas about *ku*.

> Gonyo was the disciple of Master Joshu, in China, in the ninth century. This story makes him seem a little stupid. Yet, he was an authentic disciple. He was very well respected, but it's true, he was a little strange. He was known to walk around with two tigers at his side and a snake wound around his waist.
>
> So one day, Gonjyo went to see Joshu and said to him, "I have come with nothing. What should I do in such a situation?"
>
> Another master, like Obaku or Baso, would have shouted or even slapped him. But Joshu was very gentle. He told him, "Just throw it away."
>
> Gonyo replied, "But I just told you that I've come with nothing. So what do you want me to throw away?"
>
> "Throw it all away."

Don't carry any burdens. Many people who think and say "I have nothing" lead a have-not life. And they carry this have-not with them, even into death.

∽

Most people seek the truth and want to get rid of illusions. Zen says, neither *ku* nor *shiki*.

Instead, go from *shiki* to *ku* and from *ku* to *shiki*. Go from thinking to not-thinking and from not-thinking to thinking. This is *hishiryo*-mind. Be flexible. Go with the flow. In the end, abandon even Zen, even Buddhism. And then there's just the ring of the Way, unconsciously, naturally and automatically.

10

If your mind remains tranquil, it vanishes like a dream.

People who practice zazen experience this.

Here are some other translations of the tenth strophe. First, a version by D.T. Suzuki:

If the mind is at peace,
These wrong views disappear by themselves.[9]

The phrase "these wrong views" refers to the preceding strophe, which says:

Do not run after shiki,
Do not dwell on ku.

Translator Richard B. Clarke's version is the best known:

Be serene in the oneness of things,
And such erroneous views will disappear by themselves.[10]

As with the Suzuki translation, it says: if you're calm, if instead of running after things you stay in their oneness, if you are simply One, then erroneous viewpoints will disappear.

Master Sheng-yen's version goes in the same direction:

In oneness and equality,
Confusion vanishes of itself.[11]

---

9 Suzuki, D.T., *Essays in Zen Buddhism* (Rider and Company, 1958).

10 Merzel, *The Eye Never Sleeps* (Shambhala, 1991).

11 *Faith in Mind* (Dharma Drum Publications, 1987).

∽

If your mind remains tranquil, it vanishes like a dream.

Tranquil, here, does not mean amorphous, groggy or asleep, but in the normal condition. Or again, rediscover it, come back to the original state (which of course is "you").

It vanishes . . . "It" means the *bonnos*, the illusions, the problems that we carry about with us. "It" is the mistaken viewpoint, as Sosan says in the previous ninth strophe, the mind's tendency to run after phenomena or dwell on vacuity (we might even say, "on the truth"). And when the mind functions normally, naturally, automatically and unconsciously, this mistaken viewpoint vanishes like a dream.

This, so it is said, is satori.

Master Keizan observed that when "the wind dies down, the ocean disappears." Clearly, he's talking about the mind, or about the similarity between reality and the world of appearances. He also says that, when, in the mountains, "flower petals fall in silence, everything becomes calm and peaceful." So, the wind is calm, the waves have disappeared, and there is nothing and yet everything.

Satori means losing something, losing the mind that thinks and thinks and thinks. The mind that thinks and thinks is a self-conscious mind. It's like wearing a shoe that's too tight. But once the shoe fits, you immediately forget it; you don't walk around saying, "I have a terrific shoe. Why, I don't even feel it!" It's the same with mind.

The same too for satori: you get it when you don't need it. You get it when you already have it.

∽

When the mind returns to the normal condition, it disappears. There is no mind. *Mushin.*

Everyone's true nature is absolute tranquility. It's *because* of this tranquility, and not in order to obtain it, that we practice what we practice. You don't look for fundamental tranquility; you practice it, unconsciously.

Master Dainin Katagiri said that this tranquility is faith. And, naturally, we can actualize it in our lives—in fact we all do it, more or less. But how can we actualize it, or achieve it, outside of practice? Simply by always being in the present moment. *Doshu.* And that's exactly where faith is: in the present moment. Faith is the present moment.

We have certainly all experienced this, even before practicing what we practice. In fact, maybe that's what brings us to practice together: faith in the universe—faith in ourselves, since we are the universe. But the problem is to know how not to lose this faith, how to not be affected by doubts and thinking. There are certain methods in which you count breaths, others in which you concentrate on your koan, still others in which you stop your thoughts once and for all. In any case, it's not like that in this practice. We don't stop anything at all. We don't begin anything, either. But whatever we do, we do it completely.

Faith is the essential force. With faith, you can understand the *Shinjinmei* and all the other Buddhist writings with no problem. Without faith, they're not so easy to understand.

And this is perhaps why so much has been written about Buddhism, though generally from the outside. Yet, in Buddhism, faith has nothing to do with what other religions imagine it to be. In most universal religions, such as Christianity or Islam, God or Allah becomes the object of faith, an object to which people are very attached. And this way, unity is broken. In Zen, faith has no object. It's not faith in God or in Buddha, but faith in oneness, beyond God, beyond Buddha. The object of faith and faith itself are not separate. This is non-duality. It is said in a sutra that faith is "pure awareness." That's what is taught. But whether or not the word "pure" is really understood is another matter. Pure awareness is like *hishiryo*-consciousness.

Pure awareness does not mean suppressing thinking; it's thinking/not-thinking, not-thinking/thinking. It's the normal human condition. It's the "tranquility of mind" that Sosan speaks of.

Perhaps we can establish a similarity between purity and *ku*, emptiness—not the emptiness that contains nothing, but the emptiness from which all things come. People are afraid of emptiness, of *ku*;

they're wary of it. That's why Nagarjuna, the great master and writer of Buddhism, decided to use the word "purity" instead of *ku*.

Master Ippen of the Shin School goes even further than Zen masters on the subject of faith without object. He says, "Faith is only an action of the mind, and therefore subject to corruption." He practiced faith through total abandonment to Buddha Amida. Those who practiced with him abandoned everything and were content to recite the *nembutsu*: *"Namu Amida Butsu, Namu Amida Butsu, Namu Amida Butsu . . ."* They didn't practice zazen, but they did practice recitatism. Ippen taught that one should abandon oneself, not have any mental standpoints, not exert any effort to understand, not try to measure spiritual progress of any kind. For Ippen, religious realization was non-existent. This is all very strong medicine; and indeed it is one way of expressing faith by using the eye of faith. But it's not Zen.

There are several kinds of faith. There's Ippen's faith, which is the most extreme. There's also illusory faith, which we encounter all the time: the irrational devotion of disciples who blindly follow a guru or master. Everything the guru says is true, and if the guru is against something or someone else, so are they.

A kind of distantly admiring faith also exists: believing in the teaching, but considering it to be too elevated, inaccessible. Many people experience this kind of feeling about Zen: "Unfortunately, I'm just not ready."

There's also faith based on understanding: understanding with the rational mind. "Buddhist teaching is logical, therefore I believe in it."

And then, there's faith received through true living experience, that of the practice, beyond rationality, beyond all logic. This is the faith Sosan is talking about. Faith is not something we learn from the outside, but something that comes from the inside, from experience.

∽

At any rate, the tenth strophe says that when the mind is at peace, tranquil, in the normal condition, *it vanishes like a dream*. This means being at peace with things just as they are. Unconsciously, automatically and naturally, things are already One.

Does this mean you should just stand there and do nothing?

No. You can develop faith in mind, faith in the practice, faith in the fact that we all have Buddha inside us. Faith in yourself is faith in others. To do this, you must first give yourself over to the practice—to continuous practice.

In a dojo, in zazen practice, you sit without moving, you experience the world, you experience yourself, without running after things, without running away from anything, without being influenced by your desires. It's knowing or experiencing the truth of being present now. Sitting in zazen is, in my opinion, the highest experience. Through it, you develop faith in human beings. Whatever you see, you see through faith's eyes. Whatever you hear, you hear with faith's ears.

11

If you stop all movement, your mind becomes tranquil,
And afterwards, this tranquility will provoke movement again.

This means that, when you try to stop activity, to become passive or calm, that very effort provokes movement. Here again, Sosan is talking about one's practice. People set their minds on the tranquility of meditation. The wind dies down, and then what happens? *Bonnos* arise more than ever. At that point, new practitioners often wonder what's wrong with them. Elder practitioners consciously or unconsciously understand that illusions appear even more if they try to calm their consciousness. That's one of the differences between beginners and more experienced practitioners of the Way; that is, awareness that nothing is wrong.

In the same way, in the first few years, people try to correct what's wrong by heading towards what's right. But, later on, they're disappointed and often leave the practice, because this "right" that they've tried to set up in their lives has turned out to be wrong.

Master Deshimaru said, "If you want to stop your illusions and attain satori, satori will become an even greater illusion." He also made the following profound observation: "If you start from death and go towards life, that life will be true life. If you want to stop death and you become attached to life, that life will become death."

He also talked about "falling low in order to come back up." Fall into the muddy waters, right to the bottom, and do it with a big exhalation, and that way you can come back up to the surface. He said, "You must die at least once."

When my co-disciples and I became monks, movement stopped, honors were abandoned . . . but soon, the question of the transmission—the shiho—entered our minds, and the tranquility we had known became movement once again. What should we do?[12]

[12] This question arose after the master's death: were we, his disciples, to follow and obey the Soto authorities in Japan, or were we to stay free of them?

The Way of Zen is both easy and not easy. It's like a tree without roots. Hard for some people to accept. It means always cutting away sentimentality, cutting away ideas of well-being, cutting away the duality with which we are continually confronted in our lives and in the practice.

> Master Tozan was walking in the mountains when he came upon an old man doing zazen in a cave.
>
> "Why are you doing zazen this way?" asked Tozan.
>
> The old hermit replied, "There were two cows fighting, two enormous cows, and they were so caught up in their fight that they fell into the sea and were never seen again."

The old man practiced exactly and the two cows disappeared from his consciousness. This is what having no desire means. Nothing, no mind. *Bonno* and satori are illusion. That's why you must not look for one or the other, but go beyond both of them, beyond movement and tranquility.

That's satori, the Middle Way.

12

If you dwell on extremes,
How can you understand One?

Extremes: satori/illusion, good/evil, life/death . . .

Good/evil. If you want to, you can see evil everywhere. For some people, human beings are bad, hypocritical, egotistical. Others, on the contrary, see only good—and those people certainly lead a more pleasant life.

Life/death. On one side: our world, all that is visible, all that is matter. On the other side: all that is invisible, the mind. These categories exist only in our thinking.

We see only this or that; we see only one of the two. We see only the opposition between things, filtered through our opinions and our viewpoints—because extremes, to use Sosan's expression, are also a matter of personal choice.

In Buddha's time, there were sixty-two philosophical schools of thought in existence. They were always in conflict, but they didn't clash; they disagreed, but they never resorted to violence. Today, we kill at the drop of a hat. We kill each other because we're black, white or yellow; we kill each other because we're Hindu, Islamist or anti-Islamist.

Why have we become so stupid, one might ask, or have we always been this way?

∽

In order that we may awaken from our persistent stupor, Sosan suggest that we not dwell on extremes.

This may seem obvious, but it's not easy to practice. Not falling into one extreme or the other, not falling into one way of being or the other, not seeing the world through your own concepts—this is what's hard to do.

Extremes, existence . . . Every human being has his or her own personal way of being, but it often becomes erroneous and dogmatic.

During ordinations, the master shouts, "*Dai ju fuho sanbo kaifu kyaku gen kai!*" so loudly that his face turns purple. It means, "Do not hold personal, erroneous, dogmatic opinions!" It's the tenth *kai*, the last of the monk's ten precepts, all of which come down to us from Buddha's time.

∽

In Buddha's time, the sixty-two schools were divided into two branches: *joken*, which asserted that the soul is permanent, and *danken*, which thought that death is the end of all things. These categories or classifications have always existed. *Joken* means "constant, perpetual, eternal"; it's an optimistic philosophy. *Danken*, on the other hand, means that our behavior in the present, whatever it is, has no influence on our future life.

Kodo Sawaki talked about *joken* and *danken*. He often repeated that Buddhism had nothing to do with these branches. He said—as did all masters of the transmission and Buddha Shakyamuni himself—that Buddhism is beyond that. Buddha, who studied these two ways of thinking (which are called "the two prejudices"), stated innumerable times that neither of them was in any way exact. Nor should we rivet ourselves to a point located halfway between the two. The Middle Way means sometimes going to the right and sometimes going to the left, because the Middle Way includes both.

If we do not dwell on extremes, then we can understand One. The wisdom Sosan is talking about is located in neither one nor the other. We express this wisdom morning and evening in the recitation of the *Hannya Shingyo*. *Maka hannya haramita shingyo* means, "Great sutra of the profound, essential, absolute wisdom that goes beyond."

All the masters of the transmission said that the practice of zazen is the best of all paths. This is not an extreme position, but an expression of the master's spiritual certitude. All the great Zen texts teach this non-doubt or non-hesitation. For example: the *Fukanzazengi* ("The Way is fundamentally perfect"), the *Zazenshin* ("Only zazen is realizing, only zazen is doing"), the *Sandokai* ("The smallest doubt causes a separation as great as the distance between the mountain and the river"), the *Hokyozanmai* ("No error, no doubt: such is the Dharma"), the *Hannya Shingyo* ("For the bodhisattva, thanks to this wisdom that goes beyond, there exists neither fear nor doubt").

The man or woman of the Way should go forward without doubt, without hesitation. Then, body and mind express the Way. If a master said, "The Way that I teach is okay, but there's that other one which is better," he would be a very difficult master to follow. "Master," he would be asked, "why isn't your school the best? Why is the other one better?"

At any rate, being profound in the Way means being profound in every way.

13

If you do not concentrate on the original,
The merits of both extremes will be lost.

The thirteenth strophe, like many other strophes in the *Shinjinmei*, is very difficult to grasp and comment on. We can't understand it with discriminating thinking. We can't understand it through language based on concepts, or by reading books, or by listening to lectures—except perhaps during zazen, when the words of the teaching reach our hypothalamus from the master's hypothalamus. Here is how Kennett Roshi, a British Zen master who taught in England and the United States until her death in 1996, translated this strophe:

If you are not conversant with this oneness of mind,
Both your stillness and your activity lose all their merit.[13]

This translation implies that if you don't understand the profoundness of the Way, then stillness and activity are both failures.

Now here is a translation by the academic Clarke, which is the most widely used version:

Those who do not live in the single Way
Fail in both activity and in passivity, in assertion and denial.[14]

Master Deshimaru's translation uses the expression "the original" instead of "the single Way." Whatever translation you may prefer, Sosan is telling us to concentrate on original mind, the mind from before birth, the mind after the birth of our great-grandchildren. The eternal present.

---

13 Jiyu-Kennett, Reverend Master, *The Journal of the Order of Buddhist Contemplatives* (Mt. Shasta, Calif.: Shasta Abbey Press, 1994, 3).

14 Merzel, *The Eye Never Sleeps*, 128.

When Daibai Hojo was young and practiced with Baso, he was very impressed by a mondo in which he asked Baso, "What is Buddha?"

"*Soku shin soku butsu*—Mind is Buddha," Baso replied.

Hojo had a great satori.

Afterwards, he left Baso and settled on one of the mountains nearby, where he lived as a hermit, almost an ascetic. His only clothing was lotus leaves he had stitched together; his only food, acorns and plums. He practiced alone for thirty years. His only companion was a frog who took to sitting just in front of him when he did zazen. During zazen, Hojo would balance an iron pagoda on his head and had to be careful not to sneeze or cough or fall asleep; otherwise the pagoda would tumble onto his knees, or worse, onto the frog.

One day, Baso asked one of his disciples, "Whatever happened to that nut Hojo?" The disciple replied, "He's sitting all alone somewhere in the mountains. He's still very impressed by what you told him: '*soku shin soku butsu*—Mind is Buddha.'"

"I don't say that anymore. Now I say '*hi shin hi butsu*—No mind, no Buddha.' Go find Hojo and tell him that."

After searching for a month, the disciple found Hojo on Mount Daibai (which means "big plum"), and announced, "Hey, Hojo! Baso doesn't say '*soku shin soku butsu*' anymore. Now he says '*hi shin hi butsu*!'"

Hojo replied, "Baso can say what he likes. He can say 'Mind is Buddha,' or 'No mind, no Buddha,' it makes no difference to me. I'm sticking with 'Mind is Buddha.'"

The disciple went back to see Baso and reported this exchange. Baso was very satisfied and said, "Daibai [the Big Plum] is ripe."

Thus Hojo discovered his original face: he understood that he lacked nothing; so it is said. If you have not followed in the footsteps of a master, how can you know the traceless path?

∽

If you do not concentrate on the original,
The merits of both extremes will be lost.

Both extremes is a reference to the eleventh strophe, which talks about stillness and movement, or inactivity and activity. Concentrating on original mind does not consist of concentrating on these two extremes at the same time. It's really about not stagnating in duality; because if you're stagnating in duality, how can you recognize original mind?

At the end of his commentary on the thirteenth strophe, Master Deshimaru says, "If we are not concentrated, at least during zazen, we remain either in movement or at a standstill . . . Moving and stopping are errors. If we grab on to the two extremes, how can we achieve original mind?"

In other words, activity without tranquility, or inactivity without inner activity is erroneous. Zazen is stillness, but it is not stillness within stillness. It is activity within stillness.

For people who have not been practicing for a long time, it's hard to find activity in stillness, and even harder to find stillness in activity. After a sesshin, for example, many of us dive right back into activity and their minds slip quickly backwards.

Once I read a newspaper interview with a flamenco dancer. He described flamenco as "alternating hyper-agitation and complete stillness." This is not what happens, at least not during zazen. While in zazen, we are neither in hyper-agitation nor in complete stillness. It's not necessary to ruminate on thoughts or imagination. You neither go off to the left or right, nor stay still like a corpse or a sack of rotting flesh, stuck in the middle, as Hakuin would say.

But this does not mean that one should practice both things—movement and stillness—simultaneously. While in zazen, activity is within stillness. However, when we take part in the ceremony, do *gassho* or *sampai*, it's all within activity. Don't do both at once. Zazen during zazen. Work during worktime. So, if one doesn't concentrate on the original, if he stagnates in duality, his practice will not be emptiness that becomes form and form that becomes emptiness. It will just be form, just be emptiness.

∽

Dedicating yourself to two things at the same time is very difficult. Dedicating your life to being a pianist and to being a Zen monk, for example, is not so easy. Of course, one can play the piano and be a Zen monk at the same time. But I'm not talking about that; I'm talking about dedicating oneself to something entirely. I'm talking about the total commitment that makes the Zen practice the center of your life. If your career as a pianist takes the central place in your life, then it's hard to have zazen as the absolute center. I think what one can do, if he has both tendencies (which is the case for most of us), is to find out how to unify them, while knowing all along that the two are really one anyhow.

∽

If you do not concentrate on the original,
The merits of both extremes will be lost.

In order to concentrate on the original, your energy must circulate freely. This energy is called *ki*. To practice the Way, you need powerful *ki*. And to create powerful *ki*, you must not follow your thoughts, not have obstacles or personal thoughts in your head. This is what is meant by "abandon everything," those words so often repeated. And it's all found here between the lines of almost every strophe, especially the early ones.

In an eighteenth-century manuscript on the art of *budo*,[15] there is much talk of *ki*. This manuscript describes how *ki* can be tied up by

15 The *Tengugeijutsuron* (1730).

thinking. The author, martial arts master Chissai, explains how, in the art of *budo*, the person whose *ki* is hampered by overly yin thinking is slow to draw his sword—a grave inconvenience when facing an enemy who's about to cut off your head. But conversely, when *ki* overflows, when it's too intense or too yang, it breaks up into agitation and becomes superficial and inconsistent, making you like "dry leaves swept away by the wind."

We've all had this experience: when the mind has the right attitude, it circulates without obstruction, as opposed to the mind that stagnates, stuck on one thought or another. This mind activity has no beginning and no end, like a river. It is continuous and unique. No simpler movement exists, and it is through this movement that *ki* is developed.

The *ki* in question here is *joriki*. *Jo* means, "the energy which comes from the *hara*"; *riki* means, "solidity," "strength." *Joriki* describes the energy produced by zazen.

Chissai also tells us that heart and *ki* are basically one. And in order for *ki* to be exact, authentic, unconscious, natural and automatic, says Chissan, a transparent heart is necessary, a heart which nothing can darken.

We are talking about the heart—the direct communication, person to person, heart to heart, without anything coming in between. Body and mind thus becomes a channel through which cosmic *ki* circulates—*ki*, which is then no different from *hannya*, wisdom. *Ki* is the mind's ability to react to a spiritual impetus. It's with the *ki* that we need to seek out the spiritual path and stay there. It's a spiritual impulse that we've all felt many times; otherwise, we would never have discovered the Way.

Many people entering a dojo do *gassho* to the statue of Buddha on the altar; some bow to the master's portrait. But the statue is just a piece of wood or metal, the portrait is just a photo. *Gassho* is not so much directed to an object as it is to the human heart—which is also the animal heart, and the God heart as well.

The faith we're talking about is what the masters call "fundamental cosmic energy" or "original mind." So, when you want to concentrate on original mind, you must be completely sincere . . . which is not easy.

> You may have heard the story of the Tibetans, Milarepa and Marpa. Milarepa left Marpa, his guru (that's the term he himself used) to follow someone else. At the time, he didn't have total faith in Marpa and, with the help of Marpa's wife, he stole some documents, various relics, books and images. Then he went to the new guru saying, "Here are some gifts from Marpa, who has given me permission to practice with you."
>
> The new guru accepted Milarepa because of the documents and gifts that Marpa was supposed to have given him. But he very quickly realized that something wasn't quite right with this new disciple. Milarepa was not progressing in the practice. The new guru realized that there was no reason to go on this way and sent Milarepa back to Marpa.

The meaning of this story is that, in the end, when you want to concentrate on true originality—or oneness of mind, or the unique Way—authentic faith is indispensable. And when you lie, cheat or steal, true faith does not exist. The story of Milarepa has therefore to do with true faith, the faith that goes further than God and Buddha, even beyond the words "God" and "Buddha." Faith is the intuition that the truth is present in this very moment. Faith is knowing this—and not through rational thought, but in your marrow, in your blood. Faith is what is lived, what is experienced, what is understood. It is the true understanding that is not found in words, and is not the comparative or erroneous understanding that most people have.

If you do not concentrate on the original,
The merits of both extremes will be lost.

And so, concentrate on the original; that's where true understanding is, where true faith is, where true tranquility is.

∽

Original nature, *the original* that Sosan is referring to in the thirteenth strophe of the *Shinjinmei*, is complete tranquility.

I'm not talking about the tranquility that we all experience, from time to time, when we close the door and feel happy to be home again, alone or with family. That tranquility is short-lived, limited and isolated, and it often shatters as soon as we go out into the world and come up against annoyance, deception and failure. No, here I'm talking about true, unconditional and irreversible tranquility, the kind that a person who is *mushin*—no-mind—feels every day, alone or with others.

Tranquility or original nature, the true self, has nothing to do with the Christian belief that true tranquility is found in God. For Buddhists, it's not a question of God, but of Self. And people who practice the Way of Buddha know that they are not separate from Buddha; they see Buddha within themselves.

This being so, we always come back to the same question: What is mind? Master Dogen says he has no idea . . . Just observe the dew on the grass. Maybe we can say that mind is complete tranquility. Words are never adequate to describe original nature.

∽

How do we obtain what Sosan calls *the merits of both extremes*? We obtain it unconsciously and automatically.

Remember the story of Raisan, the master who farted? He was so concentrated on his sweet potato that he completely ignored the imperial messenger and didn't even stop to wipe his nose. Concentrating on the little details, concentrating on the big ones—it's the same thing. And, Raisan's seeing no reason to wipe his nose is like Hojo's saying, "Mind itself is Buddha." No opposition, no separation. If concentration is natural and non-conscious, the merits of both extremes will not be lost.

Zazen is natural and non-conscious concentration on the original, on One. That's why you should continue zazen—I mean zazen mind or *hishiryo* consciousness—all the time, outside the dojo as well as inside.

All those who have practiced and eventually find themselves confronted with death surely ask themselves, "What was important in my life?" and "What will make me more peaceful when it's time to die?" At that moment, they surely remember zazen: "During zazen, I used my time fully and totally. All the other time—time for work, time for love, time for eating, time for drinking—wasn't really so important."

And why would you ever think of zazen when you're about to die? Perhaps because zazen mind never dies.

14

If you accept only one existence, you will fall into that single existence.
If you become attached to ku, you will turn yourself against it.

This means that, if you stick to phenomena (*shiki*), you'll end up being trapped by them. But if you run exclusively after spirituality (*ku*), you'll become its enemy.

In this strophe, Sosan explains that we must not fall into one of these categories, *shiki* or *ku*, at the exclusion of the other. But this also means that we should not confuse one of these options with reality, as Sosan says in the last strophe of this poem. And we can well understand, this is where the miseries of this world come from—from words. All the misery on this earth comes from words.

You have to study Zen writings to understand *ku*: the emptiness from which all things come, the mind, inseparable from *shiki*, phenomena. Every time the master talked about *ku*, he talked about *shiki*. *Ku sokuze shiki:*emptiness becomes phenomena; and vice-versa: *shiki sokuze ku.*

And so, this strophe talks about *shiki sokuze ku*: the phenomena that become non-phenomena. *Shiki sokuze ku*, but also, *ku sokuze shiki*. In short: don't dwell on phenomena or non-phenomena.

If *ku* is seen as the opposite of existence—in other words, phenomena—it is no longer true *ku*. In the same way, if existence is opposed to *ku*, it is no longer true existence. If light were only light, it would not be light.

The *Sandokai*, composed by Master Sekito, contains this famous verse, which evokes the same principle:

Darkness exists within light,
Light exists within darkness.

This expresses the non-duality of things. Form and non-form, material and spiritual, visible and invisible . . . one that is also the other.

That's why following *ku* is actually going against it. *Ku*: in Sanskrit, *sunyata*. For lack of a better word, it is usually translated as "vacuity." But *ku* is not, for example, the emptiness you might find in a hole. There is no inside or outside. Therefore, *ku* can be seen as God or Buddha, though it is not outside of us.

∽

It is true that the phenomenal world exists. Buddha himself said so. But everything that exists as phenomena exists only through conditions, causes and effects. In other words, phenomena exist, but they have no noumenon, no eternal substance. And *ku* has no noumenon either. There are some people who think that everything is illusion. But if you think that way, you forget that everything is mind. We say, "no substance, no noumenon," but we could just as well say that everything is noumenon. Noumenon can be God or Buddha. Hindus worship a river, the Ganges. Buddhists venerate a tree, the *bodhi* tree. So where is emptiness?

> Gensha was a disciple of Seppo. Tired of hearing Seppo say the same thing all the time, one day he told himself, "I'm going to go see another master." And he left. While walking in the mountains, he badly stubbed his big toe, and he said out loud, "The body does not exist. So where does this pain come from?" And exactly at that moment, Gensha had a great satori. Without hesitating, he went back to see Seppo: no need to change masters.

Existence without noumenon, *ku*, becomes existence. When this realization comes from the body rather than from the head or philosophical discourse or books, then this awakening, this satori, is irreversible.

∽

From the moment you try to express the non-duality of things, One appears. And in fact, this fourteenth strophe talks about One. And also, about not falling into the situation herein described; don't dwell on a single existence.

Here again we touch on the question of faith. Not dualistic faith between God and me, but, as Dogen explained it, faith which is whole, a body.

It may be hard to understand, but it's even harder to express. It is beyond words. Here's an image: a fish swimming in the water. The water is one with the fish. One cannot exist without the other. And so the fish is the water, and the water is the fish. This is the body of faith.

No separation. If you can live this in your guts, in and through your body, you will be deeply tranquil, even in the midst of conflict. Even if you find yourself in hell, inner tranquility will always be there.

15

Even if your words are correct, and your thoughts exact,
It is not in accordance with the truth.

It follows that Master Sosan himself, in composing the *Shinjinmei*, was not in accordance with the truth. And so, even if everything is correct in this poem, even if there is not the slightest error, this is not in accordance with the truth; and in the same way, neither are my commentaries on it.

In strophes fifteen and sixteen, Sosan tells us that Zen—zazen, or if you will, life—cannot be explained in words. In the *Rules for Kosho Ji*, Master Dogen, who wrote more than any other Zen monk ever did, said that books about Zen are unnecessary: you can read all the correct, exact writing on Zen that you like, but it's still not in accordance, says he, with the truth.

In terms of the fifteenth strophe, Master Deshimaru said, "Zen should not talk too much or think too much . . . Reading ten-thousand sutras, ten-thousand books, is completely useless."

This is why *doshu* is very important: how you express the Way. If you think too much, if you talk too much, this does not conform to the behavior of a person of the Way. And the opposite is no better.

Here's the story of Tokujo, the master who became a ferryman, and his disciple, the monk Kassan. One day, they had a mondo on a boat. Kassan spoke well; Tokujo threw him in the water. This happened several times, and each time that Kassan found himself in the water, Tokujo hit him on the head with a pole, saying, "Your answers, even if they are exact, are not enough!" It was like beating farts out of a dead donkey.

This verse is telling us that, however well one articulates one's words or develops one's thoughts, this is still "not in accordance with the truth." But then, what is, finally? Faith, I should think.

To better understand this question of faith, it may be useful to understand the power and subtlety of the subconscious.

In a lecture about sutras, a contemporary Swiss Zen-master Michel Bovay said, "If we are beyond words, we can understand words," adding that it's not necessary to recite the *Hannya Shingyo* in our native language [in this case Swiss German], or to understand it consciously, even though the version we use is written in Kanbun, a mixture of ancient Chinese and Sanskrit. It's the same thing for certain phrases taken from the four vows of the bodhisattva and chanted every day in Zen dojos, such as: *Shu jo muhen seigan do*, which means, "However numerous living beings, I vow to save them all." It's not necessary to translate it from any language—Japanese, Kanbun or other; it is simply chanting with a unified mind, being completely present, without trying to understand what is meant by this with one's brain. That's saving all beings. You can, therefore, say that merely thinking the sutras, beyond words, without thinking, can influence all beings on this earth.

Your subconscious is enough. It influences your consciousness. Your *mushotoku* subconscious understands Kanbun very well, and the French or English translation doesn't interest the *mushotoku* subconscious. The subconscious is not limited by language.

> One day, during a mondo, a young American asked Etienne the godo[16] this question: "What can I do to help my family? Everyone around me is suffering, sick or dying."
>
> "Chant a mantra," he replied.
>
> "Oh no!" the young American cried. "I can't do that in front of my family!"
>
> "You don't have to recite the words," Etienne told him. "Breathe it, that's enough." Hannyatara was the master of Bodhidharma, who was the son of a king from southern India. One day, Hannyatara was invited to eat with the king. "Please, Master, chant us a sutra before the meal." There was a long silence. "Okay, it's

16 Etienne Zeisler, see Glossary.

> over." "How's that possible?" "Every time I inhale, I recite ten-thousand sutras; every time I exhale, I recite another ten-thousand." The king was happy.

This is what abandoning language means. And this brings us directly to strophe sixteen.

16

Abandoning language and thought
Will lead you beyond all places.

Abandoning language doesn't mean not talking anymore, just as abandoning thinking doesn't mean not thinking anymore.

Today, many people think there should be no oral teaching given during zazen. Several years ago in Paris, a disciple rather aggressively insisted that, in ancient times, masters did not talk during zazen. He was supported by a fellow practitioner, who assured me that, in ancient Chinese and Japanese monasteries, disciples didn't utter a word during the three months of summer camp.

Concerning this matter, here's what Master Dogen said during one of the ninety-day summer retreats that he led with one or two of his disciples: "People today say that the ultimate truth cannot be explained in words. Words, they say, put us on the wrong track . . . People today think that monks should remain completely apart from other people.[17] Who says that this ninety-day retreat is a wordless proclamation? Please, show me a true retreat led by Shakyamuni Buddha that was speechless."

Japanese philosophy professor and Zen monk Kazuo Morimoto sent one of my co-disciples an article he had written on the celebrated philosopher Derrida's essay, "*Comment ne pas parler*" ("How to Not Talk").

My friend said to me,

"Can you believe that? A whole piece on how not to talk!" Then he admitted, "I didn't understand a word of it."

I said to him, "Give it to me. I'll understand it."

I read it. I didn't understand a word of it either. It was very complex. Morimoto seemed to be more professor than monk. But the article's conclusion was easier to grasp: "Derrida is seeking to shed light on the

17 The monks were expected to remain in isolation somewhere, and this way keep their mouths shut.

fact that, in the end, we cannot avoid speaking." The last sentence of the article, a quote from Derrida, states that "the real world, without beginning or end, never stops talking about Itself."

Today, there are Zen practices that allow no talking whatsoever. But that's not the Zen we practice here. And anyway, Zen uses everything: words, shouts, gestures, silence, the *kyosaku*, the *rensaku*, whisky, meat and tofu. It's important not to entertain illusions about anything. No ideas at all. *Maku mozo*.

Maku mozo is one of the well-known quotes illustrated on the *kyosaku* stick and it means, "No illusions." The Chinese master Daikaku answered every question with, "*Maku mozo*"—like Gutei, who always answered by holding up his thumb.

Words are necessary; otherwise, there would be no reason for an oral teaching to exist. Language can illustrate, and Zen teaching often uses this technique. But you have to be very careful not to get attached to words, not to take them too literally.

> The emperor liked his prime minister, whose name was Kiyu. Although Kiyu was a little uptight about the purity of speech, the emperor respected him. He performed his ministerial role perfectly and was completely honest. The emperor was elderly and did not want to continue leading his empire. He had a young fiancée and wanted to go off quietly somewhere with her. And so, he thought that Kiyu might take the situation in hand. One day, he summoned him to the palace and told him: "Kiyu, I have known you for a long time. You are very honest and very competent. You are even capable of leading a nation. Therefore, I am considering entrusting my empire to you."
>
> "What? Entrust me with your empire?"
>
> "Yes, I'm telling you Kiyu, you can have it all!"
>
> Kiyu put his hands over his ears and said, "You hurt me with these words, Emperor! Your words have dirtied my ears!" And he headed straight for the river.

> A farmer whom Kiyu knew well was passing by, bringing his cow to market. He got to the edge of the river and saw Kiyu washing out his ears in the water.
>
> "What are you doing there? Why are you washing your ears?"
>
> "Today, I am truly furious. It so happens the emperor wanted to make me his successor. He offered me his empire! My ears have been dirtied, and so I am washing them."
>
> "Rats," said the farmer, "I wanted to let my cow drink from this clear water, and now you've gone and soiled it!"

Words and ideas can imprison people like birds in a cage.

One day, one of Buddha's disciples asked him this question: "Why does an ignorant person make discriminations while a wise person does not?"

Buddha replied, "Because the ignorant person is attached to names, signs and ideas."

For example, the ignorant person thinks that hell is a place where you're punished, and that nirvana is a place where you're blessed. The awakened person, so it is said, understands that these are just states of awareness, manifestations of states of mind. Unfortunately, it's because of this lack of understanding that we witness so many atrocities in the world. People become fanatic about the words of Jesus, or the words of Mohammed. Ironically, if we took away the words of Jesus, I don't know what would be left of Christianity. Yet, I believe that if we took away the words of Buddha, Zen would still exist, exactly as it does now.

∽

So, abandoning language means being beyond words, beyond language itself, beyond all places. Speech/no-speech, thought/no-thought . . . don't stop there. Don't get stuck on anything, taking one side or the other—either words or silence. *Funi*, not-two.

Silent is the cherry blossom
In this early April,
Rose is the color of spring.
Without thought,
The music of the wind in the pines
Plays its splendid melody.

That's satori. It's like a fish swimming in water, or a bird flying in the sky. Here's a poem by Master Dogen:

As the water is clear right through to the bottom,
The fish which swims realizes the fish itself.
As the sky is wide and spreads to infinity,
The bird which flies realizes the bird itself.

Master Deshimaru wrote this poem on the first rakusu he gave me, before my bodhisattva ordination. I had worked with him for hours to translate it from the Japanese, trying to understand what he wanted to express. Many other translations existed, but none of them interested him in the least. I showed him one translation (by F. Franck), which he brushed away, though it was pretty enough:

I see the birds flying in the sky,
They fly on and on
Never reaching the boundary of the sky.

As if the sky had boundaries! That's what our practice is like—beyond all places.

17

If you return to the original root, you touch the essence.
If you follow enlightenment, you lose the original source.

One is expected, at least in the beginning, to look for the roots, and not the leaves. But what is the root, the source? Where is it? Where is the source of a river? The source is in the current. The source is indeed not just here, it is also now.

And what are the leaves? The leaves, contrary to what is usually proclaimed, are satori, nirvana, awakening. Verse seventeen contains the kanji *sho*, which is generally translated as "enlightenment," and also as "shining phenomenon." And those are the leaves. But beware, follow them and you might wind up in a mental hospital. Once I read an article about people who went mad following satori. It was written from a Soto Zen standpoint. And, in fact, Master Deshimaru and Master Dogen are saying the same thing.

During sesshin, after many days of intensive zazen, your mind becomes a little like a mirror in which *ku* is reflected, and *shiki* too, the "shining phenomenon." Yet, this "shining phenomenon" has no influence, because it passes. Everything passes. In a word, "it" passes, there's no more separation.

ᔓ

The root also means the root of our thoughts, which is *ku*. Our thinking comes from *ku*, and sometimes that thinking becomes action. But often, by the time we're into the action, we've forgotten the source.

People make decisions and don't remember them; they make promises to themselves, then forget them; they begin a job and pretty soon they don't know what made them get into it; they make a vow—*the* vow, *kan*—and, little by little, they forget. They forget why they practice.

It's often said that you should forget, forget, forget. Dogen himself said it. But you shouldn't forget everything. The great vow is very important. All buddhas make this vow, and bodhisattvas too.

In the same way, you always hear "*mushotoku, mushotoku,* no goal"—but, within *mushotoku* there's *ushotoku,* goal. Great goals do exist, not just little egotistical goals, like, "I'm going to become a good person. I'll never be angry or jealous again." But goals like, "I'm going to save others from my anger, my judgment, my disappointment." But, little by little, you get distracted, you forget these great goals. You see a couple of trees and think that's the whole forest.

Anyway, we also have to come back to our roots, the roots of our beginning. When we first came to the dojo, we all had a goal. If we practice the right way, this goal, perhaps ill-defined at first, will become more and more precise, more and more defined. Otherwise, how can we do it? How can one continue? *Kan,* the vow, the promise.

It's very difficult to practice for a long time without having secretly made that vow.

18

If you are enlightened in all directions, even for an instant,
It is superior to ordinary ku.

Out of the seventy-three strophes of this long poem, the eighteenth is one of the most complicated, and perhaps one of the most difficult to understand, even for those who've been practicing a long time. That's Buddhism: in the end, it can't be understood.

Unlike many other strophes in the *Shinjinmei*, in which Sosan expresses himself in concrete terms, this strophe may seem somewhat abstract. It deals with *ku*, the void from which all things come. There's no appropriate word for *ku* in English. Sources such as the *Shambhala Dictionary of Buddhism and Zen*[18] translate it as "emptiness." But that's not really correct, because emptiness always carries a sense of "nothing" as opposed to "something," whereas *ku* includes everything, all phenomena (*shiki*), including those of the mind. The void, the *ku* that I'm talking about, is *ku* and *shiki* working together: *ku sokuze shiki*—non-form becomes form; or, if you prefer, non-phenomenon becomes phenomenon; or, even more simply, non-form *is* form, non-phenomenon *is* phenomenon. And, of course, vice-versa: form (phenomenon) is non-form (non-phenomenon).

However, people who don't practice Mahayana Buddhism have a very different idea of *ku*; for the scholar who studies and comments on Buddhism, for example, *ku* is something else. Allow me to observe that, in general, these specialists are looking outward, while people who practice Mahayana correctly are looking inward. If you only look outward, you see only external emptiness and, because of this, you can't see the source of things. It's like the scientist who studies a chair's composition

18 Fischer-Schreiber, Ingrid, Franz-Karl Ehrhard and Michael S. Diener, ed., *The Shambhala Dictionary of Buddhism and Zen*, trans. from the German by Michael H. Kohn (Boston: Shambhala, 1991).

with a microscope and discovers, in the end, that there's nothing—in a chair, not even any substance at all. This discovery—the *ku* of nothing—can lead the thinker to adopt the exteriorized outlook of nihilism. But this is not our teaching, nor is it Buddha's.

Here's what Master Deshimaru says in his commentary on strophe eighteen: "If we look inside ourselves, into our minds, there is no longer *shiki* or *ku*; and all the speeches about *ku*, about Buddha, about the Dharma, all these discussions about Buddhism, are totally ineffective. The issue in Buddhism is to return to the original ego, the original mind, without discussion or language."

So, as long as enlightenment is directed towards external things, you can't see the source of things, and you remain at the level of the "ordinary *ku*," as Master Sosan is wont to say in this poem.

The Japanese *kanji* for this term is *zenku*, which Master Deshimaru defined as "pre-*ku*." Thus, it is necessary to understand that ordinary *ku* can also mean the *appearance* of *ku* or the *thought* of *ku*.

Ordinary *ku* is therefore external, outer emptiness, or, if you prefer, the emptiness of forms exterior to oneself. It is the intellectual (we could say, the mundane void), and not inner, authentic *ku*, the *ku* that really concerns us, the *ku* we should contemplate, the *ku* that includes all other *ku*, and the *ku* that, in the end, is us, since we are everything.

To put it another way: Look inward, and we go beyond the emptiness of the things of this world.

∽

If you lack adequate self-knowledge—so it is said—you will understand only the ordinary and not the authentic. On the other hand, if you are *enlightened in all directions, even for an instant*, it is superior to every appearance (of *ku*), every thought (of *ku*).

If you are enlightened in all directions: in other words, inside as well as outside. In his commentary, Master Deshimaru says, "You must not reduce your problems to ego, hate, love, ugliness, beauty, notions of big, small, dark, light [...] You should not see them from the outside with a dualistic vision, but in all directions, within yourself."

And thanks to this inner vision—thanks to this authentic *ku*, which enables us to open our eyes to see directly what being is—the small self dissolves in an instant, and we can see being in its entirety; we can see it here and now, because it's the reality of the moment that is being transmitted. Indeed, there is no other reality: we do not exist in the past, or in the future. And so, as Sosan puts it in the sixty-fourth strophe, one instant becomes ten-thousand years.

This also means that the transmission from Buddha and Bodhidharma exists outside of time and space. In Zen practice, we have the essential expression *i shin den shin*: from heart-mind to heart-mind. "From my soul to your soul." And that's what has been transmitted down to our time. You can't get ordained by mail-order. Although you are given a kesa or rakusu at that moment, it's not the actual cloth that's being transmitted; although the *ketsumyaku* you receive at that moment is only paper, though it is written in red, which symbolizes the blood and the body—in other words, it comes from the inside, from heart-mind, and not from anything else.

True Buddhism did not begin with external things: special robes, sutras or other writings; it began when man first looked inside himself. That was the beginning of the practice of the Way. And with the arrival of Bodhidharma in China late in the sixth century, this inner regard began to develop through a physical, human practice—body to body, body-mind to body-mind.

19

Change in ordinary ku
Requires the birth of illusions.[19]

Ordinary *ku* is *ku* that is exterior to us. We could actually say false *ku*—false, because it is dependent on the changing conceptions created by our personal consciousness. Thus, *change in ordinary ku requires the birth of illusions* means that ordinary *ku* is a *ku* that depends on our illusions, in other words, on language and thought.

Whether we use English, French or Sanskrit, as soon as it's about *ku*, it becomes ordinary *ku*. Same thing if we say or think *ku*: it becomes illusion. Why? Because our personal consciousness is once again creating categories.

It's like wanting to think *hishiryo. Hi* is "beyond" and *shiryo* is "thinking." When you try to do it deliberately, "thinking beyond thinking" becomes an ordinary, even a speculative, way of going about it.

Once, during a summer retreat with Master Deshimaru, a professor came up to me and said, "I understand everything the master is saying. *Ku, mushotoku*—it's easy. But I haven't grasped *hishiryo* yet. Could you please explain it to me?"

Impossible. All explanations are necessarily limited to the domain of concepts; they are, of course, changeable, since they are created by us. But, they still come from our small minds.

∽

Change in ordinary ku
Requires the birth of illusions.

---

19 Richard B. Clarke's translation: "The changes that appear to occur in the empty world, We call real only because of our ignorance."

As was just said in the above opening lines, all our personal coming and going, all our stories of love or failure in love, everything we think is real and that we get attached to—all of that requires the birth of illusions.

In the Zen world, it's fairly common for disciples to want to get out of their attachment to existence—which they put in the same category as visible phenomena—and move towards the idea of non-existence. But being attached to this supposed invisible non-existence, this *ku*, of emptiness, and telling yourself, "that's where true wisdom is," is still the ordinary, false thing. This, then, would be only the appearance of emptiness, the idea we form of it. And according to strophe nineteen, we get stuck in this appearance.

> From 1971 to 1982, Master Deshimaru taught every day at a Zen dojo on the rue Pernety in Paris's 14th arrondissement. One day, as I was leaving the dojo, I met a Rinzai monk. I didn't know he was Rinzai, but he was very impressive-looking—big and strong, his face clear and direct. He wore the full monk's habit—black kolomo, white kimono—and other things too, belts and sashes. I can still see Master Deshimaru coming out of the dojo and catching sight of this spectacle. His reaction was completely different from mine. He looked at the monk severely and made him come to his room. I saw that he wasn't pleased, but I didn't really understand what was going on.
>
> The next day, Master Deshimaru talked about this monk in the *kusen*, saying that he had understood nothing about Buddhism, never mind Zen. Then, he spoke directly to us in these terms: "You must have confidence in yourselves and not only follow form. You must understand more deeply than other monks. You must not make mistakes. If someone wears a monk's robe, you should not make assumptions based on his appearance. If someone lives in a monastery, you should not follow him in his error, influenced by the

> size of the monastery." This Rinzai monk, all decked out in a special *kolomo*, with a special belt and straw sandals, certainly seemed to proclaim authentic *ku*. But, apparently, there was nothing authentic about it. In any case, Master Deshimaru never put stock in appearance or age or clothes, but in what is invisible, ageless and permanent. For him, all the rest was just illusion.

All the masters tell us that we shouldn't be taken in by the appearance of things. And so, we learn not to rely on images, even subtle ones; otherwise, we'll think they coincide with the objects we're trying to represent. But an image is only an image, and in the end it represents nothing—nothing but ordinary *ku*. It can't capture Buddha-nature, which is in each of us, and which has no image or face.[20]

Maybe that's why Soto Zen attaches no importance to images or statues, such as a Buddha statue on an altar. Just as Buddha asked his disciples not to worship his person, so we do not worship Buddha or the master. When we do *gassho* towards the altar when entering and leaving the dojo, it's not for the statue of Buddha, or for the photos of the master. So, what are we doing *gassho* to? We do *gassho* to what is highest in us—that is, the human heart.

ᔓ

In his commentary on strophe nineteen, Master Deshimaru wanted to show the difference between ordinary *ku* and authentic *ku*, or impermanent *ku* and permanent *ku*—a difference that the strophe itself does not entirely elucidate. To illustrate this, he compared Hinayana consciousness (that of the Small Vehicle, which adheres above all to following the rules and precepts) and Mahayana consciousness (that of the Great Vehicle, which does not confine itself to rules, precepts and

20 Then the Blessed One addressed the bhikkhus, saying: "Behold now, bhikkhus, I exhort you: All compounded things are subject to vanish. Strive with earnestness!" See http://leedsbuddhistcentre.org/the-last-days-of-the-buddha/

sutras, to speeches and lectures, but only extends to Buddha-nature, which is unlimited, infinite and inexplicable.)

So, it can be deduced by this, that between what is relative, changeable, based on a viewpoint connected to specific places, customs, political circumstances and time periods; and what has been perpetuated until now without change—is the authentic essence that has survived to this day.

The difference between ordinary *ku* and authentic *ku* is like this: Times change constantly, as does the surface of Buddhism. Take for example the attitude towards women in the sangha. In the ancient times of primitive Buddhism, this attitude was completely different from what it is today. "Now that women have [the right to enter the homeless life]," said Shakyamuni Buddha, "the holy life will not last long, the true Dharma will last for only five-hundred years."[21] These ideas, which may seem shocking today, were formed in a particular context and related to the moral constraints of the period. It should be noted, however, that despite Buddha's reluctance to accept women into the sangha, he was nonetheless the very first spiritual leader to do so. After his death, women were, in fact, quickly excluded again. Over the centuries, they have been by turns admitted and rejected.

And so, if authentic *ku*, this essence I'm talking about, keeps the image or tone of ancient times or the morality of past eras, it's only ordinary *ku*; it's only the surface of things. It has nothing to do with the authentic mind that has come to us without change.

∽

If one establishes a parallel between ordinary *ku* and Hinayana, it's because Hinayana Buddhism holds to the idea that we must do precisely what is said in the sutras.

I think that, when Buddhism gets stuck on the words pronounced by Buddha 2,500 years ago, the ordinary Buddhist today is not taking

---

21 Schumann, H.W. *The Historical Buddha* (London: Penguin/Arkana,1989).

into account the fact that life in India at that time was very different, and that the first rules, the precepts, were adapted to the mentality of the people of that precise time period and that particular continent.

In Buddha's time, people lived outdoors, survived by begging, and did many other things that are no longer done today, such as contemplating corpses in cemeteries.[22] The monks of Buddha's sangha were very rude, primitive in their manners, and even obtuse. They had to be educated, which is why rules were established that were much stricter than those of today. Besides the fact that Buddha was not in the least satisfied with their behavior, he also had to take into account the reaction of the villagers, who called the monks sitting in zazen "those dumb pigs." So, he told his disciples that, when they assembled, they should recite the rules he had formulated for them. That's what they did, and it greatly impressed the ordinary people—more than seeing them sitting in zazen. The rules forbidding the consumption of alcohol, for example, were established because one or two monks were found dead-drunk in the village. But it's ridiculous to take that and proclaim today, "You shouldn't drink alcohol. Buddha said so!"

Here's an image from the *Shobogenzo*: a samurai on a boat inadvertently drops his sword into the water. He immediately takes out a knife and marks, on the edge of the boat, the exact spot where the sword fell, so he can find it again later.

This is a metaphor for ordinary *ku*. When the samurai marks the edge of the boat to show the spot where he should be able to find the sword, it's his personal consciousness acting, which doesn't take into account the passing of time, the water, the ever-changing river. Looking for a sword in water using a mark made on the edge of a boat is the same thing as saying, "Buddha said it 2,500 years ago, so it's still the truth." It's impermanent, ordinary *ku*.

The point is, if it's not experienced personally, if it's not lived firsthand, then it's not the zazen of the present moment.

---

22 Mahakasyapa, Buddha's first disciple, was known for this. Contemplating corpses was part of his teaching, called "The Thirteen *Duthangas*," the life of a beggar, a simple life.

Many current masters, even Zen masters, follow the sutras to the letter: "Buddha said this, so we must do it." They say they practice the pure teaching of Buddha. They recommend, for example, abstaining from alcohol and cigarettes. And what's more, monks are totally celibate, otherwise they're excommunicated. They also conduct prolonged fasts, and when they allow themselves to eat, it's always vegetarian, also on pain of severe reprisal and even banishment.

Near the end of the last decade, the International Zen Association received a letter from a disciple of a very famous Zen master. It was a "message for the new century." It told us that we—that is, especially the Deshimaru sangha—should abandon drinking and smoking and learn to live simply in our daily lives; this way, even we could heal and fulfill our ideal of compassion.

In our sangha, we don't allow any alcohol during sesshin, and outside of that, you shouldn't drink too much anyway; do as Dogen says in the *Fukanzazengi*: "Eat and drink simply. Reject all commitments and abandon all business. Do not think, 'this is good, this is bad.' Do not take sides for or against."

> During a recent summer retreat at La Gendronnière Temple, a young practitioner asked me if I could establish a separate table for vegetarians, since "people were fed up with people who always eat meat."
>
> "Always eating meat?" I replied. "But how's that? There wasn't any meat at all." "What do you mean there wasn't any!"
>
> Yesterday, he had found a tiny piece of *lardon*, ham, in his soup.

None of this has any importance. It's the inside you have to develop and deepen, not the surface of things, not to be the ordinary man or woman; it's the inner resolution we have made in secret, the *kan*. *Kan* means not getting stuck on a *lardon* (or more broadly, on being a vegetarian). This way, you can live authentic *ku*, the essence. This essence came through Bodhidharma, passed through Eka, Sosan, Eno, Nyojo,

Dogen, Keizan, Kodo Sawaki, Taisen Deshimaru and his disciples, and has come to us today—this essence which is nothing other than Buddha-nature.

And this transmission of Buddha-nature, which is not ordinary *ku*, this essence directly lived by Bodhidharma, did not stay locked up in India,[23] as many a believer asserts; it did not remain fixed in time; it was not content simply to go from Kapila, Buddha's birthplace, to Kuchira, where he died. On the contrary, it went through all the patriarchs, all the changes of time, all the changes of place, without changing one iota.

By comparing Hinayana and Mahayana, I think that one can say that Mahayana—that is, Bodhidharma sitting with no goal—perpetuates Buddha-awareness with exactitude. It's the experience that we have in the here and now. Mahayana, as opposed to Hinayana, is therefore the direct realization of the Buddha-nature that Bodhidharma speaks about; a realization that is inexplicable and does not depend on the birth of illusions or on changeable concepts created by our personal consciousness.

Only that which is ordinary can be explained; the essence of things—unlimited and infinite Buddha-nature—is inexplicable.

---

23 and China and of course Japan.

20

Do not seek the truth;
Simply be free from prejudice.

You might consider this strophe as a mantra to protect your mind. And if you do what it says—if you don't seek the truth and you stay free of prejudice—you're protecting not only your own mind, but everyone else's as well.

Anyone who has practiced zazen for two or three years or who has received the monk's or nun's ordination knows this. It's not hard to understand: we should stop seeking the truth; otherwise, we're heading straight for a dead-end, and without any means to back out. And, we also know perfectly well that prejudice is not a good thing.

But even people who have been ordained for twenty, thirty, forty or a hundred years do not always know how to put these instructions into practice. For example, you often hear, "Don't run after anything." But, once again, it's easy to say; and yet, suddenly to stop running after things is not the answer either.

Generally, in life, you run after illusions like happiness and success. You run after phenomena, *shiki*. You run after women, you run after men. You run after sex, love, family, money, power. And if you don't run after these base illusions, you run after other ones that you think are the truth. If you're not chasing women, you're chasing *mu*—nothing. It's the same.

In Zen, we like *mu* and we run after it in one way or another. You do zazen and use it as a method or a means not to run after illusions. You observe and observe and observe yourself. But if you can't manage to really forget yourself, then you fall into the opposite trap. You say to yourself, "Now I understand: nothing exists. I'm like Buddha: *mu*. When I do zazen, I'm in absolute, true reality."

> So, the master asks his disciple, "How's it going? How are you feeling today?"
>
> Disciple: "I'm fine. I'm nothing."
>
> Master: "Oh yeah? Nothing?"
>
> Disciple: "Yep. Nothing. What do you think, Master?"
>
> Master: "Drop all that nonsense!"
>
> Disciple: "How can you ask me to drop 'that nonsense' when I just told you I already have?"
>
> Master: "Well, in that case, you still have to throw it away."

Neither seek the truth nor flee from lies, because, from a higher point of view, even the truth is prejudice and illusion.

The masters of the transmission insist on telling us that existence is only a phenomenon that comes from the cosmic system, and that truth and illusion are just two shadows in a mirror. And these two shadows, the shadow of truth and the shadow of illusion, come from our personal consciousness. Your desire becomes a vision—my desire, my vision, my shadow . . .

The master wants us to be neither with *mu* nor without *shiki*. He wants us to understand that thoughts in themselves are not a burden; but, running after them, or running away from them, even a little bit, becomes a big burden, which completely obscures the practice of the Way.

To seek the truth, you have to go from thought to thought; and going from thought to thought—to use an image from ancient Zen—is like leaving your house and going where "the grass grows," the grass of your thoughts. Zen masters are always telling us to let our thoughts pass. Today, and a thousand years ago, they were saying the same thing, always the same thing: "Don't complicate your life, go directly to the source." At that time, they often used the terms "east, west, north and south." Master Tozan said, "You must go neither west nor east, but rather head straight towards the place where, for ten-thousand miles, not a single blade of grass exists." "Go neither west nor east" means we should abandon ourselves, and our awareness, which is steeped in prejudice.

In strophe fifty-nine of the *Shinjinmei*, Sosan refers to *hishiryo*. It's the first time in the history of Zen that this word appears. *Hishiryo* means thinking not-thinking/not-thinking thinking. If you do this, says Sosan, your mind won't even have time to create prejudice.

People who live at La Gendronnière Temple say, "Come to La Gendronnière, it's better than Paris, it's better than Berlin, better than Amsterdam!" Well, that's not true. Other people say the opposite: "Paris is better than La Gendronnière. There are more activities, a lot of lectures on Buddhism. And the traffic jams and pollution aren't so bad; they make us stronger!" This is also not true. Some people are looking for heat and go to the tropics; others are looking for cold and go to the North Pole. They say the heat, or the cold, is good; or the opposite—they want to avoid one or the other.

> One day, a disciple asked the master, "When it's cold or hot, what should I do to avoid the cold or the heat?"
>
> The master replied, "Why don't you go where it is neither cold nor hot?"
>
> At this point, the disciple could have had satori, but such was not the case, and he insisted. "Where, master, is this place that is neither cold nor hot?"
>
> The master replied, "In winter," the master replied, "let the cold kill you. In summer, let the heat kill you."

That's what not seeking the truth and not being prejudiced means. No need to escape the heat, no need to escape the cold; no need to escape unhappiness to look for happiness. It's *sandokai*: *san*, "difference"; *do*, "equality"; *kai*, "meeting" or "conjunction." It's being intimate with everything. And we cannot teach, we cannot give or receive, if we are not capable of becoming intimate with everything, including pain and suffering. That's the beginning of the practice and the source of compassion.

Zen teaching, the practice of zazen, is the greatest intimacy that exists.

But you won't find this intimacy if you're looking outward (and we're almost always looking outward), because then the light emanating from you is focused exclusively on your personal desires. In the end, the house is dark.

So, the sage, who doesn't run away from or chase after anything, is always trying to change people's awareness, their way of seeing things. He says, "Turn this light inward, naturally." And if people are listening, and are willing to practice, their minds turn around, completely and effortlessly. Because, although it may require practice, looking inward with your mind requires no effort at all; it's not like turning a crank or climbing a pole using your muscles.

One single look: Gutei's thumb.

∽

"Be in harmony with the cosmos," Master Deshimaru often said. "Being in harmony with the cosmic system is true wisdom," he says, in his commentary on strophe twenty. But egoism and individualism are obstacles to this harmony, this wisdom, this satori, because it's the small mind that runs after the truth, not the cosmic mind, not the great mind that Sosan is talking about, and in which you must have faith. That mind never runs after anything.

Neither for nor against. Like nature: *inmo*—just this. That's true wisdom, true freedom.

Simply be free in the present moment; in other words, not attached to what's happening here and now, what's happening within change. And everything is change.

It is said that as soon as you're free within impermanence, as soon as you become intimate with *mujo*, you're practicing the Way of the masters and patriarchs.

In the dojo at La Gendronnière Temple, there's a wind-bell hanging from the beam just next to the master's seat; it's called a *furin*. Master Nyojo, Dogen's master, wrote a poem on this subject:

The furin hangs in the sky, in the cosmos;
It is free.
When the wind comes from the East—

Okay, it rings, ding, ding, ding…
When the wind comes from the West—
Okay, it rings, ding, ding, ding…

It's another way of saying:

Do not seek the truth;
Simply be free from prejudice.

21

Do not dwell on opposites.
Do not seek out dualism.

This strophe warns us against getting stuck on a relative viewpoint. No duality, no preferences. That's a leitmotif in Zen. You find it everywhere, in all the poems, all the writings.

Buddha, Zen ... it's all very simple. But lapse into dualism, lean to one side or the other, and Buddhism becomes very complicated. So, keep away from ideas of left, right, correct, incorrect, good, bad, me, you. Don't run after the truth; don't be attached to One, don't be attached to Buddha-mind, to zazen or to the posture. I remember one female disciple who was always saying, "It's the posture that interests me. I only feel good when I'm in the posture. All the rest is of no concern to me." This woman is no longer practicing today.

Running after the posture is no different than trying to get away from noise—that, too, is a preference. "Shunning noise," said Obaku one day, "is like throwing out the flour when making bread." True silence has nothing to do with the idea of escaping noise. True silence is when your thoughts go away—because thoughts are not quiet. Most of the time, even if you're not talking, even if your jaw's not moving, the words keep coming.

Here's a poem by Master Deshimaru:

In silence, immortal silence swells.
Joy comes without speaking.

∽

Do not seek out dualism.

Historically, there's been a lot of talk about duality. Shankara, a great eighth-century Hindu master, founded the School of Non-Dualism.

Its philosophy stated that only One exists. Other schools supported the theory of pure dualism, saying that One cannot exist without Other, that a river needs two banks, that a baby needs a man and a woman in order to be conceived.

Today, we see everything through the prism of dualism: good, evil, right, wrong, object, subject . . . For the ordinary mind in the ordinary world, this kind of dualistic thinking can be necessary. I was once asked if observing was a dualistic act: "Isn't observing necessarily observing someone or something else?" was the question.

> Early on in my Zen practice, I invited a friend to come to the Pernety Dojo in Paris. She was a psychologist—very curious, very intellectual. At the time, very little was known about Zen and zazen in Europe, and psychologists in general were suspicious. When she came, I was *kyosaku*, which meant I sat facing the others and got up to correct people's postures. So, I saw that it was very hard for this woman to keep looking inward during zazen. She wanted to see what the other people were doing. She was sitting facing a window and was looking at the other people in the reflection in the glass, to be able to come away with a pre-conditioned notion of the place and the people. And during the mondo, she looked at the person asking the question, she looked at the master, she looked at the other people's faces, she studied their reactions and noted them down in her mind for later. Actually, due to the grandly unusual events unraveling before her Judeo-Christian vision—sitting motionless in front of the wall with fifty or sixty others dressed in black, chanting together the Heart Sutra in Kanbun, and listening to the strange Japanese master in *mondo*—she was really wondering if she hadn't gotten mixed up in a suspicious sect, and if we weren't all a little nuts.

Some people practice subject-object duality, in which observing is a completely dualistic act. But for the person who has deeply integrated the practice into his or her life, observing is not necessarily a dualistic act. Observing is just observing. The person who observes is just observing, the person who hears is just hearing. The observer is *ku*. The hearer as well. *Ku* is the Way, the cosmic truth. From this non-dualistic state of mind, true creativity and humor can spring forth naturally. With non-duality, your mind becomes quick, keen and, at the same time, calm.

I've seen a number of social activists come through the dojo. People who want to save the world. They usually get frustrated with zazen. They say that, at least as activists, they're doing something, instead of sitting around facing the wall. This said, some people who work for the betterment of the world are completely sick themselves. And that's no way to help. It's better to adopt a non-dualistic outlook: by helping even just one person, even myself, I'm taking care of life in its totality. Because one person is all people.

This goes back to the Buddhist idea of *bodaishin*, Buddha-mind. It's not an individual mind, but the universal mind. Buddha-mind penetrates you and me—it's *ho ten*, the Dharma changing me, as opposed to *ga ten*, my ego changing the Dharma. It's like wearing the *kesa*. The Dharma is the Buddha-mind that changes me, changes you, changes us, changes the whole world.

In Zen, to talk about this mind, we have the metaphor of the moon reflected in water. The moon shines on the water of the lake, the wind blows in the pines. A poem from the *Sanshodoei* by Master Dogen says,

Without muddiness
In the water of the mind,
Clear is the moon. Even the waves break against it
And are changed into light.

Observing is just observing. If you just observe, just listen, just see, you cannot be disturbed; nothing exists that is separate from Buddha-mind or that can perturb you. Then, "even the waves break against it and are changed into light."

∽

Do not dwell on opposites.
Do not seek out dualism.

Master Dogen used to say, "When opposites arise, *bodaishin* is lost."

In the West, God and the ego are separate, whereas Zen is based on the harmony of the ego with everything that exists—with humanity, but, more profoundly, with Buddha. "Buddha" has a vast significance. It means not only Shakyamuni Buddha, not only the buddhas of the past, or the future buddha, Maitreya, but also, the mind of every great master right down to the present time. Practicing zazen is becoming Buddha. If you manage to let your thoughts pass, you notice this Buddhahood. You notice it when you stretch your spine, when you pull in your chin.

Bodaishin is Buddha-mind concentrated in the ego in the present moment. It's Buddha in each of us, here and now.

So, no duality between Buddha and the ego. Without *bonnos*, the illusions of your ego, you cannot know awakening.

It's hard for people who doubt to accept the idea that we are One and that the ego is in unity with the cosmos; but, deep down, you have to have the certitude that you, I and the cosmos have one and the same root (in Zen, as you know, we're not interested in the leaves, but in the roots); and this certitude is faith in mind, which is not-two—*funi*.

If your mind separates you from Buddha (or God, if you prefer)—which is frequently the case—it is no longer the mind of faith that I'm talking about. And remember, it's not a matter of faith in *something*—in yourself or in Buddha—but faith without object. This is exactly the attitude of *mushotoku*: no object, nothing to obtain. If the slightest notion of gain exists, the obstacle in your consciousness becomes very large.

∽

One translation of the *kanji* "zazen" is "two people on one zafu." Two opposites becoming a unity. The first time I heard this, I was very surprised; but today it seems perfectly obvious: of course there are two people. Two minds—little mind and big one. "Two people"—this also means you are not alone, but alone with others. You are completely alone; you are born alone and die alone, and this practice with others is just that, to rediscover this solitude among others; and, from there, we can be together intimately. Our practice is to be with others in silence, in *ku*, in nothing.

This zazen of not-two makes everything that is hesitant, vague or indecisive in your mind and your life disappear. Your concentration becomes strong and sharp, naturally and effortlessly. And from this two that becomes One (and not even One—because Zen, starker than all other paths, ends up rejecting non-duality too), wisdom flows.

22

If you still have the slightest notion of right or wrong,
Your mind will sink into confusion.

This strophe simply means that, from the moment there is right or wrong, there is confusion. I would add that, from the moment there is right or wrong, there is doubt—self-doubt. And because of these doubts, we adopt definitive positions: "I'm for, I'm against," "This is good, that's bad," "There's a man of satori! That other guy is really pathetic."

> A wandering practitioner said to a master one day, "I only believe in ancient Ch'an."
>
> "What do you mean by ancient Ch'an?" asked the master.
>
> "I had satori on my own," replied the wandering practitioner, "not through zazen, not at all through the practice. I had it by myself, directly from the cosmos, with no intermediary. I've been going from place to place, looking for a Zen master who could confirm my satori, but unfortunately, I haven't found one."
>
> The master in question, an authentic master of the transmission, replied, "I myself have not had satori. So, how can I certify you?"
>
> The wanderer, who knew everything, was suddenly filled with confusion.

∽

It's a mistake to choose too much. And anyway, bad can become good. One morning in the Paris Dojo, for example, there was no *genmai*, because the person in charge of it was on vacation. No problem: we were able to do zazen a little longer.

Don't choose. Choosing is an obstacle that blocks you from entering the Way. *Genmai*? No *genmai*? What does it matter?

The world of transmigration, *samsara*, is not only the world after death; it also functions in this very lifetime, precisely because of this choosing. That's why we're always coming back to the posture, to the exhalation, to observation: with zazen, our personal consciousness, the one that chooses, can tire itself out and leave room for cosmic consciousness. It is said that, at this moment, cosmic awareness and the ego merge.

23

Two depends on One;
But do not be attached, even to One.

All dualities come from One; so drop that too. Don't even hang on to unity.

In Christianity and most other religions, there is One, the Absolute, God. But in Buddhism we don't worry about this question: God, no God . . . If you believe in God, that's fine. If you pray to God, that's fine. But while you're sitting with others, facing the wall, don't get stuck on anything, not even on God.

At this time, we're in one thing, then another. This is normal. We're concentrating, but we don't stay with concentration—we also move on to observation. During zazen, the hypothalamus (instinctive brain) opens up, but we also have a frontal brain, and we go from one to the other. For it's impossible to experience both phases simultaneously, any more than you could inhale and exhale at the same time. First one, then the other.

Staying with One, whatever that One is (and there are all kinds of Ones), means grabbing onto something, tying up your hands and feet. Almost everyone is hanging on to something: an idea, or even onto God, the highest One; but it's the same—it's still stagnating on a thought.

Your mind doesn't need a set of tracks. It's not a railroad. Swami Prabhavanda said, "If living by rule alone ensures excellence, if it be virtue strictly to follow the rules, say then, who is a greater devotee, a holier saint, than a railway train?"[24] No, the mind should be more like water, which flows freely and effortlessly. We don't practice to win or lose, to get to the next station or get away from the previous one, but to go deeper into the Way.

---

[24] Isherwood, Christopher. *My Guru and His Disciple* (New York: Farrar, Straus, Giroux, 1980).

Master Fuyodokai said, "*Shukke* [literally, 'home-leavers'] should despise the dirty work of the mind [the small mind, obviously], be beyond life and death, stop the activity of the mind and reject all complicated relationships."

Because, in the final analysis, what's important in this practice (and, in everyday life as well) is not to let your mind get stuck on anything. This way, you develop a light mind, free and detached. This doesn't mean indifferent; on the contrary, when you're not attached to One, compassion can appear.

"Even if a voice or a color seduces you, you must be like someone who plants flowers in stone," adds Fuyodokai. In other words, don't grow roots.

Zen Buddhism "specialists" think we want to become One—one with flowers, for example, one with everything that is One. But that's not exactly so; it's not Dogen Zen, and it's not the Zen we practice in the Deshimaru sangha. If we want to become One, it's a matter of personal will, and that's not the authentic teaching, that's not being led by the cosmic system. In fact, in Rinzai, they even say, "When you see Buddha, kill him," which means, "Don't hold an illusory belief in a Buddha outside of yourself."

Don't be attached to Buddha or to yourself. Don't be attached to One, either. This is absolutely Zen teaching: neither two—neither the right head nor the left head, neither good nor evil—nor One. In other words, not even the middle head, not even One, not even cosmic mind, not even God, not even Buddha.[25]

∽

Two depends on One;
But do not be attached, even to One.

[25] "I beg you," says Fuyodokai in his Gion Shogi, "throw away the two heads, and the middle one as well."

Here, *Two* means *shiki*, phenomena, substance; *One* means *ku*, emptiness. But *ku* is not oblivion. *Ku* is like the light that creates all colors, contains all colors, is all colors, but does not take on a single hue.

The passage often cited from the *Hannya Shingyo—ku sokuze shiki, shiki sokuze ku*—is usually translated as "emptiness equals phenomena, phenomena equal emptiness." I have always found this idea of equality superficial. With this interpretation, you could easily fall into a kind of nihilism—thought bereft of meaning. However, if one understands that *ku* is not equal to *shiki* and *shiki* is not equal to *ku,* but that *ku* is in itself *shiki,* then, one can understand that things—*shiki*—therefore, can be neutral, but are not necessarily nothing; and yet, their essence is always *ku.*

So, don't be attached to things: to the earth, rocks, rain, sun . . . Don't be attached to existence or non-existence, don't hold onto the slightest notion of material and non-material, or Dharma and non-Dharma.

Of course, differences exist; and, of course, similarities exist. But don't be attached to either difference or similarity, and don't even protect One.

24

If no mind appears,
Phenomena will be free from error.

Strophe twenty-four is the continuation of strophe twenty-three.

If no mind is created or realized or manifested by thinking, or even by non-thinking, then, there is no error. We could also say that, if no dualism and no monism are created, then there is no error. Or, if nothing is created, then there is no error.

Scholar R.H. Blyth translates the first line of this strophe as, "When the mind is one and nothing happens . . ."[26] "Nothing happens" is not an expression used in Zen practice, and besides it has a nihilistic connotation. But we can also understand it as the fundamental truth that "nothing increases, nothing decreases." This is undivided mind: there's nothing missing and nothing extra.

Sometimes, putting things into different words makes them easier to understand. So, I have tried to reformulate strophe twenty-four in various ways:

If the mind is not set in motion,
Phenomena show no flaw.

Or,

When the mind functions on the Way, without disturbances,
nothing in this world can throw it into error.
And when nothing can throw it into error,
phenomena cease to exist, or do not exist in the same way.

---

26 Blyth, R.H., *Zen and Zen Classics,* Vol. 1 (Tokyo: The Hokuseido Press, 1960, 73).

Or,

When the mind does not appear,
The ten-thousand dharmas are flawless.

Or, even better,

The ten-thousand dharmas are no longer troubled.

Or,

When the mind is unified, without being attached to anything,
The ten-thousand things are harmless.

Or,

When you no longer have even the idea of mind,
Then, there is nothing lacking or extra in this universe.

And finally:

When your mind is no longer disturbed,
The ten-thousand things no longer need to be rejected.

∽

This strophe is easy enough to understand. The mind that is set in motion is small mind: the one, for example, that lives only in the past or the future, or knows only success or failure. It's the mind that follows its thoughts. And when thoughts come up, the imagination starts working and *bonnos* appear.

> A samurai came to visit a Zen master to ask him a question that had been tormenting him for a long time. Naturally, this samurai didn't practice zazen, but the

way of the sword. His question seemed completely sincere.

"What is hell?" he asked the Zen master.

The Zen master told him he didn't feel like answering that question right now.

"Why not?" asked the samurai.

"Because you're too stupid."

"What do you mean, too stupid?"

"You're too stupid. You wouldn't understand."

The samurai was offended. He was probably imagining what his lord, the shogun, would think if he saw him just then. So, he tried to ask his question again, but the master cut him off.

"What could you possibly understand? You're a cardboard samurai! A loser!"

At that point, the samurai really got mad. "And you! What are you? A good-for-nothing parish priest! A boot-licking Buddha-lover!"

"You're just a coward!" laughed the Zen master.

"That's it," said the samurai. "I'm cutting off your head!"

He began to draw his sword. The master, completely unfazed, laughed even harder. "With what—with that rubber sword?"

Trembling with rage, his face dripping sweat, the samurai raised his weapon over his head. Just as he was about to strike, the master pointed at him and said:

"There. That's hell."

When small mind appears and starts following thoughts and *bonnos*, it can sometimes go as far as murder. The mind is moving, following something, fixing on an idea and chasing it down. When that happens, illusions appear, and stronger than ever, at that.

Look at yourself. Look at your mind and follow your thoughts. Think, for example, of your favorite subject: sex, your husband, your wife, your children, a nice steak. Follow, say, a girl, for a little while, and you'll quickly notice that your illusions increase. Then, stop following the girl and follow your exhalation instead: long, deep and calm. The girl disappears, along with your mind.

The mind that disappears is the mind that ceases to appear. It's *mushin*, no-mind. This doesn't mean there's nothing there. Phenomena still exist. The earth is still here. But there are no more errors. Nothing missing, nothing extra. Just things as they are: *inmo*.

To avoid the continual appearance of small mind, we practice letting things pass, letting go. Zazen is the practice *par excellence* for letting go. When a master teaches, he always says, "Let your thoughts pass." All you have to do to let your thoughts pass is to sit in the correct posture, not to lapse into sleep or agitation, and to simply exhale slowly and deeply,without forcing; and, at that moment, you no longer follow your thoughts.

"Letting your thoughts pass" doesn't mean you shouldn't think or have a viewpoint. The mind that does not appear, that lets things go, is not a paralyzed, frozen mind, but a fluid mind that flows from change to change.

Letting your thoughts pass simply means practicing the Middle Way, which is not something lukewarm, situated between two extremes. The Middle Way is not *shiki* (phenomenon, form) or *ku* (emptiness, non-form). It's *shiki sokuze ku, ku sokuze shiki*: *shiki* becomes or is *ku*, and *ku* becomes or is *shiki*. This is not abstract; it is directly related to our existence as individuals.

The Middle Way is to surrender yourself. Surrender to what? Some people surrender to God or Buddha, but God or Buddha isn't what's important. As has already been said, they're just concepts, forms. Our practice isn't really interested in forms. What's important is the act of letting go, the act of *shin jin datsu raku*: throwing down body and mind.

> One day, one of our co-disciples wanted to do an advertisement for the Paris Dojo. He wanted to photograph someone in correct posture, preferably a young woman,

> and then use the picture as publicity. So, he decided to contact a modeling agency. He studied the photos they offered, and said, "That one."
>
> To see if the young woman in question (a typically thin blonde) could get into the posture, he had her come to the dojo. She had never seen or imagined the zazen posture in her life. She was shown how to cross her legs, how to tilt her pelvis forward, how to hold her head and hands, how to pull in her chin. We were all dumbstruck: she did it absolutely perfectly—and on the first try! Knees firmly rooted in the *tatami*, top of the head pressing the ceiling . . . We took the photos.
>
> Afterwards, we studied the pictures. The model seemed completely concentrated on her *tanden*, her shoulders were relaxed, her gaze was turned inward . . . but something wasn't right. Maybe she didn't have enough *ki*; maybe she didn't have enough faith in what she was doing. We couldn't express it in words. But it was very interesting. Her posture was exemplary, the form was apparently perfect, and yet, beyond that, there was something missing, or something extra, a mistake, a fault, and it didn't work, and yet we couldn't say exactly why.

Later on, we used the photos a little; they seemed to draw people who were not really interested in the practice, but more in the idea of it all: pretty blonde sitting there, waiting for you. However, people who were already practicing and knew the practice well were not happy with the photos, and especially the women. In the end, we completely stopped using them.

Drop everything—form and non-form—and practice the Middle Way. Neither *shiki* nor *ku*. That way, you can observe all your problems and conflicts from a much higher point of view.

∽

In ancient times, the Middle Way was considered to be the Pleasure Way, meaning that it does not create suffering. This is not the Zen teaching. Contrary to what one might read in books about Buddhism (especially ancient Buddhism), don't run away from suffering. Don't look for *samadhi,* either. Don't practice to improve your health or to find calm and tranquility. Just practice *shikantaza*: silent sitting, concentrating with no goal or object, *mushotoku.*

I think that if mistakes are made in zazen practice today, they are often connected to the notion of pleasure: the pleasure of the state of *mushin*, no-mind; the pleasure of the state of *samadhi.* Of course, pleasure is useful: it motivates us, it pushes us to participate in days of zazen and sesshin. It's obviously a pleasure that goes beyond the pleasure of eating or making love. But, in the final analysis, it's still part of the same illusion.

You have to be careful not to let yourself be fooled by the pleasure of the here and now; otherwise, you can be sure it won't be long before mind appears and is set in motion, and you won't be on the Middle Way anymore. The Middle Way, Zen, is not the Way of Pleasure, even if it is pleasurable. "Zen," said Kodo Sawaki, "means losing yourself, losing everything." Thinking you can obtain something, or get any kind of benefit from Zen, is just superstition.

∽

The *Avatamsaka Sutra*, a Mahayana sutra, tells us that "everything is mind." This sutra tries to show us that mind, Buddha, and sentient beings are the same thing; it teaches us that the whole universe is a single mind, or more precisely One Mind. Everything depends on mind—not only big things, but the small as well. If you always eat too much: mind! If you never eat enough: mind! Is alcohol medicine or poison? Is money a treasure or a curse? Is Allah greater than Buddha, or is he not? It depends on your mind.

Only in the human mind can phenomena appear as errors or show faults. No error is possible if mind is not set in motion. However, as soon as mind is set in motion, everything changes, everything reacts.

Even plants and flowers react to mind when it appears. They react to whatever isn't in the normal, original condition—not just the human condition, but the universal condition—because, according to the *Avatamsaka*, the whole universe is a single mind.

This is no abstraction or vague philosophical theory; this is an integral part of Mahayana teaching and directly concerns everyone. If the whole universe is a single mind, how, for example, does one see oneself in the midst of everyone else? How, in this world, does one see other people inside oneself?

People who criticize those who practice are, ipso facto, those who criticize from the outside; thus, their criticism can only be heard as mere judgement. Now, if you really want to criticize somebody, the criticism should come from Buddha, from the buddha inside you, and not from your personal notion of things, Buddhist or otherwise. A person who criticizes must first be able to discern the other person's mind. It's not a question of his mind being good or bad or right or wrong—you'll never harmonize if you think in those terms—but a question of the mind that appears, rather than the mind that does not appear. That mind that appears sees other people's faults; and other people's minds see yours. That's all. But that mind which does not appear is really something else.

∽

The mind that does not appear is no-mind, which signifies, more prosaically, the mind that is being led by personal awareness. This doesn't mean, however, that you should do away with personal awareness and become a no-mind zombie.

Following your personal awareness leads to complications, which become more and more pronounced and can eventually cause mental problems. We're all familiar with this process, in ourselves and in others; and what's more, it's this excessive awareness which, in the end, drives away the people around us.

Don't let yourself be guided by your personal awareness: that's the teaching of the twenty-fourth strophe. And the work that falls to each of us—master, monk or simple practitioner—consists of not feeding personal thoughts and not having an awareness that comes from the ego.

This doesn't necessarily mean that you shouldn't be guided by anything. The master-disciple relationship has existed since time immemorial, and understandably so, for the master is understood as the universal in all of us: the undivided mind, with no inside or outside. Finally, this is what we can follow fearlessly, because this is the mind that does not appear and is not set in motion.

That's why it is often said in Zen, "Don't be influenced by the environment; be influenced by the cosmic system instead." Be guided by the sky, by the earth, by the cosmic order, instead of by your personal awareness.

"The cosmic system guides our lives, but these days," says Deshimaru in so many words, "we think too much with our personal consciousness." So, what should we do? How do we think not-thinking? How do we not-think thinking? Because, if we think: "I shouldn't think"—that's the mind appearing and being set in motion.

"Unconsciously, naturally, automatically," says Deshimaru, "I know I repeat it a lot, but it's very deep."

During zazen, unconsciously, naturally and automatically, thoughts come up, then disappear. This is the normal state, the normal condition, and it's not at all the same as following your personal consciousness. Here's a story which says the same thing, though much more subtly:

> Hotetsu was a disciple of the Rinzai master Baso. One day, Hotetsu was sitting in front of the dojo, fanning himself with a fan. A monk appeared and questioned him. (At that time, monks asked each other a lot of on-the-spot questions, especially in Rinzai Zen.) "Since wind blows everywhere," says the monk, "and its nature never changes, there is no reason to use a fan. So why, master, do you do so?"
>
> What the monk was saying is that the nature of wind is everywhere, air is everywhere, and so he—the monk—didn't understand the master's efforts to fan

> himself. He was, presumably, referring to the master's Buddha-nature.
>
> "Though you know that the nature of wind never changes, you do not know what 'blows everywhere' means," replied Hotetsu.
>
> The monk was confused by that remark and he said "Now, what does that mean?"
>
> Hotetsu's answer was to continue fanning himself.

I think there are many ways to understand this exchange. It's *gyoji*, the continuous practice—continuing what we are doing, without goal. It is a metaphor for the Way, for cosmic energy. Cosmic energy—the wind—is everywhere; Hotetsu continued to fan himself and nothing was disturbed. Phenomena show no fault. That's what it means not to be mentally attached to structures; it's the mind that does not appear.

But, if you don't welcome this wind, this cosmic energy, if you don't practice it with and through your own body, you cannot receive it. Only when you live in unity with the cosmic system can you be happy and free.

25

No error, no Dharma;
No Dharma, no mind.

That's the literal translation of the Japanese *kanji.*

This strophe of the *Shinjinmei* is very powerful. It shows us Zen as steep as a cliff: it goes straight to the point. This is where the Dharma ceases to be necessary, where cosmic order and universal law become useless.

If there is no error, says Sosan in this strophe, *there is no Dharma; and if there is no creation of Dharma,* he goes on to say, *there is no mind.*

When error does not exist, the Dharma is not necessary, nor is order, or universal law: no God, no Jesus Christ, no Buddhist teaching.

Strophe twenty-five may seem harsh. From a Christian standpoint, it could even be interpreted as blasphemous: you say "no God," and immediately you're labeled an atheist. Yet, it's another way of educating, teaching and giving, because "no God," like *No error, no Dharma,* simply means that there's no mind plunged into illusion, no stupid mind.

Most Western cultures have religions with holy days, like Sunday or the Sabbath. But other cultures are different. Native Americans, for example, have no particular holy day. There isn't even any religion as we know it, because they don't need any. No need for a holy day, no need for a church. It's the same in Zen. We don't need a Buddha statue: a big stone would be enough. We don't need a dojo: we can practice where we want. This doesn't mean that we don't need to be educated through a practice. Native Americans receive an education every day; they practice all the time. For them, all life is sacred; their whole lives are a practice. It's the same in Zen.

And so, far from being severe, atheistic or even nihilistic, this strophe is actually an expression of great compassion. It's not talking about nothing; it's talking about the essence. This essence has no noumenon. It is *ku,* empty, essence without noumenon.

No error, begins strophe twenty-five. No fault, no special essence. In other words, there is no God, no Buddha, that exists outside of us—which, in my opinion, goes deeper than any other belief.

"No special essence" means always coming back to yourself. Come back to the zazen posture, which follows the cosmic order, naturally, automatically and unconsciously. Come back to the position of your hands, the position of your eyes, the observation of your thoughts.

In the end, there is no Buddha, no master. As the anarchists say, "Neither God nor master." No mind—*mushin*.

Master Dogen explains that *mushin* is the source of all minds, of all forms of mind. He also says that the true Buddhist mind—in other words, an undivided mind—lies beyond discriminations and oppositions.

This is the inner revolution, the 180-degree turn that frees you from yourself, and that is neither positive nor negative. Is freedom from yourself—from your ego, your small ego—a positive thing? Maybe one could say that being happy through your breathing is not something positive, because the idea of positive and negative is always a concept that springs from the small mind.

The fundamental root of Buddhism is *kakunen musho*. *Kakunen* means "infinite, open sky"; *musho*, "no holiness, no madness." There is no more holiness in silence—which we sometimes call "golden"—than there is in the sound of a hammer. With silence, you can hear your breathing; with the noise from a hammer, you can hear the hammer and the nail. It is said in the *Diamond Sutra*, "When the mind dwells on nothing, true mind appears." This is the teaching, this is what we should practice—with our breathing, with our postures, with our bodies. It's the state of *hishiryo*—beyond thinking, beyond mind.

Hishiryo is a concept that is very present in Buddhism, especially Zen. Master Kodo Sawaki once said: "You should be like a dead person in a coffin. When everything disappears, consciousness vanishes."

This means dropping your *bonno*, your illusions. Drop everything: Buddhism, Zen, even zazen. Forget the self, forget the mind.

Go beyond the buddhas and the patriarchs of all time,
says Master Dogen,
Do not be attached to south or north or east or west.
Eat the rice cake with the intuition of the wind and clouds.
Attack and strike the sage.[27]

Master Dogen's "Strike the sage" was perhaps inspired by Master Rinzai, who said, "Kill the Buddha." He may also have been thinking of the monk, Fuke, who ran through the streets clanging his little bell and singing,

Strike the light when it approaches shade.
When it comes from the south, the north, the east,
the west, the eight directions,
I attack like a whirlwind.
I strike it with my broom.
Ding! Ding! Ding!

> Eno was born in Canton, in southern China. One day, he heard a monk reciting the *Diamond Sutra*: "When the mind dwells on nothing, true mind appears." He was inspired to seek the Way, and, on the monk's suggestion, went to see Zen master Konin, who lived in the Eastern Mountain Temple.
>
> He arrived at the temple and Master Konin asked him, "Where do you come from?"
>
> "From the south," answered Eno. "The south?" said Konin. "Oh my poor boy, I'm afraid you don't understand a thing!"
>
> "It's true, I come from the south," replied Eno, "but do remember, Master, on the Way there is no north or south."

---

27 *Eiheikoroku* by Master Dogen and translated by Master Deshimaru (Edition Intégrale, 1991).

So, there is no measure, no Buddha, no Dharma. It doesn't matter if you come from the south or north, east or west, because the real question Konin asked Eno had not to do with either north or south, as Eno was wont to believe, but "How far are you from your original nature?"

∽

In Buddhism, south, north, east and west don't mean anything. They're categories, relative expressions. Buddha, Dharma, and even sangha are just nice words. For a lot of people, they're comforting, but in reality they're empty of noumenon. They're just fingers pointing to the moon.

Here's what Master Dogen says in his *Zazenshin*: "The essence of Zen is transmitted from buddha to buddha and master to master. It is fulfilled without conceptualization and accomplished without causality."

When a disciple—monk, bodhisattva, layperson—practices seriously, every day, then words like "buddha," "dharma" and "*ku*" are just concepts. Whereas, perhaps, for someone who does not practice, but teaches nevertheless, "Buddhism" and "Buddha" are reality. That's why the more you practice Buddhism, the harder it is to talk about.

And so, we have the expression *tokusho*, which means "a place beyond verbal expression." This has nothing to do with the scholar, professor or writer, who earns his living by putting everything into words. So, to continue in this manner of placing the scholar and the monk back to back: for the former, words are reality, or almost. For the latter, not at all. For him, Buddha turns the flower in his hand and Mahakashyapa smiles.

∽

No error, no Dharma.

No Dharma, no mind. No *ku*, no *shiki* . . . What is it? Here's another poem, this time by the monk Ryokan:

Wherever I am, I am home.
It is no different than Bodhidharma's Mount Sung.

Riding out the changes that each new day brings,
I spend the years of my life in calmness and freedom.

This is the normal condition, the original condition, what *is*. "Riding out the changes"—*mujo*.

People who deeply understand *mujo* are never unhappy. Because, for such people, every thought is a good thought. The content of the thought is not good or bad, but every thought in itself is a good thought. Why? Because the man of the Way, the woman of *mujo*, simply sees the thought appear, then disappear. That way, wherever they are, they are home, riding out the changes that each new day brings.

This is *doshu*—the expression of true freedom that explodes right before our eyes. As Yoka Daishi said concerning the very same strophe:

This opinion, this expression of non-fear,
Explodes like the lion's roar.
It bursts the brain
Of the hundred animals who hear it.

26

Following the object, the subject vanishes;
Following the subject, the object collapses.

Although the *Shinjinmei* is more poetic than many other ancient Zen texts, certain strophes aren't very poetic at all. When Master Deshimaru translated them, he wasn't worried about poetry. This is especially true for strophes twenty-six through twenty-nine, which deal with *subject* and *object*—typical Zen terminology. If you want to understand Buddhism, if you want to be able to teach it, you must really grasp this question of subject and object.

It has been said that this strophe is a koan. But I don't see why, since it can be more or less explained, whereas a koan is inexplicable. For example, how do you explain the sound of one hand clapping?

∽

When the subject disappears, the object disappears as well; when the object disappears, the subject disappears too. Or: when the thought disappears, the thought object disappears as well, and vice-versa.

Master Dogen taught that all our thoughts are illusory. They rely on objects or symbols. And when you don't have those mental objects inside your mind anymore, your *bonnos*—illusory forms—disappear. *Bonno soku bodai*: illusion becomes satori.

> Ryutan had been tending with his master, Tenno Dogo, for three years. One day, he told him: "Up until now, Master, you have taught me nothing."
>
> "What?" replied the master. "In all the times you've come here, when did I not teach you something?"
>
> "Oh, really? You taught me something?"
>
> "Every time you served me tea, every time you brought me something to eat, I bowed my head." Ryutan

> began to think about this. So the master added: "When you look, just look. If you try to understand, you'll never make it."

The disciple who tries to understand is the subject that appears, a mind that manifests. As soon as there are no more mental objects in his mind, then this subject, this ego, disappears. There are no more illusory thoughts, no more "faults."

In a way, strophe twenty-six echoes strophe twenty-four, which says, "No mind, no error." Here, it's "When things don't exist anymore, neither does mind; when mind doesn't manifest, things don't manifest either."

> One night, Master Nansen decided to visit two farmers living near his hermitage. He made his decision all alone at home, and mentioned it to no one; but the next day, when he arrived at the farm, to his great astonishment he found the farmers, and an enormous feast, waiting for him.
>
> "Who is this meal for?" he asked with surprise.
>
> "It's for you, Master!" replied one of the farmers.
>
> "But how did you know I was coming?"
>
> "Late last night, an earth god announced your arrival today. So, we prepared this meal."
>
> "I am ashamed," replied Nansen. "My practice must be very poor if the gods are able to spy on what happens in my head!"

In Buddhist legend, there are several kinds of gods who have no trouble entering the heads of people (even monks) who are not sufficiently attentive to the functioning of their minds. Ashamed that these gods were able to see his mind when it moved, Nansen returned to his hermitage, where he meditated on this question for a long time. Maybe he re-read strophe twenty-four or twenty-six of the *Shinjinmei*, which had been composed one hundred and fifty years before he was born and was known by all the masters of that period. Whatever the case may be, he began to practice seriously alongside his disciples. He practiced letting his thoughts pass—*mushin*, no-mind—so well, that they died before the gods could see them.

And then, one day, the gods came to see Nansen. But they couldn't find the master, although he was sitting peacefully at home in zazen. Nansen had become invisible to them. And why was he invisible? Simply because his mind was not moving. It did not manifest anymore in any way. He was not at all influenced by the environment or attached to any kind of mental object.

Imagine that such a wise person would be inclined to think about this question of moving mind at the moment of his or her death. In any case, if you have a lot of mental objects when you're about to die, it will be difficult for you to control the direction your mind will take after death.

Your karma always leads you in the direction of your strongest desires and attachments. Generally, this is the baggage, the accumulation of mental objects, that you carry around in your head for your whole life—often, right up to the moment of death, and especially for those who commit suicide. This personal karma will control your impetus and direction, even after death.

So, how can you be free when you're about to die? How can you be free in this lifetime? How can you be free here and now? How can you not be bound hand and foot by mental objects, desires and attachments?

∽

When the gods went into Nansen's house, they couldn't find him—even though he was sitting there in front of them. He was sitting without anything.

And so, when you understand strophe twenty-six, you can also understand the exact attitude of mind during zazen. The subject (the self) that vanishes when following the object (the outside), and vice-versa, is the fluid mind that does not dwell on anything, going endlessly from non-form (*ku*) to form (*shiki*) and back again.

This strophe is the mind during zazen. When "one" disappears, "other" does too. The subject disappears with the object; the object disappears with the subject. Imagine, for example, that you're sitting in zazen and you hear music. If you go with the music—not running away from it, not running after it—then the music disappears. There is no separation between subject and object, no dualistic relationship. Is it God or is it not? Better than that, look into yourself. Go nowhere but into yourself. That's God. That's Buddha.

There's no point in making a separation between zazen and daily life, either, or between inside and outside the temple, or between the dojo and the street. Though the street may avoid the dojo, the dojo—the practice—does not avoid the street. It doesn't run off to the Himalayas. The practice changes the mind. As it happens, the world—the whole universe—is contained in the mind. The mind changes, the world changes. And when the mind vanishes, the object, the world, vanishes as well. There's no separation between mind and world.

This is what you can experience during zazen. After one, two or ten years of practice, what happens? *Mushin*, no mind. Individual karma is cut. It's Nansen without anything. It's true freedom.

∽

Following the object, the subject vanishes;
Following the subject, the object collapses.

Subject and object fall together.

Here are a few paraphrases I formulated of strophe twenty-six:

When things cease to exist, mind does the same.
When mind disappears, things do the same.

∽

When thought objects disappear, you disappear.
And when your mind disappears, its objects disappear.

∽

No more subject, no more object;
No more object, no more subject.

∽

The observer disappears after the observed. And vice-versa.

∽

When your skull, filled to bursting, empties itself, Your mind is simply a vehicle
from which thoughts appear and disappear.

∽

No more cosmos, no more spectator;
No more spectator, no more cosmos.

Subject means "ego," "personal consciousness"; *object* means "environment," "cosmic consciousness," "other existences." So, strophe twenty-six is expressing the harmony between the ego and the cosmos.

In his commentary on the *Shinjinmei*, the master says, "When our ego has noumenon, the environment—in other words, the cosmic system—appears." "Noumenon" is a synonym for "substance." "When your ego has substance"—but, this is obviously an illusion, since the ego has no substance. Let's say, "If you think your ego has substance, and you function with this idea, then the cosmic system appears."

"When our ego has noumenon, the cosmic system appears." Now what does that mean? The cosmic system suddenly appears: this is the subject manifesting and, by so doing, it creates the object. Sosan here tells us that when the cosmic system does not appear, the subject vanishes, following the object, and vice-versa. If the subject does not vanish, if it keeps the substance of its ego—in other words, when the ego is really the ego—then the object, the cosmic system, appears. And not only the cosmic system, but everything—God, Buddha, me and other.

On the other hand, if you don't look at the world through your ego, then nothing appears; there is no cosmic system. Why? Because, there is no more subject and, therefore, no more object. Kodo Sawaki once defined satori as a thief going into an empty house: there's nothing left to steal.

ංං

Men and women of satori, of awakening, of the Way, never see the cosmic system appear. They don't function with the idea that the ego has noumenon. They don't look at the world with their egos. They don't talk about the cosmic system, or about satori; they don't say, "The cosmic system is like this or like that." In fact, they don't even know they have satori. This reminds me of a saying attributed to Dogen's first master, Eisai: "Only cattle and cats know they are Buddha."[28]

Someone I knew once overheard Zen disciples talking together in a café. They were talking about ordinary things, she told me, not at all about life, morality, good or evil. She seemed very disappointed. She would have preferred to hear a discussion about philosophy or religion. But they just went on talking, she said, about "the unimportant everyday things" of daily life around them.

Be this as it may, satori comes from the outside. For example, when Buddha Shakyamuni had his great satori, the entire universe had it as well; there was no more separation between the cosmos and himself, between the universal and the particular, between subject and object.

Funi, not-two, is the unity between satori and the functioning of the cosmos. Shakyamuni saw the morning star and, in that instant, he experienced supreme satori, the supreme vehicle. And this supreme

---

28 In reply to a question asked by the young Dogen concerning Buddha-nature and satori, Eisei replied, "All the Buddhas in the three stages of time are unaware that they are endowed with Buddha-nature, but cats and oxens are well aware of it, indeed!" Yokoi, Yuho, *Zen Master Dogen* (Weatherhill, 1976).

vehicle is not the vehicle of the bodhisattva. It's not the vehicle of the *shomon* either, or that of the *engaku*. This vehicle that we try to practice is not the vehicle of celestial beings either, the *devas*. Nor is it the vehicle of men and women. This vehicle is not something we can grasp through thought or non-thought.

This supreme vehicle, this satori, as grandiose as it may sound, is nothing other than our true original nature, which existed before our life on earth and will exist after it. It is nothing other than the mind, beyond the personal, beyond the person, beyond subject and object, automatically, unconsciously and naturally.

That's why all the masters of the transmission say that zazen is satori. Master Dogen was always repeating that zazen and satori are not different; that satori does not come afterwards, nor does zazen come before. And Master Deshimaru's commentary continues this way: "The forgetting of the self through personal will is very difficult to accomplish. But, by concentrating on the posture and breathing, we can abandon our personal consciousness." That means that you cannot forget your self, your ego, through self-will. Harmony between the self and the cosmos can only be realized unconsciously and naturally, outside of conscious will. *Following the object, the subject vanishes*, and the small ego becomes the big ego, the cosmic ego.

Unlike many other masters, Master Deshimaru didn't often talk about reincarnation. Here's what he said one day in the dojo about death and rebirth: "When we die, when our breathing stops, if our last thought follows the cosmic system, our consciousness is in union with it and our imagination can reach the depths of the cosmos."

27

The object can be fulfilled as a true object through its dependence on the subject. The subject can be fulfilled as a true subject through its dependence on the object.

The next three strophes are closely linked to strophe twenty-six, and also talk about subject and object. They are completely interdependent.

If you know how to decode them, the *Shinjinmei* strophes are not as complicated as they may seem. In general, they describe the awakened mind. Here, it's the mind that makes no discriminations and yet sees all differences in a perfectly clear way.

∽

Strophe twenty-six said that when the mind (the subject) disappears, the object disappears too, and vice-versa. In strophe twenty-seven, Sosan goes one step further and tells us that the object is the cause of the subject.

The word *subject*, as we've seen, is used in the sense of "ego," "self" or "personal consciousness." It's the subject that has the possibility to see, hear, smell, taste, touch and think. *Object* can be understood as "environment," "other existences," or "the cosmic system."

So, the object appears as it does because of the subject.

Our co-disciple Etienne Zeisler once said in *Teisho*, "When we are alone, the need for an object disappears. If we are not looking, the object does not become concrete." In other words, there is only a true object if a subject appears.

> Or, if you will, by manifesting ourselves, we create things; and things, by manifesting themselves, create us! So, myself and others have, therefore, only a relative existence. Now, imagine what that means—it means that you, who love yourself, love all mankind. Love, too, is relative, like almost everything else. At least in the

> mind. One day, Akbar, a Mughal emperor, drew a line on a wall. After this, he called the wisest men of his entourage and said to them, "Without touching this line, make it smaller." The entourage, wise as they were, did not understand. They thought it was impossible. But suddenly, one of them by the name of Birbal, the wisest of them all, stepped up and drew a second line that was slightly bigger. And so, without being touched, the original line became smaller.

This is our existence, always relative.

For example, hearing, or rather listening, creates sound: mind, the subject, creates noise and noise creates mind. Rain, wind and sun are indeed rain, wind and sun. If mind is mind, it's because of rain, wind and sun. It all depends on the other.

But for someone abandoning themselves completely to the exhalation, noise does not create the person practicing, anymore than the person practicing creates the noise. For that person, there is no rain and noise. There is nothing. Everything disappears. This is *mushin*, no-mind. So, what's left? Zazen? No, not even that.

Here's how Master Ejo describes it: "If you abandon yourself to the exhalation and let your inhalation fill you up in a harmonious coming and going, there remains only a zafu under the empty sky. The weight of a flame."[29]

Now, that would be a fine thing, were death to be nothing but that.

∽

Sosan tells us all this; and besides, I think we've all experienced this ourselves. In Zen, we call this certification: when the subject, the disciple's mind, is certified by the object.

---

[29] Koun Ejo, *The Komyozo Zanmai*. See: *The Song of the Wind in the Dry Trees* (Prescott, Arizona: Hohm Press, 2014).

Mahakashyapa's mind was certified by Buddha turning a flower in his hand. Master Deshimaru's mind was certified by his master Kodo Sawaki. And what's more, this certification of the disciple by the master occurs outside of any structure, religious or otherwise.

We could also say that satori is "he who is certified plus he who certifies"—in other words, the person who experiences (i.e., the subject) plus the experience itself. Therefore, it's never the subject by itself, but subject and object, subject and cosmic system, subject and all phenomena.

I've never heard of someone sitting with legs crossed, head straight on shoulders and eyes cast down, who at that very moment had satori. And what's more, without anyone else, or anything at all . . . no, I've never heard of that.

What happens is that, by looking into yourself, you forget yourself. And it's then that you can awaken to the ten-thousand dharmas. Follow your exhalation, practice *mushotoku*, no object, no goal, let your thoughts pass . . . and then the cosmic system (the object) can penetrate your personal consciousness (the subject)—unconsciously, naturally and automatically.

Buddha, when he had his satori, was practicing zazen under the *bodhi* tree. He was practicing *shikantaza*, following his breath, nothing more, nothing less. And that's when he saw the morning star. It was certification by the object, by the cosmic system. It was the transmission, the *shiho*. It was the object that came to meet the subject, or, we could say, which entered into the subject. This has nothing to do with psychology, or even Buddhism. It's simply transmitted experience.

> One day, a monk said to Master Joshu, "The moon is shining in the sky." (At that time, a lot of talking was done in symbols or metaphors. The shining moon is satori, or Buddha-nature.)
>
> "You are under the roof (in other words, you are on Earth)," replied Joshu, "and the moon is in the sky."
>
> "How, then, can I come into contact with the moon?" asked the disciple.

"The moon will come to meet you," said the master.

∽

And so, looking into yourself does not bring about realization, and satori doesn't come from the inside; it comes from the outside—the exterior. And he who claims to have had satori by himself, all alone, means precisely that: a personal satori.

You often hear expressions like, "certified by the object," "certified by the cosmos," "certified by nature." There are many Zen accounts of monks who have satori by observing something, or hearing an external noise: they look at a star or hear the sound of the river in the valley, and they have an awakening.

At the simple sight of a peach blossom, Master Reiun achieved satori.

Sotoba had satori contemplating the mountains and hearing the sound of the valley. He wrote this poem immediately afterwards:

The sound of the valley is a great lecture.
The color of the mountain is the true Buddha.

> Kyogen was a disciple of Isan, and a sutra specialist. One day, Isan said to him, "Talk to me about the self. Please, Kyogen, explain to me what self existed before the birth of your parents." Not knowing how to respond, Kyogen went back to his sutras; but he could not find the answer there. In despair, he took all his books and threw them into the fire. Someone asked him, "Whatever are you doing?"
>
> "A painting of a rice cake cannot satisfy hunger!" he replied, the books burning in the fire. "From now on, I will spend my time working in the kitchen and making rice cakes." And that's what he did for years.
>
> One day, he told his master Isan, "I am completely stupid! Please, Master, tell me a word that will show me the path and open my mind."

Isan replied, "Sure, I could tell you something. But if I do, later on you'll reproach me for it." Unhappy and at a loss, Kyogen left Isan's dojo and went into the mountains where he built a hermitage and grew bamboo.

Later, when he was sweeping the floor, a pebble knocked up against a stalk of bamboo—clack! It was exactly the right moment: when a chick is ready to be born, its mother breaks the shell, and so it was with Kyogen. He did *sampai* in the direction of his master (Isan's dojo was situated at the foot of the mountain, on the other side of the valley) and said, "If you had given me an answer to my question, I would never have had satori."

Then he wrote this poem: *My actions leave no trace. This is the true Way.*

Strophe twenty-seven is therefore the realization of the body through all phenomena. The morning star, the peach blossom, the voice of the valley, the sound of the pebble against bamboo... and, for the man or woman of satori, for the awakened mind, there is no more sep- aration, no more subject-object duality. Here, we attach much importance to phenomena. The approach to life is not the same as in Christianity, where we are told what we have to do, how to do good, how to help. In Buddhism, it's more a matter of profoundly and intuitively understanding the nature of phenomena—how things work—and thus do what is necessary naturally and unconsciously.

This brings us right to strophe twenty-eight.

28

If you wish to understand subject and object,
In the end you must realize that both are ku.

In order to grasp the two aspects that strophes twenty-six and twenty-seven talk about—subject and object—one must understand that their origin is always one: one single and same *ku*.

Object and subject are separate in duality: "You are under the roof and the moon is in the sky," said Joshu. Clearly, this duality is necessary: without it, we wouldn't be able to talk; without such words as "good" and "bad," we would be incapable of expressing ourselves; without the opposition between good and evil, for example, we wouldn't be able to write books.

We are also very different from each other, and Western culture (novels, films, etc.) speaks of nothing but this difference. Since we're not really interested in similarity, we forget about it.

The purpose of strophe twenty-eight is, therefore, to bring the two aspects of duality back to one unique and identical *ku*, without denying them; because as Sosan tells us, in the final analysis, difference is reduced to sameness.

Men and women are different. In the martial arts, a man is never made to fight a woman. It's the same in sports: women are ranked in a separate category. Nevertheless, both are originally identical and similar. And this is the mind of *ku*, the mind we experience during zazen: One mind. In true religion, one practices the essence, the root—where body and mind, man and woman, are identical; where differences are erased or fade away.

In Zen practice, for example, we go from *shiki* to *ku*: *shiki sokuze ku*. *Shiki* becomes *ku*.

Zazen after zazen, we return little by little to the normal condition; bit by bit, the problems we were carrying around in our minds at the beginning of the practice (or as some say, the training) lose their importance; thoughts decrease, and the subject/object duality becomes much less pronounced. And when we return to our daily life, even if differences reappear—*ku* becomes *shiki*—one no longer falls into confusion.

So, in the dojo, who's stronger on the zafu: men or women? There's no difference, no duality. The original is One.

But saying that difference ends up being reduced to sameness does not mean that everything is the same, or that we are all alike. It's easy to say, "We're all brothers and sisters." But it's not true. How can we be brothers and sisters when we are Afghani or Chinese and not American or French? When we are black and not white, when we believe in one faith and not in the other? Now, where are our "brothers and sisters" to be found among all these limitations? Well, while most of us practice *self*-identification, the monk practices *non*-identification: no nationality, no color, no particular belief. And this is what is called "without limitation."

So, in the end, what is difference? What is duality? What differentiates men from women, or a buddha from a demon?

There is no answer to this question, for true spiritual understanding goes beyond differences. Man, woman, buddha, demon: it's the same thing. This is the true teaching that all the patriarchs transmitted.

To return to the strophe in question, here is a poem by Master Ikkyu that says the same thing as strophe twenty-eight, but more poetically:

Rain, hail, snow and ice
Are different from each other,
But once they fall,
They form the same river in the valley.

Self, others, subject, object: one unique and identical *ku*. So, don't create separations between subject and object, between yourself and others. Stay away from nationalism and other such categories.

∞

> Ungo Doyo had been following a Buddhist master for several years. At his side, he studied the sutras and the patriarchs' writings. One day, he said, "I'm sick of all this! Why would a normal man remain bound up by all these rules and laws?" (Many monks who later became masters—Dogen, for example—asked themselves the same question.)
>
> Ungo left to live alone in the mountains. He did zazen in a hermitage and lived in complete ecstasy. His practice became so pure that nature took care of him: celestial beings came to bring him food. He didn't eat much meat, didn't smoke, didn't make love. All he did was samu and zazen.
>
> One day, a monk passing through spoke to him of Master Tozan, one of the most famous Soto masters of the time. Ungo decided to go visit him in his dojo—just like that, no reason (he wasn't a Zen monk yet, but he was already practicing *mushotoku*).
>
> Upon seeing him, Master Tozan asked, "What is your name?"
>
> Ungo replied, "My name is Ungo."
>
> "Beyond this name, who are you?"
>
> Ungo, who was not stupid, replied, "Beyond, even Ungo cannot be named."
>
> Tozan smiled and said, "It's the same response that I gave my master, Ungan. If you like, you can stay here."
>
> Ungo stayed for a while. One day, he asked Tozan, "What is the significance of the patriarchs' teaching?"
>
> Tozan replied, "Later, when you are back in your hermitage, if someone asks you this question, what will you answer?"

In other words, he who does not know readily explains Buddha-nature—there being no other way to explain it, in fact. Only know that it *cannot*, and *never will be* explained, let alone known. Nonetheless,

Ungo Doyo was awakened by these words, and he went back home to the mountains and began doing zazen again. The nature of his zazen, however, completely changed. And from that moment on, the celestial beings who used to bring him things to eat stopped coming.

What happened? Before his encounter with Master Tozan, Ungo Doyo was nature's very object; and nature took care of him. Now, he *was* nature ... and he had become invisible because of it.

One unique and identical *ku*. This is the state of non-separation, non-identification. It is also the source of real love.

∽

So, don't be separate from other existences, from things, from the cosmos. Don't be special—on the contrary, as the Taoist master Chuang Tzu said, "Be ordinary."

Satori isn't interesting at all, even though people attach enormous importance to it, talk a lot about it and even write books on the subject. Kodo Sawaki warns us that "having a satori or two is no better than a fart." What's important is what happens afterwards. After Buddha had satori, he went off in search of companions—companions in satori, in other words, people he could share with. "Without companions in satori," he said, "it is very difficult to go on living."

But satori itself does not distinguish you from others in any way; on the contrary, you lose what you have, the tigers and birds forget you, and you become nothing. What you have found, however, is the normal condition—one unique and identical *ku*.

I've already mentioned the story of Master Gozu, who received flowers from the birds and was protected by tigers.

> One day, Gozu met Master Doshin, and, like Ungo Doyo with Master Tozan, had satori after a mondo. What happened then? Exactly the same thing as with Ungo: the birds stopped bringing him flowers and the protectors, the tigers, left him. This story happened

> in the 600s. Some two centuries later, a monk asked Master Joshu, "Why did the birds stop bringing flowers to Master Gozu after he met Master Doshin?"
>
> Master Joshu replied, "One gets tired looking for firewood and carrying water."

This exchange has stayed with me forever. Indeed, maybe that's true Zen. And "ordinary" doesn't mean common, banal or unoriginal, but simply realizing that "the two are originally one," that "the two are one unique and identical *ku*."

This is how, in Buddhism, we go beyond the borders and boundaries of subject/object, and beyond the boundaries of the individual. We even go beyond the center. The origin and original nature of all things being *ku*, there is neither dualism nor monism. No left, no right, and no middle either. And so, the idea is deeply and immediately to understand contradictions and differences; not to worry about them, not to deny them—because they do exist—but, simply go beyond them.

∽

Here is Ryokan's death poem:

> *The maple leaf falls*
> *Showing now one side*
> *Now the other.*

Sometimes, you have to make a decision. But that doesn't mean choosing one side or the other. It's not easy, because our minds are always in duality. Contradiction reigns between the frontal brain and the instinctive brain, and between left brain and right brain. But the broader your mind, the easier it is to accept contradictions and transcend them. Then, it's no longer a question of rationality, but a question of faith. This is what all practice is about: going with faith beyond dualism and differences. Which brings us to strophe twenty-nine.

29

A ku *identical to both*
Includes all phenomena.

In *ku*, in emptiness, two (object and subject) are the same (*funi*) and contain all phenomena.

This strophe is a big Soto Zen koan, the source of Zen, which is: *shikantaza.*

This strophe develops and deepens strophe twenty-eight. It describes the mind—*ku*—that does not discriminate but nevertheless sees all phenomena clearly. This is not easy to apprehend; but if one really understands what *ku* is, it becomes less complicated. And obviously, one must study the meaning of words like *ku* and *shiki* in order to find out what Sosan is saying in this particular verse.

∽

So, what is *ku*?

Literally, the Japanese word *ku* means "sky." It is often translated as "emptiness," "vacuity" or "nothingness"; but, because *ku*, like the sky, is not empty, containing the mountains, oceans rivers, streams, you, me and everyone else, it—*ku*—is the essence.

One of the buddhas said, "There is no *atman*." *Atman* is Sanskrit for "the immortal self," something like the soul, something absolute, an absolute consciousness, God. Saying that there is nothing absolute, nothing with substance, does not mean that, in the world of *ku*, the existence of things is denied. It's very important to understand this, because, if you think that things don't exist, you can easily fall into nihilism, which says that nothing is real, everything is empty. In fact, Zen has often been accused of being a nihilistic philosophy, especially in the West when the Christians began to discover Buddhism. But that's not the case.

So, what is real *ku*? Real *ku* is not *ku*. Impossible. Real *ku* is obviously *shiki*. This isn't a paradox, or a contradiction, or an attempt to be enigmatic; it's pure lucidity. It's what Sosan is saying in this strophe, that *ku* is not only One. Because, in *ku*, the two (subject and object) are inseparable and indistinguishable; both include all phenomena.

Strophe twenty-nine shows us the interdependence of all things; each thing, each person, is the entire world. Our minds must include everything, because the truth is not found in one thing and not the other.

A wave, for example, is not separate from the ocean. It contains the ocean within itself. But, on the whole, there is no difference, no distinction. The wave and the ocean are the same thing. The wave is the ocean and the ocean is the wave. You can't distinguish between them; one can't exist without the other. And yet, the wave disappears, while the ocean remains forever.

We know all the stories of people who get attached to phenomena—you just have to look around, or better yet, look inside yourself. Today, we know the *shiki* side very well: we want to succeed, we want to get things. And when it comes to getting things, we can be very clever. Even the mere wanting to progress in zazen is wanting to get something; it's separating *shiki* from *ku*.[30] "I'm not progressing. I've been practicing for ten years and I'm still just as selfish."

In any case, people who are attached to either *ku* or *shiki*, who run after the world or who run away from it, are not so different from those who hang on to their thoughts, to phenomena, to things. Because, when you become attached to something, you deny the other side—and you lose everything.

∽

And so, there's no need to distinguish between *shiki* and *ku*; light contains all colors, but is itself colorless. No need to distinguish between the

30 i.e., separating phenomena from emptiness.

sound of words, noise, the wind in the pine trees. No need to distinguish between immaterial and material, because material is immaterial in its essence. When you look at something very closely, you see molecules; but if you look even closer, you see nothing: *ku*. No need to distinguish between life and death, because there's no difference between them. By deeply understanding this, you can be happy in life and in death.

In the "*Genjokoan*" chapter of the *Shobogenzo*, Master Dogen talks about the relationship between life and death. He uses the example of wood and ashes. Wood, the tree in the forest, becomes ashes; and when the wood has become ash, it cannot go back to the state of wood: it's over. Life becomes death. "Ashes do not return to wood," says Dogen. In the same way, your death as an individual never becomes your own life again.

Yet, Buddhism does not say that wood comes first and ashes follow, nor that birth comes before and death afterwards. You're not a person before and a pile of dust after. This way of seeing the world is strictly personal. Because, though the wood and the person carry within them a before and an after, they belong to a dharmic dimension that is situated beyond you and me and beyond before and after. "We must understand that wood remains in its dharmic position of wood," says Dogen.

On one hand, there is continual change, *mujo*, the impermanence of all things; and, on the other hand, there is non-birth, non-death, eternity, *ku*, essence without noumenon. This is not contradictory, because both sides are true. Nor is it life on one side and death on the other; *ku* is not one thing and *shiki* another.

∽

Here's a poem by Eno, the sixth patriarch:

Sitting or lying, this whole pile of stinking bones—
In the end, what does it mean to you?
The body comes and goes,
Original nature always stays the same.

Of course, as individuals, we die—we return to *ku*, to the cosmic order; and, from there we don't come back—no more "*ku* becomes *shiki*." This is death. And yet, from a wider perspective, Buddhism and Zen tell us there is no death. Our life doesn't end with our skin. Emptiness and form are not in two separate places: *ku* exists in *shiki* and *shiki* in *ku*. So, no death, and likewise no birth.

This being the case, one can understand the importance of the idea of karma in Buddhism, and the extreme freedom that is associated with it. In effect, because there is neither birth nor death, each of us, at any moment, can transform and cut our own karma.

Nihilists, on the other hand, proclaim that since nothing exists, in the end there is only death. By this, they disavow the karmic consequences of their actions. But there can be no nihilism if we say that *ku* "in and of itself" (*sokuze*) is *shiki*, and that *shiki* "in and of itself"[31] is *ku*: a *ku* identical to both includes all phenomena. Then, subject and object are one and the same *ku*; and, when subject and object become one, Sosan tells us, everything is included.

To put it another way, when you lose the particular—the self, the subject/object duality—you obtain the whole, the totality. This is the loss we experience directly in deep meditation, in zazen.

This is a loss. Things are taken away, removed. All the useless baggage we've been carrying around with us is set down. And, after years of practice, one realizes that by losing oneself, he receives everything. Then, he finds his true nature, which is always different from one person to the next.

When the monk Dogen returned from China after having studied for three years with Master Nyojo, the committee of officials who met him when he got off the boat in Hakata asked him, "What have you brought back from China?"

"Empty-handed, I return with nothing."

And because they did not understand, he added, "Eyes horizontal, nose vertical."

---

31 *Sokuze* in Japanese.

∽

Some people who know little, talk with a certain trepidation about this meditation without object, worried that if they practice it for any length of time, they might very well go and lose themselves. "I won't be me anymore!" It's something they really are afraid of.

It's true. The teaching and the practice can be frightening: they're afraid of *ku*. People feel as though they're facing oblivion, on the edge of a precipice, and they're not ready for it. They want to go slowly, step by step; they want to climb the ladder progressively and not be catapulted all at once to the top of the mountain. Many Rinzai practitioners, for example, see the practice as a ladder to be climbed rung by rung, koan after koan (two thousand in all), after which they're at the top: it's the so-called great awakening of Buddha. But is it really?

In any event, there's no reason to be afraid. Afraid of what? Afraid of losing your incompleteness? Afraid of dying? In the end, isn't that our practice: dying?

Going to sesshin is a good way to practice dying. Sesshin means taking away something special, taking away every idea, abandoning every thought—the negative and the positive. And abandoning your thoughts—that's "dying." Dying to yourself, to your own ideas. And living in this way, dying can be very pleasant, indeed.

"Zazen," Kodo Sawaki said, "is getting into your coffin." It was seeing the world from the viewpoint of the coffin that interested him. He said, "Look at the world and yourself from the inside of your coffin and you will see that all the things you took so much to heart were not so important." But because we've lost contact with our true self, we have lost faith. And without that, our lives remain torn between contradictions. But touch this true self, this true mind, and then doubt and fear vanish, leaving room for faith.

What's important is to understand, in our guts, what *ku* means, and to have faith in that, to practice the Way according to this teaching. Have faith in the fact that we are just a particle of *ku*—the emptiness from which all things come and to which all things continually return—and we are unlimited.

Here's a poem written by a Buddhist monk named Jo Hoshi,[32] who was executed in 414 for having refused to obey an order from the emperor. Jo Hoshi wrote this poem the morning of his execution:

Originally, the four elements have no master.
The five aggregates (skandha) are essentially empty.
I now confront the sword with my head;
Let's do it like hoeing the spring breeze.

---

32 Seng-Chao in Chinese (384-414). Highly talented Buddhist monk. The emperor had ordered Seng-Chao to return to lay life and to serve him as the imperial secretary. Seng-Chao refused and was executed. He was thirty years old.

30

Make no distinction between subtle and gross.
There are no sides to take.

This strophe describes the state of mind—the unconscious, automatic and natural state—of the man or woman of the Way. It's the unifying thread in the life of the sage and the artist.

Make no distinction between subtle and gross. Don't discriminate, don't choose: that's not complicated, and most of us have heard this teaching before. But putting it into practice is another thing entirely.

It means, for example, not making comparisons. Because, when you compare yourself to other people or to yourself, you're only producing *subtle* or *gross*. People who have been practicing for many years are very familiar with this phenomenon.

The practice of zazen itself often becomes a means of discrimination. In the dojo, you look at another person out of the corner of your eye and think, "Oh, he's always moving, but I'm hanging in there"; or, "I'm better than her, my posture is better, my understanding is superior"; or the opposite: "I'm suffering like a dog and I can't help moving, while he isn't budging an inch!"

It's inevitable to react this way in the beginning; at that point, this type of discrimination can even help you. In the very beginning of my practice, for example, I couldn't accept the fact that everyone else could do zazen without moving, without any apparent difficulty, whereas I was having a lot of difficulty. Looking at the others, I judged myself inferior, and this comparison motivated me—even if it was a gross point of view.

And then, like many people, little by little, I went from this gross discrimination to a refined, subtle discernment, in the sense that I no longer looked at other people much, but at myself instead. Observing yourself is a subtle practice. But this new way of seeing can also become a form of discrimination; because, in looking at myself, I began to compare myself to me. Many people suffer from this subtle discrimination, which is based on mistaken opinions. You often hear practitioners say, "In the beginning, I was progressing on the Way, I was improving, I was going somewhere. But not anymore. Now I have the impression that I'm stagnating, that I'm going backwards." So, some people ask themselves, "Why aren't I progressing anymore? Am I observing myself correctly? Maybe I am progressing and don't know it? Or, maybe I can't go beyond a certain level and I'm sliding back."

But what happens with years of practice—and on the condition, of course, that you practice regularly and correctly—is that you stop comparing yourself to yourself (even if you continue to observe yourself). Because little by little and unconsciously, you understand *mushotoku*, "without object"; you don't fill your thoughts with a goal anymore—the one, for example, about becoming a better person; you're no longer preoccupied with the idea of awakening . . . and all the discriminations, all the comparisons fall away by themselves, unconsciously and automatically.

∽

Looking at yourself directly during zazen is not that difficult, but freeing yourself from your personal conditioning, your habits and your personal viewpoints is another matter.

So, *make no distinction between subtle and gross*. If you make no distinction between differences, judgments, opinions and values, you will be free from all constraints; you will no longer be tempted by your preconceived ideas, your prejudices, your erroneous opinions; you will simply stop choosing with your personal consciousness. But if you throw yourself into your thoughts all the time, you will be led to make endless choices, or, in Sosan's words, to always "take sides."

People often say, "If you don't have an opinion, if you haven't taken a side, then you're lost." But that's just conventional wisdom. "Ah, he's so intelligent! She's so beautiful!" Or even cruder: "He's such an asshole! She's such a dog!" On the contrary, do what Sosan says: stop discriminating between subtle and gross. He is. She is.

A field, seen from up close, is full of bumps; it's not completely even. But if you move away, it becomes infinitely flat, like a lawn. In the same way, you think one thing is profound and subtle, another thing simplistic and gross. You may acquire, say, a taste for oysters, and a disdain for meat and potatoes. But gross or subtle, in the end there's not much separating them.

"What nationality are you? How old are you? Are your parents still alive? Do they have money?" Are these questions gross or subtle? When a monk arrives at a monastery, the master doesn't ask these kinds of questions. He says, "Hello! The pure wind caresses the spotless moon; the stream girds the mountain's waist."

The Way, like the field, does not change. It is always there, under your feet. It's just *you* changing—you and your illusory viewpoints, you who are endlessly torn between right and left, pulled by karma, continually slipping from gross into subtle and back again. Some of us spend our lives juggling our reflections on right and wrong and good and bad, always wanting explanations.

Ordinary people, driven by their karma, live in the world and also in time. They live in transmigration, the cycle of births and deaths, *samsara*. The advantage of becoming a monk or nun and practicing zazen is that you are directly confronted with your karma, and, through zazen, have the possibility to cut it and get out of transmigration.

Our job is to cut karma. When we're in zazen, we create very little karma, because we don't speak or move. The karma of the mouth and the body are momentarily suspended. In daily life, on the other hand, we never stop talking; and even if we don't really mean what we say, we say it anyway, and the karma of the mouth gets going.

Karma is typically human; so, in order to not create karma during zazen, you have to follow the advice of Ota Roshi, one of Kodo Sawaki's disciples: "Do not bring anything human into the heart of zazen." To avoid initiating this karma of discrimination, he said, "simply cut off your head and place it next to you during zazen."

Far from being harsh, these words reflect infinite compassion—a compassion that applies to all human beings, even though each one has his or her own characteristics.

For example, there are people who always think in terms of political or social events: they think about Christmas or the New Year; they think about a football game, the lottery, the holidays. Others think only in terms of judgment: they spend their time criticizing, finding other people worthless. Still others think exclusively about their family, their wife, their husband, their friends—I know a woman who only thinks about her boss. Some only think about sex, others about food, or clothes—they're always asking themselves what they're going to wear today—leather pants? jeans? pimp shoes? cowboy boots? And then there are those who only think about themselves: "What do these people think of me?" "Those people don't like me!" "Do they find me attractive?" "Was my lecture good?" "Is this teaching okay?"

All these states of mind resemble each other very closely; it's always a matter of discriminating points of view belonging to people who have completely "taken sides." These people believe themselves to be in the normal condition, but that's not the case at all.

Another way of discriminating is the one that consists of always thinking about the future ("With all the money I'm going to win in the lottery, I'll be able to have a lot of fun!") or endlessly projecting into the past ("Why did I waste all my money on that stupid lottery ticket?") which amounts to the same thing.

One of the most common characteristics of human beings is always being caught up in the past—always wanting to go back there—so much so, that we're never in the present moment, and our aspiration to the Way dries up. This is why zazen is absolutely indispensable: to understand in your guts that it is the path itself, here and now, that is important.

When he was dying of cancer, Zen master Reikai Vendetti described how he had learned to "get out of the past and jump with both feet into the here and now"—and I suppose he did it through the practice of zazen. He also said that he asked himself, "Why was I born? Why am I going to die?" Now those are some important questions! "But now," he added, "it seems much more important to me to be in the present, to follow the present moment."[33]

---

[33] Vendetti, Reikai and Luc Boussard, *Pèlerinage chez les maîtres éminents* [*Pilgrimage to Eminent Masters*] (Paris: Editions Sully, 1999, 137-9, 152).

∽

No longer picking, choosing or discriminating, no longer thinking about the past or the future, no longer feeding those ideas of "who am I?"—Buddhism teaches us that this is what the practice leads us to in the end, and that, with time, all these reflections fall away, and there is evolution and transformation. *Shiki sokuze ku, ku sokuze shiki*: non-form becomes form or phenomena, and vice-versa. And it's not a closed circle in which you go from *ku* to *shiki* and from *shiki* to *ku*. It's not a simple symmetrical relationship between *ku* and *shiki*, but an evolution: *ku* is developed and transformed; it grows and expands.

You understand through your body; you understand *ku*, which is nothing other than yourself. And the question "Who am I?" falls away all by itself. You're no longer interested in your little being. With the practice, you even begin to understand the other person's point of view, and to embrace it unconsciously.

I think this understanding is absolutely necessary. Obviously, it has nothing to do with psychology or those little manuals about "How to Behave," "How to Make Friends" or "How to Be Loved." Understanding others doesn't mean making friends in the sangha, getting close and seeing each other all the time.

Remember Master Fuyodokai, who said, "Don't spend your daily life for your own benefit, don't just be interested in your own health. Cut off both heads, and the one in the middle as well." Which means, don't love this, don't detest that. It's true, we often go towards what we consider to be good for us, while fleeing from what we judge to be bad. Don't look for what is good, beautiful and profound; don't run away from what is stupid and ugly. Don't love the right head and don't hate the left head. Same for the head in the middle.

The more you practice zazen, the less you follow your personal thoughts and the less you have these problems of choice. The more you practice, the less you worry about your little well-being.

> For a long time, Vasubandhu, though he had many disciples, did not have the official transmission from

his master. He ate only once a day, always before noon, always sat in meditation, never slept and never neglected to make offerings to Buddha day and night.

Yet, he still did not have the *shiho*.

One day, Vasubandhu's disciples went to find Jayrata to talk to him about it. After explaining all of Vasubandhu's good actions and qualities—that he was pure, celibate and vegetarian, and that he was already famous and had many more disciples than Jayrata himself—they asked the old patriarch, "Why, under these conditions, do you not give him the *shiho* ?"

Jayrata replied: "Your master is far from the Way. Even if he continues like this for many *kalpa*, it will always be a source of illusions."

"How can you say that about such a deserving master?" he disciples wanted to know, very surprised.

"I do not seek the Way," answered Jayrata, "and yet I am not plunged into error. I do not make offerings to the Buddha, nor do I hold him in contempt. I do not practice long hours of meditation, nor am I lazy. Without choosing, I eat what's in front of me. I am neither modest nor greedy. Wanting nothing at all: this is called the Way."

∽

Make no distinction between subtle and gross.
There are no sides to take.

If you can get the meaning of this strophe into your guts and understand it, not with your head, but through your body—through the *hara*, the *tanden*, and through zazen—you will never again be overwhelmed by attacks or criticism, you will never again be unhappy when faced with hate or scorn, nor happy, faced with love or veneration. These things will simply no longer touch you at all. This is what Fuyodokai meant when he said, "Even if a voice or a color seduces you, you must be like someone planting flowers in stone. Even if you see honors arise, they are just dust to clear out of your eyes."

Be rootless. That's the meaning of the thirtieth strophe.

31

The substance of the great Way is generous.
It is neither hard nor easy.

The thirty-first strophe of the *Shinjinmei*, which is almost the center of the poem, is one of its most famous and most poetic verses.

The great Way is wide, vast, generous—*generous* meaning "cosmic," "unlimited."

We often hear that zazen is the door to the Way. But I don't think that's a very good image. The Way is big—so big, so wide, that it has no door. And there's no place where you could put one. Can there be a door to the cosmos? How could the Way have a door when it has no way in and no way out? What good would a door be, knowing that no one enters and no one leaves?

The great Way is the normal, original condition of the mind. How can you enter or leave the normal, original condition?

It's your face before the birth of your parents, before the birth of your grandparents and your great-grandparents, before the birth of Charlemagne, before the birth of the cavemen, before the birth of Adam and Eve. You may think you weren't there, but in that case, you wouldn't be here today. That's what *the great Way* means.

Generous also means "universal," "all-inclusive," "not limited."

The Way, especially the Way of Zen, is completely free. Many people picture it as a clearly marked path, like the jet trail of a Boeing, or the tracks of a train. They follow very strict rules and live like locomotives rather than sages.

The Way is not pinned down by any rule, or situated in any set place. In fact, it's not anywhere. You can't find the Way in a bookstore. You can't find it in a university. You can't find it in Goethe or Bukowski or Picasso. You can't find it in the artist's studio, or in books on Zen. Yet many people prefer to study Zen, to have contact with it through books, rather than to practice it.

> Sekko was a painter in ancient China who adored painting paper dragons. He spent all his time talking about paper dragons and collecting them.
>
> A real dragon heard about Sekko and his paper imitations, and thought, "If a real dragon like me came to visit him, he could paint the real thing and he would be very happy." So the dragon went to see Sekko.
>
> But he was mistaken. When Sekko saw him—"AAAAAAAH!"—it was a terrible shock.

The phenomenal world is not reality. Reality is simply here, now. This is what you confirm during zazen by continually coming back to your posture and breathing. In order to come back to your own body—which is not really yours—it's important not to follow your thoughts.

Presence is what's real, not the phenomenal aspect of the body. Universal, original nature constitutes reality. That's why it's not necessary to be an admirer of dragons—or of monks. Be the dragon itself, and you will never again be frightened by one.

This is how the great Way is vast, generous, universal, cosmic, free, unlimited. Here are so many words, because the Way is everywhere, not just in the dojo; because it includes existence and non-existence (*shiki* and *ku*); because it is everything, and it is nowhere.

So don't look for it. You're wasting your time. It's like looking for air.

∽

The substance of the great Way is generous.
It is neither easy nor hard.

The thirty-first strophe echoes the first strophe in the *Shinjinmei*:

Practicing the Way is not difficult,
But you must not love, or hate, or choose, or reject.

In this poem, Sosan often comes back to the question of choice. Choosing makes life difficult, though it's not always easy to avoid selecting or choosing. We're always taking sides, defending personal viewpoints on one subject or another. But these kinds of discussions limit life. They do absolutely nothing to create an *i shin den shin* connection: heart-to-heart communication.

One day a monk asked Master Deshimaru to talk to him about space. "Everything exists in space," said the master, "but where does space exist?" The monk could not reply. The master said that these kinds of questions are pointless. They are concerned with division or quantity, and in fact only hinder us.

The same goes for another question that many people used to ask themselves about Master Deshimaru: Was he an authentic master or not? "He can't be a master—he drinks," said some. Others said, "Sure, he's a master—at least when he's in the dojo." Still others wondered, "But is he really *my* master? Wouldn't I be better off going somewhere else?" Since at the time there was nowhere else to go, these people stayed by him. But when he died, most of them left.

Always picking and choosing. Maybe it's normal, in the beginning; but later, if you practice sincerely, you don't think about those kinds of questions anymore: "Is he my master or not?"

∽

For years now, in the United States, there's been some debate in Zen circles about whether or not to wear black robes, chant the sutras in English or in Sino-Japanese, wear the *kesa* or *rakusu*, or even receive the ordination. This debate has come to France, where an elder disciple of Master Deshimaru, who has become a fervent advocate of the Westernization of Zen practice, renounced his monk's ordination because of his ideas of what defines a monk. For example, "All monks have always lived in monasteries, and since I do not, I am not a monk." This person is forgetting that his own master, Deshimaru, never lived in a monastery, and that his master's master, Kodo Sawaki, was called "Homeless Kodo" because he traveled so extensively to teach the Dharma outside of the Japanese temple system. When you pick and choose like this, the Way is not very generous, great, wide or vast. If, on the other hand, you stop choosing between this and that, then your doubts will disappear and true practice can begin: *funi*, not-two.

Because the Way, in and of itself, is neither hard nor easy. The practice is neither hard nor easy, even if you sometimes suffer during zazen.

Each of us carries our difficulty within us. Difficulty (or non-difficulty) is all in your head; it just depends on you and where you are. Things become hard or easy when, for example, you set yourself a goal on the Way, and you measure the distance that separates you from that goal: "I'm not ready yet. I'm practicing, but I'm not quite there yet."

> One day, a young man who practiced *kendo* went to see a great master and asked to become his disciple. The master looked at him and said nothing. The young man was somewhat disconcerted, but he was very eager.
>
> "How long do you think it will take for me to learn your technique?" he asked.
>
> "Oh, about ten years," replied the master.
>
> "Ten years! That's too long! If I train and work twice as hard as everyone else, how long will it take?"
>
> "Thirty years," said the master.
>
> "Oh, master, you're joking! I'll do anything to learn your *kendo* method, anything!"
>
> "In that case," said the master, "it'll take you fifty years."

What is the goal? What distance separates you from it? Are there signs to show you the way?

No. There are no signs, nor is there any distance to cover or time to transcend. There is no goal, because you are the goal. Right where you're walking, right where you are: that's the goal, that's the Way. The Way has never changed. It's under your feet, and you cannot walk anywhere else.

"Where do you come from?" the master asks the monk who arrives at the monastery gate.

"I'm from Paris," or "I'm from Brooklyn," the monk generally replies. And the master slams the door in his face.

This kind of exchange is quite common in Zen. It almost always takes the form of a mondo between two people: the disciple who is sincerely seeking the Way, and the master who wants to help her and always asks questions that bring her back to herself.

This teaching has always been protected and preserved—but not like preserves in a jar, which always end up going bad. You can't use other people's discoveries just as you find them, like taking a jar off a shelf. Times change, circumstances change, languages change. Master Kodo Sawaki took the expression of the Way out of the antiquated context it had fallen into and brought it into modernity. Master Deshimaru and others of his generation transplanted it into a Western context. And now it's up to us to make it understandable for today's generation.

From the beginning, it has been up to each of us, constantly, to rediscover this teaching, to make an effort again and again through an authentic practice, continually to embody the Way anew through the practice of zazen.

In his commentary on the *Shinjinmei*, Master Deshimaru says, "We must create our path. But the source, the origin, is unique: zazen."

In zazen, when your hands slide forward, you bring them back in against your abdomen. When your body slumps, you pull your thighs and waist upward, you stretch your spine and the back of your neck. That's zazen. Zazen is action—action in the present moment.

I think that's what Buddha was showing us when he said that everyone could do what he did . . . everyone could become like him. In Zen, you don't even have to believe in Buddha; simply believe that we are all Buddha; that today, here and now, we all have the possibility to become men and women of satori, men and women who are fully awakened.

So, in the end, why not be calm? Why not be free? That's *the substance of the great Way —do*—which is neither easy nor hard but consists simply of knowing how to be awakened in your everyday life.

PART II

The style of Part II differs from Part I in that these commentaries were composed as a written text by the author. The spontaneity is more in the tone of conversation rather than the spontaneity which occurs during zazen. Here, the author has no restraint of language; it is as if he were talking to friends over coffee. So, the tone can fluctuate from satirical, to serious, from impertinent to benevolent all in the space of a few sentences. After decades of practice, the author is able to manifest his feelings of anger, disappointment and frustration while still managing to express the magnitude of the practice as shown in this ancient Zen text. In this way he offers a sympathetic voice to the modern reader as well as his fellow practitioners.

32

Narrow minds founder in doubt,
The faster they want to go, the slower they go.

Or as translated by R.H. Blyth:

Small views are full of foxy fears[34]
The faster, the slower

While Ch'an master Sheng-yen translates it this way:

With narrow views and doubts
Haste will slow you down.

A basic characteristic of narrow mind is doubt. Narrow mind always doubts, and this is because it thinks only of itself (and that's good enough reason to doubt, I should think). Remain in such a mind, it is said, and you will never really succeed in your practice or in anything else you might wish to undertake. However, to sit for many years in meditation and yet to still entertain doubts concerning yourself and your own capacity to continue this practice on a regular basis for the rest of your life, without goal or self-benefit, is completely normal, even for a monk of long standing. That's *one's-self*-doubting. But to entertain *other-self*-doubting, about the teaching, or even about the master himself is, as Sosan says in so many words, to leave you in a very bad way. From going very fast you will find yourself going very slowly indeed, and—as it's very difficult to remain at a standstill for long—maybe even slipping backwards.

Unfortunately, most people who are seeking the Way look for something that wouldn't take them too long to obtain, like ten years

---

34 The term "foxy fears" in Japanese is *Kogisu* which means "to hesitate, to doubt like the fox."

maximum (though it would be more appealing were it to take just one or two years), as the *budo* aspirant mentioned in Strophe 31, "Why, then I'll do anything, Master," promises the aspiring samurai, "anything to learn your method of the sword!"

To look for something with this type of goal or expectation in mind is to limit yourself to your own personal senses—or even worse, to limit yourself to something which is "right for you," or at least which "*feels* right for you." Alas, it generally follows that, "the faster you go the longer it will take."

Indeed, going that slowly, it will take you, not ten years, not one lifespan, but eons of lifespans, and no ordinary human would even dream of taking on such a huge enterprise. But Sosan isn't talking to ordinary people, nor to the "narrow minded." Nevertheless, most of us hope to "get it all," or at least a good share in the profits. And, looking from that angle, the faster you run the better off you'll be, that's for sure. Goes without saying . . .time is money. But remember, the moment we limit ourselves to such a notion, using the time dimensions of the ordinary mind, the way we learned them in school—a few years, ten years, a lifespan—it just won't work for finding the Way.

ꟷ

"*Buppo mujen*" are the words inscribed at the entrance to temples and dojos of ancient China, and it means, "The Way is infinite and eternal." To understand this, better to go about the process slowly, I should think. And if death gets to you first, then maybe death is a necessary step. What is meant here is that, maybe, for one to really realize the Way, even death will prove to be not enough.

Every morning for many months, on my way to the dojo, a young guy who wanted to walk with me and ask me questions about Zen Buddhism joined me. It was the wrong moment—on the way to the dojo, the sun hadn't yet risen, and this guy was insistent on getting all the information he could, even on such complex matters as *ku* or emptiness. "Please tell me, what is *ku*?" he asked.

"Look at the moon in the sky," I said, and pointed to the moon. "Have you noticed that it's still there even though it's almost six A.M.?" He figured this to be a koan I was giving him, and he looked up at the moon, then at his wristwatch, and said, "*Et alors*?"

"*Alors*, if we don't move faster we won't arrive on time, that's what!" I said.

He was a likeable guy, had been around for about eight months and was in the dojo every morning, dead on time. Clean cut. Well dressed and well shaved. But, it was clear that he wasn't really interested in knowing either about *ku* or about koans. Besides, he had no sense of timing. "In the morning we can walk together, sure. But quietly; that is, without all those questions." But he was in a hurry and wanted to know as much as possible, before it was too late. The thing is, he had decided beforehand that he would practice for one or two years maximum, and this is what he did. In two years he never missed a single early morning zazen, and he even stayed for *genmai,* the rice soup we served after zazen. He never talked about himself (though it was rumored that he worked for the police, in the anti-sect section—in Renseignements Généraux, more simply known as the R.G.—and was investigating us for possible perverse or sectarian practices. Who knows, maybe this explains his high-speed accumulative way of thinking).

Anyway, he quickly learned the basics of the posture and the breathing, though he never did grasp the basics of mind, and that because "mind" didn't interest him at all. So, of course, he kept away from such concepts as *hishiryo* (beyond mind). He did learn a lot about the history of Zen, the lives of Kodo Sawaki and Deshimaru, karma, the precepts, the Chain of Causation, vegetarianism...Then one day, directly after *genmai,* he rose to his feet and announced to the thirty-or-so practitioners present that he was stopping zazen. "In my two years of daily sitting with this fine congregation, I realize that I have nothing more to learn from you and from this practice, interesting as it is." Surprised by this sudden declaration, we all remained silent, waiting for more. He went on: "Quite frankly, your practice of meditation is too slow for me and for my own temperament. *Ceci dit*, I wish to thank you for your patience and understanding, and to thank you for the daily meditation practice in the dojo I shared with you all." He did *gassho* at the door, said loud and clearly, "*Et bonne continuation*!" waved again and left. That was it and no one ever saw or heard from him again.

Narrow minds founder in doubt.
The faster they want to go, the slower they go.

∽

When you realize that, at the pace you are going, you will never get enlightened in your whole lifetime, you inevitably lose courage, slow down and finally give it all up. Like the long-distance runner who hasn't stopped running once in two years, and who realizes that something's wrong: that however hard he (or she) tries, he (and she) are never going to make it to the end. Then, winded, tired, bored and demoralized, they become suspicious of the honesty, the authenticity, of the practice (in this case zazen), and also of the master and of the entire sangha about them, and start thinking that they might try something else, something that might bring them, if not success and recognition, at least a sense of, say, personal self-fulfillment. This sickness is so current in the senghas and might result in the final aberration of Zen in the West,[35] if the mind of "nothing to obtain" (*mushotoku*) is not successfully and continually transmitted to each new generation.

Coming and going in this manner means starting all over from scratch each time. First, you learn by heart the sutras we chant, like the *Hannya Shingyo* and the *Bussho Kapila*[36]; but when you decide to go to the Tibetans, for example, you must then set about learning the *Vajrayana* tantras and so much more as well. All this requires a lot of time and work—and especially for someone doing it in order to *get* something (or say, at best, to *become one with* the great and mysterious

35 In Japan this has already happened, with their father-to-son *shiho* transmissions and so on.

36 *The Heart Sutra* and the Mealtime chant.

wisdom hidden away in the middle of the mountain, though more likely in order to be graced with a feeling of personal fulfillment). This is a very slow way to go about your practice. So slow, in fact, that you will give up the search and even the practice itself. One more ordained monk or nun of the Way grinds to a stop at the dead-end road.

If you practice Tibetan Buddhism, the concern for progress is not the same, because Zen and Tibetan practitioners don't worry about the same things. Whatever failure the Tibetan lama proves to be in this world this time round, he or she knows full well that they can always try again, in another lifetime; if, of course, after all those worthless lifetimes they have already spent on this earth, they would still *want* to try it again . . . one more time.

Narrow minds founder in doubt.
The faster they want to go, the slower they go.

In any case, whatever the reasons for questioning one's own practice, and perhaps even leaving it to try the other one next door, be it Tibetan Buddhism or Zen or the like, it's still "narrow mind" that makes us continually come and go and makes it seem so worthless. Whatever the reasons, doubt is the instigator, and that's the worst. The practitioner doubts the master and wonders if the master is the "real thing," or just another impostor? At that point, practitioners begin to doubt everything around them, even the practice itself. They doubt zazen, they doubt meditation, they doubt the sangha, the Buddha and the teaching all together. They are paralyzed by doubt and can't move anymore.

If you're not careful at the beginning, then that's how slow the going can become. In fact, you are going so slowly forward that you even start to go backward, and without even realizing it either. Before you know what's happening, you're out in the cold; you're off the path; you've forgotten everything, even the seated posture, even the teaching. Nothing remains.

Two years or ten, in the dojo every day, and yet it will take him or her (me or you) eons before they will enter into this world of the buddhas and the saints.

33

If you adhere to a narrow mind, losing all moderation,
You will veer onto an erroneous path.

The very idea of going fast or slow on the Path leads us into error. And it begins the moment we want to go somewhere. To want to go somewhere means to want to arrive somewhere, like maybe going through a gate to get there, like going from one world to the next, from say, a bleak desert of ignorance and delusion into the luscious green landscape of the awakened mind, somewhat similar to that long-desired place of peace and happiness. And if this were true, and if there were a place like this to go to, what a waste of time and energy it is trying so hard to get there, when you could use your time and energy to get there immediately and directly and without wasting a single moment, just by sitting the right way in zazen.

"Why would you want to throw away your zafu," Dogen once said to a monk, "and travel to other countries?"

People who spend their lives running from place to place, practicing here or there, going from one guru to the next, from one method to another, from one lineage and one tradition to another, always looking for something fresh and new, for another, different answer, for another explanation, for another finger pointing to another moon, as if the first finger didn't suffice, they will become stuck for sure, finding themselves without faith in any thing—not in Buddha, any more than in themselves.

Here are three other translations of this same strophe 33 worth noting for their different ways of seeing and expressing the same thing:

When we are attached to this idea of enlightenment,
We lose our balance and inevitably enter the crooked way.

Clinging cannot be limited;
Even to be attached to the idea of enlightenment is to go astray.

Clinging, they go too far,
Sure to take a wrong turn.[37]

One master has one way of saying things, another has another. But this doesn't mean that you should accumulate, or even pay heed to, the different ways things are said, or even the different ways the masters may say them. Otherwise, you are only accumulating knowledge and sophistication around the same old thing.

This approach to the understanding of Zen, and the understanding of the different masters themselves, could very well lead you to a professorship somewhere, or even to writing a bestselling book on the subject. But it's still "taking the wrong turn," as Hae Kwang says in his commentaries to this strophe, and not really how you take the Great Way; nor is it how you take the way to wisdom.

> One day master Tozan asked his monks a question. The *shusso* had to give Tozan ninety-six answers before Tozan finally agreed with him and said: "Why didn't you say so before?"
>
> I don't know if the *shusso* really gave Tozan ninety-six answers during that same single exchange, but as the story goes it was indeed ninety-six and the ninety-sixth answer was the right one. The *shusso* got satori.
>
> Another monk who was present had heard all the answers except the last one. He was the *tenzo* and he began to harass the *shusso*. "Please tell me, *shusso,* what was the ninety-sixth answer?" But the *shusso* always refused to answer him. Nevertheless, for three years the *tenzo* remained obsessed by his desire to hear the ninety-sixth answer, as though his life depended upon it, and he kept asking the *shusso* for the answer, but to no avail.

---

37 Blyth, Clarke and Hae Kwang respectively.

One day the *shusso* fell ill and was bedridden. The *tenzo* entered his room and said: "For three years I have been very polite and sincere when asking you to tell me what was the last answer you gave the master. But now, *shusso*, now I will get you to tell me by more drastic means!" This said, he pulled out a kitchen knife and threatened the *shuso* with his life: "TELL ME THE ANSWER OR I WILL KILL YOU!"

The *shusso* was cornered in his bed and he was very frightened. The *tenzo* had gone completely insane! So, he said, "Alright, alright! Please don't kill me and I will tell you!" Then he added, almost as an after-thought, "But you know, *tenzo*, even after I give you the answer, you still won't have gotten what you are looking for."

The *tenzo* suddenly understood. The truth had come to him like a bolt from the blue, and he put away his knife and *in a complete change of mind* he did *gassho* to the *shusso*, turned away and never bothered him again. In any case, whatever it was he had understood, he no longer needed to know the ninety-sixth answer.

And so, if you do not take heed and, as Sosan says so well,

If you adhere to a narrow mind, losing all moderation,
You will veer onto an erroneous path.

34

If you express it freely, you are natural.
In your body, there is no place to go or stay.

One of the better-known translations of this strophe was by the scholar and writer R.H. Blyth:

When we are not attached to anything, all things are as they are;
With Activity there is no going or staying.

Beautifully said! But it doesn't say much for zazen does it?

Blyth was an English teacher who went to live in Japan in the 1930s. He spent the war years interned as an "enemy alien," and it was there that he came across some books on Zen. Blyth didn't have a Zen teacher; he didn't have a Zen practice, either alone or with others in a dojo, or even in a prison cellblock. It was solely from the books that he developed his understanding of Zen, and yet, indeed, a very deep understanding at that. But there was one thing he didn't want to hear about, and that was zazen. He didn't like zazen, nor anything connected with it, like dojos, temples and monasteries.[38] But he liked everything else around it. He wrote some fine (though sometimes not so fine) pieces on the anecdotes of the ancient Zen masters and on the teaching itself—for example the 34th strophe of Sosan's *Shinjinmei*—as having nothing to do with the practice of zazen.

Deshimaru's translation, on the other hand, comes across as a statement of *how* to take the Way—with this body, naturally, rather than with this mind. Not with thoughts, not with words, but with the *kikai tanden*, the *hara*; in fact, "there" where body takes mind, and not where mind takes body, whether you are attentive to it or not.

---

38 "Life in a Zen monastery," wrote Blyth, "however earnest and active it may have once been, was always a farce." Blyth, R. H., Zen and Zen Classics, Vol. 1 (Tokyo, The Hokuseido Press, 1960, 18).

And anyway, how can one really express Zen in writing? Both Bodhidharma and Eno the 6th Patriarch said it themselves: Do not count on the sutras for the truth. Sutras and all other writings are not complete—that's what they were saying. And this, regardless of how scholarly, learned or even sanctified the authors themselves may actually be, they are not complete.

I would occasionally work with Master Deshimaru on his English translations of Dogen's and Wanshi's poems. He would give me his version and I would take it home and study it, or sometimes I worked with him directly and we would eventually come up with a final version.

One complicated poem had taken us almost a full week—one verse was particularly difficult for us (about the fish becoming the sea and the birds the sky). Then, while working with Sensei on another text about a year later, we came across the very same verse elsewhere, and a translation was again necessary.

"We've already done that one, Sensei," I told him. "I'll just find the passage and we can copy it over again."

"Not necessary," he replied without lifting his eyes from the text before him.

He didn't want to see the old version; he didn't want to trouble himself, or more likely he didn't want to look backwards. That is, he didn't even know how to look backwards anymore. He was who he was today and not yesterday, and he made me think of master Wanshi himself while composing his *Zazenshin*. Or of Fuyodokai composing his own *Gion Shogi*. Anyway, we set to work, the same poem once again, though actually a different poem entirely. Different and yet the same. Deshimaru was always creating; he was free and spontaneous with his work, with his translations of the sacred Zen texts, much as with everything else he did, in translation or otherwise. In fact, even while translating the sutras, nothing affected his spontaneity.

Expressing the Way freely is not just limited to written or spoken words, nor to the reading of the sutras, in translation or not. Expression concerns the body: how we *express it freely*—how we express it with our bodies and our posture, and not necessarily in movement; not only in the dojo, but everywhere.

"Being natural" means, for example, having a natural posture. This may be difficult at first, but soon you—your body—realize how natural the zazen posture really is, contrary to what people who don't know the practice often say of it.[39]

One day my friend Stevens and myself were talking about what's natural for the body and what is not, and at that I showed him the seated posture.

"You call that natural?" he said.

"Sure, for the body," I replied. "Put the body into great stress, like have it sit for a long time without moving, and you'll see for yourself what's natural for the body and what's not."

"Oh yeah?" He didn't believe me. "I'm sure you could sit just as well and just as long, if not longer, in any other sitting position you might come up with. Why, I bet I could outdo *you* sitting motionless on this couch here, than you could outdo *me* sitting on that cushion of yours."

"Oh yeah, my eye," I replied.

He sat down on the couch.

"Make yourself comfortable, 'cause it's not going to be easy for you," I laughed (it was as though being "comfortable" had anything to do with it, I thought). But he was very strong, in good health and he had the determination of a rodeo bull. Yet even so, he couldn't sit on the couch doing nothing all that time without moving, not for very long at any rate. Nevertheless, he was very sure of himself, and he stretched out on the couch, his heels on the ground, toes pointing skywards, elbow on

---

39 "The zazen posture taken up by the Zen adepts today is no different in mind and body than is the posture of sitting at attention in the army," observed Alexandro Jodorowsky at a conference on *Spirituality and the Tarot*, he gave in Paris in the early 1980s. He had just come from visiting Deshimaru at the Paris dojo on the rue Pernety, and he had only this observation to make to the large audience before him. To better make his point, he sat down on a cushion, on the stage, crossed his legs, saluted the audience with two fingers of his right hand to his forehead. Then, hands closed into two fists, he placed them on his lap, and took on the look of a martial arts expert on the *qui vive*. (It seemed to me, at the time, that he was just covering up where he had failed in life—he himself once followed a true Zen master—but maybe not.)

the armrest propping up his head ("just in case the going gets rough," he muttered, a moment of doubt crossing his mind). Well, after a while I could hear him breathing. First it was slow and steady, then it speeded up and got very loud and jerky; back bent, head falling forward, sweat dripping off his chin; we'd only been sitting thirty or forty minutes and he was a pathetic sight, lumped over and gasping as though he was going to die on the spot. "Okay okay, you win! I give up!" he grunted and fell off the couch in utter fatigue, both physically and mentally.

True enough, it's not easy to sit facing yourself without moving when you've never done it before and don't know what it's all about. It's not only hard on the body, but even harder on the brain, maybe giving you the feeling that you're going crazy or something.

Sitting straight is a natural way to hold the body. If you lean to one side, you'll end up falling over, and that's not natural: what's natural is to be centered. Same with the head, same with the shoulders. The shoulders falling naturally, not forward, not backward, but downward. And this is just part of it.

If you express it freely, you are natural.
In your body, there is no place to go or stay.

"*There is no place to go or stay*" is to return to the normal condition of body and mind; this is not only the beginning of the practice, it is the beginning of everything. And it's not a matter of mind control either.[40] We often say that you should control yourself, always control yourself. Yes, but always controlling yourself is not really the normal, natural behavior of anyone, nor of life in general. This is not free expression. What's natural is not control but being *beyond* control, beyond even the thought or desire to control. In the end, by not trying to control mind, mind is controlled.

40 Takuan, *The Unfettered Mind* (Koddansha International, 1986, 39). "The effect of tightening up on the mind is to make it un-free. Bringing the mind under control is a thing done only in the beginning."

To return to the normal condition of body and mind means to function naturally, unconsciously and automatically, without trying to control anything; this is to be in harmony with the Way. Only in this state can our true nature—the true nature of all things—appear.

"If you express it freely" is another way to say "if you are free in your body and mind"—free from ideas, free from emotions, and finally free from all mental interference. This is the freedom Sosan refers to in the next line: "*In your body, there is no place to go or stay.*"

In fact, "*In your body*" can be understood as meaning "in your mind," in your true mind. And this is why it is activity and movement—as when seated in the posture. Here in the posture there is no place to go, no place to stay, the practice itself being neither coming nor going; and this is zazen body—activity and movement.

Once again, this is hard to explain with words, but Blyth does so, quite well, when he says in his own translation of the above verse, "*With Activity there is no going or staying*":

> Buds open in the spring without straining; leaves fall in autumn without reluctance. The seasons come and go, years and centuries—but not the Activity, not the Great Way. There is no presence or absence, no increase or diminution."[41]

∽

In zazen, you're like a spinning top. Your mind moves. Your body moves, the blood, the lungs, the diaphragm, the ten-thousand thoughts. Everything moves. But you can't see it moving. As Takuan says: "We cannot see him, but he can see us." We cannot see him because he is not resting, not stopped on anything. "And this," he says, "we call pure movement in immobility." And again: "The mind that does not stop at all is

41 Blyth, 79-80.

called immovable wisdom." And further on: "In Buddhism we abhor this stopping. We call this stopping affliction, *bonno*." And again, "the mind of attachment arises from the stopping mind. So does the cycle of transmigration. This stopping becomes the bonds of life and death."[42]

Pure movement, pure movement in immobility is like a spinning top. Stillness in activity. Stillness is not something that comes to a stop, like a stopped car at a red light. For though the body does not move, the unobstructed mind, unlike the parked car, can go anywhere; for indeed it follows the ten-thousand thoughts. This is the activity of zazen mind. Though the body appears not to move (the legs, arms, hands, tongue, and eyes have come to a complete stop), the mind is utterly fluid: it goes to nowhere, comes from nowhere, and stays nowhere. This is the activity of zazen.

It is said that (in the Kodo Sawaki-Deshimaru lineage) you don't count your breaths, you're not supported by koans, you don't contemplate the sunrise, you don't visualize anything, you don't even think of doing good. You just have no object—no better place to get to, no one person either to respect or to love, not even Buddha, not even God. Simply to sit, simply to be, without any of this coming and going.

---

[42] Takuan, *Unfettered Mind*, 20, 26, 35, 74.

35

If you trust nature,
You will be in harmony with the Way.

This strophe is very simple, and completely echoes the preceding one. I quoted it when I conducted a marriage ceremony for a close friend, now dead. He wanted me to marry him and his girlfriend in the manner of the Zen tradition. But when I replied that in Zen we don't marry people, we only bury them (which is the truth), he suggested that I forget the Zen tradition and marry them anyway. Besides, as he and she could not get married legally—he was wanted by the authorities[43]—and could not very well get married in a church, he asked me to officiate for him, and this is what I did. So, we created a marriage ceremony for the occasion and I chose this strophe, because it talks about trust, about big mind and about no separation.

Here's Blyth's translation:

Obeying our nature,
We are in accord with the Way

And here is Sheng-yen's:

Accord with your nature, unite with the Way,
Wander at ease, without vexation.

The difference between the Blyth, Sheng-yen and the Deshimaru translations has basically to do with the meaning one gives to the word

43 Robert Desroches, involved in the famous Spaggiari prsion escape, and before that for his activity in the OAS (l'Organisation Armée Secrète) in Algeria in the 1960s.

"nature." While Deshimaru speaks about nature in general, Blyth and Sheng-yen talk about *our* nature, i.e., our own individual natures.

Nature, of course, can mean different things to different people. It could mean: nature, as in living beings. "The true way of human beings."[44] Or it could mean the landscape, the trees, the river and the mountains. And again, nature could mean the original character of every living species, what the cosmos has already given us, our original energy, our *ki*. To say it differently, buddha-nature, awareness, the cosmic order.

However one may wish to understand the deeper meaning of nature and the Way, it is true that we are always being told to have faith in our very own nature; this is a fine thing to have, but how to be in harmony with the wind in the trees, with the flow of the river or with the flux of the ocean . . . this we are seldom taught to do. We just know it, or we don't.

> A sailor was crossing the Pacific Ocean on a freighter. He was at the bow of the ship when he was overcome by a wave and thrown overboard. It was dark out and no one noticed that he had fallen into the sea. It wasn't until eighteen hours later that his cabin-mate realized what had happened and informed the Captain. A long time had gone by, but you never know... Miraculously, they found the sailor. Thirty-six hours later. It was a miracle. He was floating on the waves, dozing among the swells. The crew threw him a ladder and he climbed onto the bridge.
>
> The Captain, amazed by the sailor's ability to remain so calm and collected for so long a time and not to have drowned from sheer panic and fatigue, later approached him and asked, "Sailor, how'd you do it, can you please tell me that?"

---

44 Masao, Abe. *The Eastern Buddhist Review* (Spring '93, 44).

> "Well you know Captain, it was pretty easy, I mean, since I figured I couldn't get anywhere by swimming," he replied, "I decided there was nothing else for me to do but to float on my back and give myself over to the ocean and to the powers that be, that's all."[45]

Not complicated. The sailor had entrusted himself entirely to the ocean and that's what kept him afloat. This man was in harmony with nature and with the Way. He trusted the cosmic order, and not his own personal consciousness. And so, he survived.

∽

If you trust nature...

The title of this long poem, the *Shinjinmei,* means just that: to have faith in mind.[46] To have faith in your original nature is no different than to have faith in, to trust in, the original nature of every living being and in the innate nature of all things, human or otherwise.

There is no separation, and this is the deep principle Sosan is talking about. *Genshi,* he calls it.[47] The fundamental essence. If you trust this, says Sosan, you will be in harmony with the Way.

"What is the true self?" a monk asked Master Joshu one day.

"Spring, summer, fall, winter," he replied.

---

45 For a different version of this story see *Tricycle Magazine* (Summer 1994).

46 *Shin* means "heart/mind," *jin* means "faith" and *mei*, "record."

47 *Gen* means "deep," and *shi*, "principle."

36

Sanran[48] *opposes the truth;*
Kontin *is weak.*[49]

Sanran means a distracted, overactive mind. Mind in this state does not rest; it is unstable and perpetually seeking, fleeing, anxious and noisy. And so, it opposes the truth. This is the first line. The second line says the opposite. And yet ... it says the same thing. On one side we have the overactive mind and on the other, the mind sunk in torpor.

Bound by thoughts or bound by dullness, one goes against the truth. One opposes what is obvious, and this is what is weak.

The continually changing state of mind, the mind that is always swinging from *sanran* to *kontin* and back again, is not only symptomatic of most people today, it is symptomatic of our entire civilization. For the mind that is excited and unstable is just about the same as the mind sunk into the darkness of Hades. To denote this latter state of mind, psychotherapists might use the expression "depression" and sometimes even diagnose it as "mental illness."

The Buddhists call it the mind that doubts, disbelieves and is suspicious, and Zen master Sosan simply calls it the mind when it is "weak." And each state can last as long as it is allowed to last—a short time or a long time, depending upon oneself. For some reason, however, it always seems to begin with *sanran*, at least when it comes to the practice of zazen. One always begins the practice in a state of *sanran*. One sits with

---

48 *Sanran*: *san* means "dispersed," and *ran* means "thought or thinking"; and *kontin* means "sinking or falling into darkness, sleep"; *kon* means "darkness" and *tin*, "the mind falling into dullness." Interestingly, these two terms *kontin* and *sanran* not only existed in China in the Sui Dynasty (the late 500s), but were both widely used in those times as well.

49 In another translation of this here second verse, Deshimaru says: "*kontin* escapes it."

one's eyes wide open, looking at the wall and wondering what this is all about, while one's mind is all the while working overtime, and nothing can stop it.

Sure, you're up on top of the waves thinking up all kinds of things, both good and bad. But then, sooner or later, and as if from sheer mental exhaustion . . . as Deshimaru would say, "his" (meaning "this practitioner's") eyes would begin to close and "his" mind to sink down "like a stone sinking into water." Here is the other state of mind. You (the practitioner) sleep all the time. After you've been sitting regularly for four or five weeks, months and even years in an overactive mental state, you drop off into sleep. As much as you were overactive during these last months and years, now you are just plain tired . . . and all the time, at that. And even when you step forward in *kinhin*, you do it like a sleepwalker. You hardly follow or, in some cases, hear the master giving the teaching; you don't even notice the ringing of the bells, though perhaps you do hear the drum signaling the end of zazen. And later, in the dressing room after zazen, you say (if you're still curious enough): "Well, what did the master talk about today?" But fortunately, this state doesn't last forever. It's one thing to have perseverance, and if one of these days you're lucky enough to come out of *kontin* without immediately going back into *sanran* again—that is, if you are no longer escaping from anything, not even from your own mind, and no longer running after it either—then this is awakening, satori.

But this doesn't mean that you shouldn't sleep in zazen or anywhere else, or, on the other hand, be active (during zazen or even not during zazen); it is the same finally. A person can be asleep without being in *kontin*—really asleep yet be quite awake. Same for *sanran*: a person though highly stimulated in the brain, can still function actively and constructively in life, in the dojo and elsewhere, without having a scattered mind and also without blindly running after one's thoughts. Being highly active in the brain and being scattered in it are not the same. And again, a person cannot be scattered in the brain and at the same time be in the present moment. If you are going from thought to thought, without a break, it is extremely difficult, if not impossible, to be really present, much as it's impossible to hear the sounds of the world around you, or even the sounds of yourself, when you are plugged into your music, listening to your CD's or reading your e-mails, answering telephones, speaking to the media. There is no wisdom in this and no rest anymore for anybody.

Sanran *opposes the truth;*
Kontin *is weak.*

As everyone presumably knows, our society and most of the rest of the world, is always in a perpetual state of *sanran*: no rest, no stability, but always on the run, always seeking, fleeing, anxious and noisy. It's the same with our statesmen and our leaders. Imagine trying to run a country . . . or the world . . . with minds stuck on the treadmill? Making endless world decisions, signing international contracts and making business deals, delivering goodwill speeches, all day long, without ever sitting down and meditating? At least without really looking at *themselves*, but rather only looking at others, as if through a telescope? Therefore, our leaders are never speaking from their own hara or hypothalamus but only from their own party politics, an egocentric viewpoint that can never give us any real visionary solutions. But, quite the contrary, they give us a hell-like pit hole to fall into at any moment.

We find *sanran* everywhere. We live it in our daily lives, all the time. And yet as Sosan says, this is not the truth. Everything has speeded up and today we are on a rollercoaster ride that only goes downwards. No-one today is at the controls anymore, nor is anyone even available for the job these days. Because everyone is elsewhere in their heads. And if one continues to remain elsewhere, that is if one continues to dive straight down into this bottomless hell-pit, one might really wonder about the consequences. That is, about the future of humanity.

∽

However, it must be said, we're all caught up in the same race. Keeping up with others is almost seen as a matter of self-survival, even for those who meditate! We practice zazen for so many years and we're still running around in a state of *sanran*, as obsessed as ever—either with sex, or power, obsessed with our very own personal problems, and with our frontal brains that never slow down no matter how much we sit! All this is a fact, old-timer that you may be in the practice. We've even known some "old-timers"—that is with twenty or more years of practice—so badly off in their heads that they even commit suicide to get away from it . . . bodhisattvas and even monks and nuns included. Poor and deluded souls that they may be.

Anyway, if all is well with you, however devastating your "problems" may be, what's not only important but absolutely necessary is that whatever they are—loneliness, failure, despair—they pass by quickly. Otherwise, it's better that you stop zazen and go to the hospital ("to the *Tibetan* hospital" as Deshimaru was fond of saying, pointing in a direction across town to where all the recently-arrived Tibetan lamas and Rinpoches in the early '70s began giving their own teachings).

What's more, these problems mentioned above are not something that is particularly hard to overcome, though perhaps you wouldn't necessarily know it at first, and that's because it's the workings of the mind, the unconscious mind, that does it for you.

So, in order to be present, you must slow down first. It's like riding a horse that's galloping out of control. You squeeze your knees together against the horse's sides, lean back slightly, hold tight on the reins and say, *Whoa-there boy!* That's not so hard to do, anybody can slow down a horse; just as anybody can be pulled around by a horse as well, after a little practice it all occurs unconsciously.

Once when I was leading zazen, I couldn't concentrate at all. I spent the whole sitting—an hour and a half—trying to will myself to do so. But because I was aware of the fact that I couldn't do it, there wasn't a minute in that hour and a half when I wasn't aware that I couldn't do it. I was so focused on my inability to concentrate that, as the leader of zazen, I didn't ask that the *kyosaku* be administered, didn't call for *kinhin*, didn't give any teaching, and when the end of zazen came I kept on sitting. My desire to be rid of *sanran* was so strong that it seemed I could go on in this manner for still another hour because, even though I was aware I was in *sanran*, I was *concentrating unconsciously* all the while, as though my will to do so—for no other reason—led me directly into the state of samadhi, the act of pure concentration without object. So, there are no rules to follow, except to be present, and not just present like a lump on a log, but present in effort without object or goal.

∽

Kontin *is weak.*

It is the same with *kontin*. You've got to apply yourself not to sleep all the time. "Man is a sleeper," Heraclites once said. Some masters of the transmission, however, don't seem to attach any importance to whether or not this is so, even during zazen. Master Bankei,[50] for instance. But others advocate trying to avoid sleeping as much as possible. In his text *Zazen Yojinki*, Master Keizan suggests several methods for not falling asleep during zazen. He lists about ten strategies—concentrating on the point between the eyebrows, opening the eyes wide, doing *kinhin*, etc.—and finally winds it up saying, "Do something, but just don't fall asleep!"[51]

> One day, in 9th-century China, in Master Hyakujo's dojo, everybody was sitting in zazen, except for Obaku who was sleeping, his head on his zafu! Hyakujo got up to get the *kyosaku*, went over and nudged him with the stick. Obaku opened his eyes, looked up at Hyakujo, grabbed his zafu and crawled over to a corner of the room and went back to sleep.
>
> Hyakujo then saw the monk beside him, sitting straight as a soldier, struck him with the *kyosaku* and said, "Look over there *Josa*[52] at how Obaku practices correctly, while you are here, just sleeping!"

---

50 Bankei, famous Japanese Rinzai master. Died in 1693.

51 Bankei, on the other hand, was once quoted as saying: "Why hit him [i.e., the monk slumped over on his zafu] when he's enjoying a pleasant nap? Do you think he leaves the Buddha-mind and goes somwhere else when he sleeps?"

52 *Josa*, friend and co-disciple in the sangha.

37

Weak mind is troubled.
So what use in being partial?[53]

The 37th strophe flows from the last line of the 36th poem, which says that *kontin* is a weak or weighed-down mind, like a stone sinking into water. And such a mind, says this strophe, though indeed troubled or weak, differs from the previous strophe in that it also speaks of mind that is partial. A troubled, weak mind is in fact a partial mind. It chooses and discriminates and is in no way universal mind.

In any case, it's not good to tire the mind by alternating between *sanran* and *kontin* any more than between aversion and affection. Don't be partial, taking sides for this and against that, and don't always be choosing. Choosing involves attachment. And the leitmotif of the *Shinjinmei* is to practice and to live without attachment, which is without choosing and without rejecting.

Being "unattached to anything" is no different than being "attached to everything"; there is simply no partiality. And what's more, to live this way does not mean to be detached from any one thing more than any other, for in fact, one is already attached to both anyway.

With a mind that is partial you become quickly weak. This is what Sosan is saying. And that's because the energy, the *ki,* can't really circulate freely anymore, although we learn in physics class to consider energy to be everywhere, and that in fact we are made of energy and only that. The four elements—water, air, earth and fire—are pure energy. That's why we must return to this body of the four elements, to its source, to that which can be called "the body of the true monk."

---

[53] "Not well, the mind is troubled / So why hold or reject anything?" (Lombardo translation.) "Discrimination's useless / So weary not your mind." (Li translation.) Both these translations are found in Mu Soeng's *Trust in Mind* (Wisdom Publications, 2004).

The true monk in zazen is nothing but a channel, without thoughts, not even religious thoughts, with nothing blocking. In this way, cosmic energy—earth energy—can flow through freely and without hindrance. Buddha . . . Bodhidharma . . . Sosan…

In the practice of the Way, we avoid maintaining notions of material and non-material, or taking positions, left or right. *Somehow.* But this doesn't mean that one doesn't make his (or her) own distinctions, let alone decisions about things. You make distinctions and decisions all the time, but are not attached to them. Consider deeply that when you don't even distinguish between dharma and non-dharma, how could you possibly make distinctions and decisions concerning lesser matters such as good and bad, left or right?

Though the teacher and scholar Confucius[54] lived in China almost a thousand years before the arrival of Zen in that country, he was well known, even in Sosan's time when this account was being frequently recounted amongst the Zen practitioners of the times. It was the story of Confucius and the bandit, and finally, what is truth and what is not.

The bandit, whose name was Koshi,[55] lived in hiding in the mountains. He was the head of a dangerous gang of thieves and killers and he was both feared and venerated by the people. In fact, what Koshi embodied in the eyes of others was in complete contradiction to Confucius's doctrine of correct morality, kindness, honesty and correct behavior.

Seeing a chance to spread far and wide his benevolent doctrine, Confucius decided to go find Koshi himself. The mounted police had been searching for Koshi and his gang for years, and sometimes if they got too close they'd lose their lives. All this intrigued Confucius, who eventually set out with a small entourage of hefty souls in search of Koshi and his gang in the northern mountains of Lu.

The way was arduous, and they were obliged to make many detours—for fear of being tailed by the police. It took the little group

54 Confucius, 557-479 BCE.

55 *Tche* in Chinese.

several weeks before they finally came across the hideout in one of the mountains.

"I am Confucius of Lu. I have heard spoken of the high vision of your General," he announced to the guard at the entrance, "and I have come to speak with your man, to inform him that I, Confucius, will plead his case before Wou and Yuc.[56] Also, I have come to instruct your General upon the noble path of right morality."

"Hey you!" called Koshi from inside the cave, "You the clever hypocrite from Lu are you? Who preaches one thing and does another? Come here to instruct me on right living, have you?"

Confucius, to all appearances, didn't practice deep exhalation, let alone "letting the thoughts pass," nor did he give himself time to take in the surroundings, to take his bearings, nor to take in the man before him, the one he called "the General," at least a little bit, and that's because Confucius was flustered and taken aback. He wasn't used to hearing such harsh words said of himself, and so directly as well, and he began to talk about, in so many words, the path of right morality—for example, that Koshi should stop robbing and killing people, and this for the betterment of himself, of his entourage and of the whole of China as well.

On this particular occasion, however, the teacher was not up to the task, and Koshi shrugged him off; he again addressed the famous scholar and thinker as a "hypocrite," pointing out that he preached one thing and did another,[57] and finally, that he lacked a deep and true understanding of life and the world to come bothering him with such a silly teaching. "You see only one side to life, you silly boy! You're just like a donkey, a burro hitched to a post, you are!" He spit on the floor.

Confucius, however, wished to talk about the teaching, about correct behavior and about being truthful to oneself, but quickly Koshi

---

56 The two leading members of the imperial court at that time.

57 Though Confucius preached fidelity between husband and wife, he himself was reported to have had 24 legitimate wives and all of them around the same time. *Zen Notes* (Winter 2003).

stopped him with a wave of the hand and said: "Get out quickly. Otherwise I cut off your head, understand?"[58]

This encounter between the two men was memorable, if only for Confucius. For had not Confucius himself recounted his adventures and misadventures with Koshi the bandit in the northern mountains of Lu, it wouldn't have gone beyond the walls of the bandit's hideout and no one would have ever heard it, neither then nor today. But thanks to Confucius's recounting of this episode, Zen master Sosan (who, interestingly, lived and died in these very same mountains in the year 606, almost eleven centuries later), was surely struck by it himself.

In any case, Confucius must have realized that to really convert an outlaw such as Koshi would be quite impossible. In fact, Confucius wasn't counting so much upon the persuasive effectiveness of his own moralistic teaching, as on the influence of his very high position in the government. He wished to impress Koshi with his power and influence and to thereby persuade him to stop robbing and killing people;

58 This same story is recounted as such in the *Complete Works of Tchouang Tseu* (1968, 237-42): Stepping down from his chariot, Confucius, alone, approached the watchman and told him: "I, K'ong K'ieou of Lou, I have heard talk of the noble sentiments of your General!" Tche hears Confucius and replies: "This K'ong K'ieou, is it not you the clever hypocrite from Lou? You who wear a hat with a thousand boughs and yourself up with leather from a side of beef! (i.e. You who gird up your fat belly with a wide leather ox-ribbed belt). You who eat without labor and dress yourself without weaving! You with your 'yeses' and your 'noes' flapping your lips while playing with words. [....] You who under the pretext of preaching filial piety and respect towards your elders, aim only at accumulating fortune in cahoots with the feudal lords, the rich and the powerful.[....]

Your words, K'ieou, I reject them all. Your Tao is extravagant and vain, deceitful and hypocritical. It cannot allow man to realize his true nature. Get out quickly, before I cut off your head!"

Confucius left, his face livid, head bowed. Returning to the Capital of Lou he told the story of his meeting with Tche (Koshi). "I ran to stroke the tiger's head, I wanted to braid his mustache, I was lucky to escape his tail."

and this alone would be a fine and noble Confucian accomplishment.[59] Nevertheless, scholar and great man that he was, he did not see, and maybe could *not* see, who was before him. And he was lucky to have gotten out alive.

∽

Anyway, this verse encourages us to practice without attachment, which is not so easy, but all the same essential to the practice. Time and again in the *Shinjinmei,* Sosan says that if you attach to something, it is a sure thing that you will lose all direction and lose the Way as well. To follow the Way is not easy. But it's possible. Whatever you do, and in whatever situation you may find yourself, you have to come back to your original aspiration, your original élan vital, your beginner's mind; you have to come back to those moments when you first made those vows, secretly, and to yourself. So say all the masters of the tradition! Then, maybe it's possible.

---

59 Confucianism was triumphant by the first century CE. Though it had to contend with Taoism and Buddhism and was often eclipsed by them, the actual government continued with Confucian principles.

38

If you wish to go by the sole and Supreme Vehicle,
You must not hate the six impurities.

After Buddha's death, many people thought that his teaching *should be followed to the letter* just as he had pronounced it, while fewer, though still many, thought that his teaching was *not to be followed to the letter.* The former came to be called the "Smaller Vehicle," and the latter the "Greater Vehicle." The Smaller one, the Hinayana, now more commonly referred to as Theravada, and thereby indicated, for some limited reason, as less great than the other one. And the latter, the Mahayana, the self-proclaimed Greater One, within which it is understood that the truth is not written in stone, but within ourselves (though not in writing). As the masters will tell us: the truth is to be re-discovered by each and every one, and all the time.

∽

"[T]he sole and Supreme Vehicle" noted in this verse is the Mahayana. Zen is the Mahayana school to which Sosan belonged. The *Shinjinmei* was written around the year 600 in China, and at that time, Theravada (Hinayana) Buddhism was very strong and very strict. Its doctrine taught, among other things, to do away with the six impurities, which covers a lot of ground, including that of individual love, sex, meat and alcohol.

This verse (and the one to follow) were presumably composed in reaction to the Theravada influences of the times. Mahayana, Sosan points out here, is not like Hinayana any more than like Theravada. It does not try to cut illusions; it does not resort to asceticism and abstinence and self-denial. In fact, the Zen of Sosan, which is the Zen of Bodhidharma, does not even try to attain a *higher* spiritual state. Besides, to attain the Supreme Way by negating things is a very difficult way to go about it; actually, it would seem, outright impossible.

How can one ever abandon something that has no noumenon and no actual substance in the first place? Certainly, struggle in itself is a necessary ingredient for all true wayfarers, but to struggle *at* it, or *for* it, even for something like zazen or meditation, is not the way to go about it. Struggling all the time is wasting that time completely.

According to Sosan, in order not to waste your time *trying* to rid yourself of some "thing" or of anything at all, just don't start by ridding yourself of it or anything at all in the first place.

It's very strong medicine, the Mahayana Zen teaching. In order to not "hate the six senses," as Sosan puts it, you must first stop refusing them, stop fleeing from them, naturally and unconsciously; and this action is not accomplished through struggle, or at least not "ordinary" struggle. Here is the making of a holy being.

So, stop hating the senses. Then, slowly (perhaps) but surely, you will be able to elevate the "phenomena of your life"[60]—upwards unto the "Supreme Vehicle." This is what strophe 38 is all about.

∽

While human beings in the West consider themselves to possess five senses, in Buddhism we talk about six. So, in Buddhism there are six sense "organs," or roots (eyes, ears, nose, tongue, body and mind); and likewise, there are six sense "objects" or dusts (form, sound, smell, taste, touch and thought); and when organ meets object, we have the six consciousnesses (seeing, hearing, smelling, tasting, touching and, of course most importantly, thinking. For without thinking none of the other senses would have any *raison d'etre* at all.

The "six impurities" Sosan is referring to in this verse are precisely that—the six sense objects, dusts or consciousnesses.

If you wish to go by the sole and Supreme Vehicle,
You must not hate the six impurities

[60] An expression of Master Deshismaru's.

It's true that in our society, past and present, cultivation of the senses is not really considered an extreme act, nor even a harmful one—French cuisine and the taste buds, prolonged sightseeing at Versailles, sex connoisseurs at the prestigious French Exchangist Club[61]; these activities have been going on forever. Epicurus only tried to remedy this deluded state of affairs by teaching that true pleasure is to be found, not in French cuisine nor in the "winebibbing orgies" as Epicureanism has been re-labelled (to better suit our own contemporary understanding of things), but rather in what Epicurus actually taught: simple plain living, and that best done by oneself, alone.[62]

∽

In any case, whatever senses people may wish to develop and to refine, be it that of taste, of touch or any of the others , that's their business; yet, of course, this way of life as experienced and developed through the senses has little to do with that of a *dojin,* a seeker of the Way.

Whether you follow the first or the second approach to the senses mentioned above (hating or indulging), and whether and for whatever reason you wish to hate (say, by simply rejecting) or to love (by running after), you're leaving traces like truck tracks on a muddy open road in rainy autumn. Furthermore, this is not how a *dojin* lives his or her life in any of the four seasons, or at least how she/he would wish to live it.

When it is neither one way nor the other, there is no trace. Not even that of purity anywhere.

∽

---

61 And again, like the hundreds of thousands of Westerners who fly to Bangkok to screw the Thailandese kids over the weekend, then fly back to their jobs on Monday morning. See: Michel Houellebecq, *Plateforme* (J'ai Lu, 2001).

62 341-270 BCE, Founder of the school of Epicureanism. His superior teaching was later debased to "eat, drink and be merry."

As for this matter of polarization, Rabelais once observed: "a man full of meat and overstuffed will have great difficulty gaining knowledge of spiritual matters." A little later on he points out that the opposite is no better: observing "the writings of the fasting hermits are as flat, meager, and sour-spittle as were their bodies when they composed them."

The best thing to do is to find true mind. This is not all that difficult, so long as it has nothing to do with increasing the senses nor with decreasing them, neither with running after nor with running away from them. It is not through the senses that you'll find this mind. Rather, it is by going beyond them and not being attached to them, precisely as Epicurus taught in his own time.

Though Gautama was known to have had the shape and form of the perfect Buddha, it's true he did say: "He who seeks me through form, sound or taste, has his feet turned the wrong way on the Path."[63]

It is said that, freeing yourself from the senses will allow you to enter into the world "as it really is," free of one's usual preconceived ideas, free from one's habitual small mind, free from common everyday "form," even free from the less-common "non-form," *ku* or *sunyata*.

∽

So, you must not hate the six senses. But how does one do that? Not by ignoring them (i.e., the sense objects), not by evading them, but by going even deeper into all of them . . . and all at once and together too. By seeing all of them with your ears, by hearing all of them with your eyes. When you listen to yourself, you aren't using your ears; when you look at yourself, you aren't using your eyes. It's not the same as a deaf man or a blind woman who learns to use their other senses to compensate for the loss of their hearing or sight: that's a result of training. In Zen, it's different. Here you don't train yourself to use anything. You simply learn to practice freedom, naturally and unconsciously, and to do this, you must practice freedom in terms of your own in-

63 From a passage in the *Diamond Sutra*.

dividual self. Do this and you will become available in the world. As I've already said, being truly detached is being attached to everything and everyone: not just to your family or your sangha, but also to the sangha of the whole world.

∽

> For many years, an old woman lodged a monk of the Ch'an lineage on her property. He lived in a hut down by the river, and the old lady fed and supported him while he meditated. But as time went by, the lady, who had not frequented the monk's company on any regular basis, began to wonder about him. About his understanding of the teaching and of how he was managing his life when he wasn't sitting in meditation or exercising himself with the sutras and the ceremonies. For someone, even a monk, to remain alone all the time . . . now that just wasn't normal. Something was wrong.
>
> So, one day the lady contacted a young woman, known for her graces and her sensual beauty and, as expressed in the ancient texts, as being "a demoiselle rich in desires."
>
> "Go see the monk in that hut, I beg of you, and kiss him. Once you have kissed him, ask him this: 'Now what?'"
>
> The girl understood, and not wanting to disappoint the lady who was certainly going to give her something for her efforts, brought the monk little delicacies to eat, served up some tea, sat beside him and chatted away flattering him all the while. The monk did not answer. He hardly looked at her, and when she leaned close and kissed him on the cheek and said, "My handsome monk, how do you feel right now when I kiss you?" he replied, "To tell you the truth, I feel no differently than an old dried up tree, than a cold rock in winter."

> The girl returned to the old lady and told her that she had indeed kissed the monk, and of how he had reacted and what he had said to her—namely, that he felt nothing for her. "He never once looked at me," she told the lady.
>
> The lady was very displeased. "That stupid monk! Sitting in my hut all these years wasting his time! And in such a worthless practice! Why, I will show him what we do with 'a cold rock in winter'! We throw it out!"
>
> Keeping to her word, the old woman chased away the monk on the spot and burned down the hut.
>
> Later, when asked why she had behaved thus, she said, "He didn't have to evince passion but he should have had enough understanding to know how to teach and help this girl in her lamentable situation."

How essential it is to teach and to help others, whoever they are! But to do so there exists only one way, as Kodo Sawaki once said: "To pass through the gate of Buddha, there is only one rule: reject nothing We dismiss nothing, we grasp nothing, we flee from nothing, we pursue nothing.[64]

[64] Kodo Sawaki, *Le Chant de l'Eveil* (Albin Michel, 1999, 208).

39

If you do not hate the six impurities,
You can become one with true Buddhahood.

This is what can happen if a man or woman doesn't hate their senses nor their objects: he or she can become one with the true buddha. Which is also called satori.

Once again, the message is clear; when you no longer run after things of the senses, the sense-objects, nor run away from them, when you don't close yourself off from the world and from yourself, you can experience Buddhahood. This is what Sosan tells us so succinctly in this strophe.

Most of us, however, are so attached to what we see, hear, smell, eat or touch that we are no better than robots, and our responses to the life around us become so rigid, automatic and ordinary. It's like going off to Monet's Giverny Gardens to look at the flowers. "Oh, look at those lovely flowers!" Or like going to the Metropolitan to hear Beethoven with the ears. "Ah, I love to hear Beethoven!" This is fine, certainly, you've got to say something; just don't be fooled by it. Don't become a slave to the labels and categories you see and hear everywhere, in the magazines, on the radio, in the gardens, at the concert, that's all. Don't be fooled by phenomena.

> Once master Isan gave his disciples the following problem to solve: "Let's say that after I die you see a cow wandering by our temple with the inscription 'Isan the Monk' written on his left flank. You might say, 'There goes Isan,' but still it will be a cow. Yet if you say, 'There goes a cow,' well, it will still be Isan too. However, if you say, 'What sort of thing was that?'—only then will you not be far off the mark."

∞

The six senses Sosan is talking about are at the core of the Buddhist teaching. We find them negated in the *Hannya Shingyo, Heart Sutra*: "*Mu gen ni be ze shin i*" and "*Mu shiki sho ko mi soku ho.*"[65]

It's not a question of whether or not the six roots and six dusts exist, *but rather how you relate to them*. And this is not a question of self-control. Though it is often said that we should learn to control our minds—the idea being that if you control your mind, you can control your eyes, nose, ears, and the rest of it. But I doubt this. I mean, does one really have control of the mind? Even a Buddha, does he really control the mind? I mean, does he control life and death? Obviously not, and perhaps this is because it's really impossible to control anyway . . . whoever and whatever you are.

Okay, but maybe if the mind can't be controlled, at least it can be transformed. Like you transform *shiki* (phenomena) into *ku* (emptiness) and into nothing else.

Everything seems the same, everything is in order: phenomena or form becomes emptiness. It's just as we learn in the dojo and in the books. You go from *shiki* to *ku* and back to *shiki* again; and the conclusion? Why, it's all the same . . . But not really! And that's because one is not equal to the other, never has been and never will be, whether you are black, yellow, white or whatever, it makes no difference. And this is because mind is not the same before as it was after.

"One is transformed into the other, and this transformation happens through zazen," says the master, "through total human encounter." Then he continues: "It makes no difference whether gods or demons appear to us. It is not necessary to pay them attention. They are only phenomena, only mental illusions. In the right posture of zazen, through *hishiryo*-consciousness, every contradiction, every opposition and every duality is immediately resolved. At once, awareness dives into the divine source."

Or as Sosan would say, "You become one with Buddhahood."

---

65 "No eyes, ears, nose, tongue, body, or mind," which also means: no color, sound, odor, taste, touch or thinking.

40

The sage is inactive;
The fool attaches himself.[66]

The sage is inactive. One hears this often. In Taoism they say *wu-wei*, non-doing, the absence of action. Some people, taking this at face value, say, "Everybody who practices knows that Buddhism is about taking action, about being decisive, about going straight ahead, not vacillating this way and that, not being weak-kneed. This is the path of the bodhisattva," they point out, "and since this is about diving into life and death, how can you do that if you are doing nothing?"

When it is said that the monk is inactive, it doesn't mean, as some may like to think, that the monk doesn't do anything.[67] Rather, "doing nothing" means that she or he is not behaving with intention and motivation, or said more simply, not running after their own personal wishes and desires. "Doing nothing" is a recurrent leitmotif of the *Shin Jin Mei*—as in, not running after something because one wants it, nor running from it because one doesn't want it. This is what ordinary people do all the time: always busy accomplishing things, running about creating families, meeting important people, earning good money, moving up in the workaday world, not to mention climbing the social ladder while they're at it. Or, on the other hand, such people may simply be escaping from it all, running away from people, running off to desolate places, and at the same time running from themselves, which is one effective way to avoid

66 Also translated as: "The fool loves and attaches himself."

67 "Even in the time of the Buddha the local population scoffed at the monks of his Sangha who sat in silence like 'lazy, good-for-nothing parasites' and 'dumb pigs.' Same as with the father who wrote a poem to his daughter, not understanding her enthusiasm for this same Sangha: Work-shy they are, a lazy bunch, /Who live on other people's gifts, / Sweet-toothed parasites all of them—/How can you like the Samanas?" From: Schumann, H.W., *The Historical Buddha* (Penguin, 1989).

one's responsibilities. For example, a man is trying to escape the role of husband, and by the same token, that of father of his children; in a word, trying to escape his most fundamental terrestrial obligations, i.e., by not paying his child support payments. We see it all the time. He avoided his responsibilities not because he was a bad person but because his gaze was not really turned inward and he did not know himself. He didn't look at himself nor was he interested in doing so. This is what Sosan points out all the time, and here lies the difference between the wise person and the ordinary. Or if you will, between the active and the inactive, the ordinary man who doesn't assume his responsibilities to the world, and the sage.[68]

∽

This notion of activity and/or inactivity is expressed and understood in different ways, depending upon who is talking—as we have just seen from different points of view, of the ordinary man and the sage. And again, if you are a follower of Lao Tzu or of the Buddha, the vision will be different. The Taoist, it is said, goes with the current, flows down the middle of the river on a raft or just on his back, right to his final destination, the inevitable big ocean. Certainly, this is quite an idyllic way to live—though perhaps not such an idyllic way to die—but in any case it's not the Buddhist practitioner, and certainly not the Buddhist monk, Zen or otherwise, who lives this way. The Buddhist monk does not head down the river, going along with everyone else, directly back into the vast ocean, into the vast communal coffin along with one's old friends, parents, grandparents and ancestors. Rather the monk rows hard and with determination, and what's more, in a completely different direction—not down the river, but across it. He wants to make it to the other shore. In Zen we call it the shore of satori.[69]

---

68 As the Taoist expression has it: "With nothing accomplished all day long, nothing is left unfinished."

69 "The other shore is not originally characterized by coming and going," writes Dogen. "'Gone' [to the other shore] means 'actualized,' truth without error. So do not think that we arrive at the other shore after practice. We have practice

The sage is inactive;
The fool attaches himself

Crossing the river without effort doesn't mean you cross it without continued perseverance. Crossing it means going straight ahead and never giving up. And this without intention or goal is what it's about. Whether or not you arrive at your destination is not the point. Just keep the destination within view, and this doesn't mean keeping it within eyesight, as you might an island on the horizon, but keep it within view as you might the path of non-fear that you are (and have always been) treading.

∞

Doubt is done away with. For this reason he can row hard all the time, even when he sleeps. For even then he always does so facing the Great Way. When he walks it's the same: how he carries himself—his head, his shoulders, even down to his hands and his very fingers even. Naturally and *unconsciously*, because he doesn't know it himself. In so doing, he does not lose sight of his port of destination and, however rough the river crossing, with all its crosscurrents, its swirls and its whirlpools, he continues, going round, over or under the many obstacles he encounters, to the other shore. Whether he gets there or not is of little importance; he is not sucked downwards with all the other living and dead cadavers into the endless ocean of suffering and death.

This does not require effort, as one might wish to understand the word, meaning some activity that requires muscle power, either in the biceps or in the grey-colored cortex. No training is involved. No preparation either. It's not like a sport in any way whatever. It's got nothing to do with business, either. Nor, for that matter, with non-sanctified meditation, the kind we see for sale everywhere nowadays.

---

on the other shore and therefore arrive there..." Dogen Zenji, *Shobogenzo*, Vol 2, translated by Kosen Nishijama and John Stevens (Tokyo: Nakayama Shobo, 1977, chapter Bukkyo.)

Thinking that you might actually accomplish something by sitting cross-legged day-in and day-out is a truly misleading teaching. To meditate without a guide, without a master, without a lineage, without a school of thought and/or practice, but rather alone in one's room doing it "in his pajamas,"[70] is perverting the teaching, and not just for him but for everybody.

ᔓ

What Sosan is talking about here has nothing to do with accomplishing anything, with getting someplace in particular. Rather, it has to do with losing. Losing everything, even your own life. Anyway, living and dying is not the question, living and dying doesn't even matter really; what matters here is that you just go straight ahead, doing what you must do, and even if it's the impossible that you must do, do it without a second thought; do it without a goal; do it without effort. Without a second thought = without effort.

ᔓ

Crossing to the other shore is not a goal nor is it a destination. It's just a direction. The action of the bodhisattva, of "diving into life and death," does not require a goal. A goal is something of one's own personal making.[71] Perhaps for this reason, in order to succeed, to attain the hoped-for goal (as was just said, inevitably of your own making), one must calculate and plot all the time. To always be working for oneself takes a lot of energy and it's very tiring. The drive to succeed at one thing or other is such a personal matter ("It's for my wife or husband, for my children, my country, my religion," and finally said more simply: "Whoever I am, whoever is my wife or husband, my children,

---

70 Says well-known hedge-fund manager David Ford. *See:* Burton, K. *Bloomberg News*. "To make a killing in the markets, start meditating," (29/5/2014).

71 "Conditioned production" as Kodo Sawaki would say.

my religion and my country, whoever I am and wherever that may be; any way you cut it, it's still *all for me*, obviously.") This approach to life makes people prematurely old and weary before their time.

What's more, if the desire to excel is for what he or she might call "altruistic" reasons, say in order "to help my neighbor" or perhaps to "help the world," it's probably not truly altruistic after all. Probably, by the word "neighbor" or even the word "world," they are really thinking of *their own neighbor*, like *their own world*, and not at all that of another's neighbor or another's world. Besides, thinking this way is bad for the brain, in the long run. This is why one's mind must be invulnerable and vigilant even from the very beginning. Zazen is a risky business and not suited to everybody.

∽

Buddhism is often seen as a fatalistic religion. "Well, there's nothing to do about it—that's just the way I am," you hear someone say with a shrug, "It's my karma you know."[72] Well, that's not really true. Karma isn't created by something done in the past, it's created right here and now. And it's this energy that is exerted, even while you sleep. Deshimaru once called life "a combat," and like all true combats, if you are not careful with your own karma—the present one, the one you are creating right here and now—it can kill you. Indeed, life can kill you easily enough.

∽

72 Even though the Japanese writer, Mishima, understood the Buddhism of his homeland and of the world quite differently than we do in Mahayana. For instance, he says he could not assimilate the Buddhist philosophy with its paralysing ideas of sin and karma, according to which everyone is born and reborn forever. *Le Japon Moderne et l'ethique samourai* (Gallimard, 1985).

A man, a woman, a devil or a deva, whoever advances without goal is not agitated; they are simply not caught up in all the many things happening about them, and certainly not in things occurring across the ocean in Far East Asia, or elsewhere. And, if such an awakened person gives money to charity for certain catastrophic earthquakes and tsunamis, it's not very often. (For if one has anything to give at all, one gives it to true seekers of the Way.[73])

The sage is inactive;
The fool attaches himself.

The sage is present, but not attached. The attached person, meanwhile, gets caught up in almost everything around them. They get stuck; even get stuck in what's happening at the other end of the world. Once that's happened, once they get stuck, how to unstick themselves is the question, very rarely resolved in one mere lifetime.

He always wanted to succeed: in school, in business, in politics, in sports, in the arts and/or maybe even in love—to excel in something. It was in his genes, "It's in my karma to succeed," he explains. Then one day, years later, he realizes that this hasn't happened, that he hasn't succeeded at all, but quite the opposite, he has failed. Even in his practice of Zen he is a failure. After this false realization—that one is a failure—one can only continue along the same path downwards, leaving the dojo, the practice and the master, disheartened and maybe even disgusted with themselves for having wasted so much time and all for nothing.

But if one has a sane eye and sees things for what they really are, from the viewpoint of non-attached self, they then realize that they

---

[73] And yet, the abbot of a Buddhist temple in Vancouver, Canada, feeling quite differently, donated "his" entire temple to the victims of the 2004 tsumani in Far East Asia. "A Buddhist monk in Canada stunned his congregation by putting his temple up for sale for $590,945. Thich Nguyen Thao: 'This is the least I could do to provide some comfort to the victims. Their need is urgent and greater than our own.'" *The New Zealand Herald* (10/06/2014).

should *go* to religion, not *leave* it! What a mistake! For it's via one's failure that one should *come* to religion, to Zen, to meditation, not *leave* it. This is the direction of the bodhisattva as well as that of true understanding. In other words, when nothing else works in life, religion is best.

∽

The fool attaches himself. A fool is someone who goes against the cosmic order, and this is not necessarily from a lack of intelligence. You can have a high I.Q. and yet nothing you do in life will lead you to awakening. If anything, it will lead you completely astray. Then too, there's the "stupidity" of the low I.Q. fellow who's not so stupid at all, but quite intelligent in fact.

One of Shakyamuni's followers was called Culapanthaka. He couldn't remember anything Shakyamuni told him, and that was in those days when you remembered everything you heard, especially if they were the words of Buddha. This was in a time before writing, so the disciples remembered all the words, as was expected of them, and to which the Buddhist sutras—that is, the words of Buddha compiled hundreds of years after his death—bear witness. For this incapacity to remember anything, Cula was considered the stupidest member of the Sangha. Yet, for all his stupidity, he was a true disciple of the Buddha. Shakyamuni didn't talk with Cula very much; it would have been a waste of time. He just gave him a broom and told him to sweep. And that's what he did. Always meditation in the morning, sweeping in the afternoon. Thus, the stupid Cula, with his effortless perseverance of the Way with the broom became a full-fledged *arhat*,[74] a sage of the no-more-learning.

---

74 *Arhat:* One who has freed his mind through perfect understanding. The highest level or ideal of early Buddhism.

41

There is no differentiation in the Dharma;
But the ignorant person hinders himself.

This verse is quite similar to the last one where we see the sage inactive, unattached and not like the fools who actively get caught up in the ten-thousand things and thereby find themselves attached hand and foot, and stupidly at that. It's the same story here but said differently.

Human beings, according to Master Sosan, perceive different dharmas[75]—the different phenomena, the ten-thousand things—and that's because they tend to choose and distinguish, and thereby hinder themselves. "The ignorant person hinders himself," he says in this verse. In Buddhism, an ignorant person is not a bad student with poor grades; and likewise, as I said in the previous commentary, an intelligent person is not necessarily someone with a high IQ who succeeds in school, becomes a top student at the university or a whiz at business, or even a great lover. Regardless of culture, education and capabilities, you are ignorant if you follow your own six senses. In following the senses, one or all of them, you quickly conclude that they (the senses) speak the truth. I'm talking about what one sees through one's own eyes, hears through one's ears, thinks through one's mind, etc., when actually the senses are what we call in Buddhism *bonno* or illusion.

The so-called ignorant person, because of their loves and hates, because of what they hear or do not hear, because of their thoughts which they regard as something real and true, is a person who ends up "hindering," even harming themselves, and others as well, and not just in mind but in body. Therefore, as intelligent as such a one may seem, one is not so intelligent as all that, because one has stupidly attached oneself

[75] Note: dharma with a small "d" means "factors of existence."

to one's self (through the use of the six senses—the last one of them being, of course, the worst, namely, conscience or thinking).[76]

However, when you sit facing yourself in zazen, you learn to go from thought to no-thought, and from no-thought to thought again, not at all consciously but completely unconsciously and automatically. *Shiki soku ze ku, ku soku ze shiki*, as Deshimaru would say. If all goes well and you don't flip out from what one might call "stupid reasoning," the bonds of attachment decrease and actually disappear. The same with "repulsion," and even "rejection" as a whole. What do you really reject in the end? And for what reason, if not a stupid egotistical one? Look at yourself, Sosan says in so many words, and see for yourself.

So, without these bonds to shackle you hand and foot, you are free to live fully, beyond happiness and unhappiness, beyond your personal desires and your personal failures, i.e., beyond your small self, the one we are talking about right now. That small self is perhaps not the most "intelligent" of people,[77] but wise nonetheless.

If you only think of yourself: about your childhood, your love-life, your work and your vacations, then you are *not* like those people who only think about others: how to get the others' approval and, of course, how to get other things as well, like status, money, and other such dharmas. For instance, the person whose life is politics and for whom all preoccupations are with the government and the law. Or again, the heartfelt people who are very concerned about the welfare of the world as a whole, and who may suffer for the tsunamis in Japan, for the bombings in Iraq, the tortures in Guantanamo, pedophilia in the Church . . . And again, the religious people who only think about spiritual matters, with their thoughts stuck upon purity and enlightenment, thinking that, for enlightenment to materialize, purity is necessary. As if "purity" comes first before enlightenment. This is why Sosan says that he who acts in like manner stupidly "hinders himself."

---

[76] The six senses: *gen ni bi ze shin I*, and *mu* or negation, i.e., negation of eye, ear, nose, tongue, body and conscience.

[77] "A strange creature, the human being; groping in the dark with an intelligent look," says Kodo Sawaki.

There is no differentiation in the Dharma;
But the ignorant person hinders himself.

Tanka[78] was a disciple of Baso, then of Sekito. Once he spent the night in Erinji,[79] a small temple in Northern China. It was in midwinter and very cold and he found himself alone in the Buddha Hall with three wooden buddha statues. Tanka took one and burned it to keep warm. Smelling the smoke, the abbot (who had a white beard and bushy eyebrows) came running. "What have you gone and done!" he lamented on seeing one of his three wooden buddha statues burning in the fireplace. "You have burned the Buddha!"

Tanka took a stick and poked in the ashes.

"What are you doing now!" said the abbot momentarily perplexed. He pointed to the ashes, "What are you looking for in there, in those ashes?"

"I'm looking for the Buddha's *sharira*. (*Sharira* are the remains, a thumb, a tooth, a tuft of hair of a buddha after cremation[80]).

"Young monk, you are crazy! That is a wooden statue, not the living buddha!" Shaking his head in both anger and bewilderment, the abbot went on: "Imagine that, trying to find a *sharira* in a wooden statue—!"

The flames from the burning statue were about to fizzle out and Tanka said, "In that case, reverend master, what do you say if we burn the other two as well?"

---

78 Tanka 739-824.

79 The temple of Huilin in China.

80 *Sharira* or *sarira*; "body" or "husk" literally. The cult of preserving and venerating the relics or remains of the cremated body of Shakyamuni (and eventually other sages and saints as well) began at his death in 483 BCE.

One of the Buddha's teeth, it is said, went to a temple in Shri Lanka and a tuft of his hair to a temple in Burma.

> The abbot stepped back, thinking to himself: "why this monk is not only infringing the precepts in a most outrageous manner, he is outright mad! I must get rid of him right away!"
>
> And that's what he did. He threw Tanka out of the temple, into the cold night. And told him not to come back.
>
> According to the temple annals of the time, the monks connected with Erinji considered Tanka as a *persona non grata* and forbade him to ever again set foot in their temple. Master Dogen saw the mishap at Erinji quite differently. "Tanka always sat in accordance with the prescribed rules," said Dogen,[81] "his study never failed to follow good manners; he was always courteous as if meeting a noble guest, holding his hands in *shashu* . . ." (hands placed in front of the chest or directly below it).
>
> And so, it came about that Tanka did not undergo any cosmic retribution for burning the buddha statue, nor for that matter anything else good or bad he might have committed then or before. While the abbot of Erinji, who lived an exemplary life in a temple, protecting and preserving the place, and in particular the temple's three wooden buddha statues, but did not see whom he had before him, suffered the cosmic retribution reserved for those heads of temples who mistake the teaching and the true meaning of the precepts—let alone compassion for others (beyond that of lip service),—that of having his beard and eyebrows drop off.

The message is simple and clear. The abbot—after having mistaken a carved piece of wood in the form of a Buddha for something sacred and holy, and even up to the point of venerating it, as so many of us

---

[81] In his *Shobogenzo-zuimonki*.

learn to do in school, in church[82]—then inevitably faces the retributive consequences of his ignorance. Even more so if he is the abbot of a temple or the bishop of a diocese.

The same mistake may be made when entering the dojo to practice zazen. We pass in front of the buddha statue on the altar (actually Manjusri[83]) and bow in gassho in its direction; and yet, if we imagine that we are bowing to the holy Buddha and not just to a wooden statue momentarily depicting his holiness, then we do not see what is really before us: neither the statue on the altar, nor the living buddhas who are already sitting facing a wall; or those who have sat, or will be sitting in the future.

It's the same confusion with the *kesa*, known as the robe of liberation received during one's ordination. The *kesa* is exactly the same one as was worn by Shakyamuni himself, though of another color. Anyway, before putting on the *kesa*, it is customary to place it, folded on top of the head when chanting the Kesa Sutra. Some people do this in the dojo, facing the altar; but it's more exact to face the wall in front of you—in other words, not to face the Buddha statue, but to face the bare empty wall in front of you.

You don't need an excuse, a special occasion, a statue, a temple or a dojo in which to wear a *kesa*, do *gassho* and recite a sutra, such as the sutra we chant during mealtime, "For the Buddha, the Dharma and the Sangha; for the innocent and those who cannot help themselves." Any object, in fact anything, is good. Anything, anywhere, and at any time. Because, spiritual or un-spiritual, material or immaterial, they are not

---

82 Elephants in Africa are being massacred—tens of thousands a year—and their ivory tusks exported to Asian countries for use as a sex aphrodisiac and also for reasons connected with religion. "When I see an elephant tusk," explains a Catholic ivory collector in the Philippines, "I do not see an elephant, I see our savior Jesus Christ." *National Geographic* (France, Oct. 2012).

83 It's the custom to place Manjusri, rather than the Buddha, on the altar in a Zen dojo. Manjusri (Monju in Japanese) is the most important mythical figure in the Buddhist pantheon after that of Avalokitesvara. He is depicted brandishing the sword of wisdom which cuts through ignorance.

just connected, they are one. Being "one" does not mean being "one" as opposed to being something else. The Way is not a matter of creating its opposite.

Therefore, one could simply say that being one is not creating two. But, this does not deny the differences that exist everywhere. In the *Sandokai,* the poem written by Master Sekito Kisen in the 8th century, it is said that differences and similarities do indeed exist, *san* meaning "difference"—existence in time and space, you, me, the others; *do* meaning "similarity" or "essence"; and *kai* meaning "fusion," "whole" or "harmony." And strung together, *Sandokai* is when difference and similarity work together in complete harmony, without separation. In the *Upanishads* they say *neti, neti*: "not this, not that," which is the same.

42

Using mind with mind:
Great confusion, or harmony?

When you begin the practice you use your mind to work on your mind, or at least you try to. But in fact, all you are doing is using *bonno* (illusion) to reduce *bonno,* and in some cases by removing it—your mind—altogether. This is not the mind of zazen. If say a thought arises, we do not try to reduce or remove it by use of another thought. This would be like trying to remove blood with blood. Shakespeare saw that clearly, so did Macbeth.

R.H. Blyth writes of mind being already free anyway. "Clinging to the search for the mind is the last infirmity of the religious soul, and the most self-evidently absurd, for why should we search for the Buddha that we have already. . . ?"[84] So, in answer to Sosan's question, using mind with mind is certainly not being in harmony with anything, except perhaps confusion.

Then there's Master Deshimaru's approach to this verse, which is again very different. He says, "when we use mind with [or 'to'] mind, dharma to dharma, this is the great encounter, the moment of deep intimacy. *I shin den shin,* from my mind to your mind." *I shin den shin,* mind which transmits gives mind.

To illustrate this point the master recounts the story of Tokujo the boatman and Kassan the monk. (And by this story he underlines the notion of "harmony," as mentioned above, rather than of "confusion.")

> Tokujo,[85] having practiced under Yakusan, and from whom he had received both the monk ordination and the transmission thirty years earlier, worked ever since

---

84 *Zen & Zen Classics* (Japan: Hokuseido Press). By "the religious soul" Blyth simply means an unhealthy, deluded fool.

85 8th to 9th Century.

as a simple ferryman. He didn't shave his head, never wore his robes and didn't have any disciples. He just ferried passengers back and forth across the river. But this didn't mean that he had given up hope of finding a disciple to whom he could transmit the essence of the teaching. He even wrote a poem to this effect:

I have waited for thirty years, no one has come.
Never have I caught the big fish.
The water in the river is too clear,
And the fish cannot swim in it.

The water was too clear and not really the place for big fish to swim in. But then one day a monk arrived at the river's edge where Tokujo sat waiting in his boat. His head was shaved and he was wearing a black robe.

"Hello, monk," said Tokujo.

"Hello, boatman," he replied. (Tokujo was known in the region as "the boatman").

"Where are you from and where are you going?"

"I'm from nowhere and going nowhere," the monk replied and climbed aboard. Tokujo pushed the boat out into the current, then asked him again, a little differently: "Well, tell me monk, who educated you?" (In other words, what school do you adhere to? who is your master? what is your practice?)

"Zazen educated me," replied the other. "I come from zazen."

"Even if what you say is right it's not complete!"[86] Tokujo shouted and using his oar as a lever he catapulted the monk overboard.

86 Certainly Tokujo was familiar with Sosan's poem *Shinjinmei* (strophe 15), already in circulation among the Zen practitioners of the day: "Even if your words are correct, even if your thoughts are exact, it is not in accordance with the truth."

> Stunned but not incapacitated Kassan[87]—for that was his name—climbed back into the boat, grabbed hold of the master and in his own turn threw him overboard. However, unlike with Kassan, Tokujo sunk right to the bottom of the river and never came up again; the master had bloody drowned!

This story illustrates, I think, the notion that "using mind with mind" can indeed be done, and in perfect harmony as well. For, at this precise moment, Kassan got satori, and believe it or not, even the *shiho,* the final (and we can even say "official") Zen transmission from Tokujo.

So, the big fish was finally caught and he became the ferryman in the master's stead. And a great one at that, as is recorded in the annals of Zen of Ancient China.

∽

However, it should be pointed out that a completely different and even diametrically opposed interpretation of this verse exists and is even accepted as the official version, by such masters and Buddhalogues such as Sheng-yen, Genpo, D.T. Suzuki and Blyth. They all by and large adhere to the following English translation by Richard B. Clarke:

> *To seek Mind with discriminating mind,*
> *is the greatest of all mistakes.*

Whatever interpretation one wishes to make on this 42nd verse of the *Shinjinmei,*[88] Tokujo in this story succeeded very well in

87 805-881 CE.

88 In the second line of this strophe in the original Chinese, we have the ideograms *dai saku*: *dai* meaning "great," and *saku* meaning "confusion," "mistake" and "error"; but, as Deshimaru deals with this second ideogram, *saku*, it can also mean both "confusion" and "harmony"; and here in this context Deshimaru took it to mean nothing but total harmony.

transmitting on to Kassan the essence of the teaching. It was the true encounter. Where the struggle of life and death begins and ends—with the arrival and blossoming of the true disciple, and the abrupt death of the master—we have an example of total harmony between two beings.

43

In the state of doubt, sanran and kontin arise.
In the state of satori, neither love nor hate exists.[89]

A Chinese Tendai meditation master, Chih-i, was already talking about sanran and kontin in the 6th century,[90] so this manner of describing the workings of the mind during zazen really dates back to the 500s and even before. Chih-I, who died in 597,[91] said that due to the great effort it requires to overcome sanran and/or kontin—that is, at least one hour a day in correct-sitting meditation—it is too difficult for most people. In fact, most people, and even those in the practice, says Chih-I, end up by abandoning themselves completely to these two highly undesirable states of mind, always running after something or away from something. It's the same situation (whether in the seated posture or otherwise), and it's this running after and running away that creates mental deformation.

Imagine that condition—always in a state of agitation and doubt (like some of the characters in the books by the writer Houellebecq[92]); or otherwise lost in disillusion, sullen, joyless. Sinking, sinking into the obscure path of doubt. Both *sanran* and *kontin* are on that same voyage, like being in that same stinking sea, one floating on top, like say the politicians, the other sinking under the first wave, like Faust or like Molloy and Malone[93] or like Oblomov, the Russian character in a book by the writer Goncharov who never got out of bed. In other words, people who sink down low and never come back. But, without dramatizing more than necessary, such an abandonment to these mental states is just

89 See also verse #36: *Sanran* opposes the truth; *kontin* is weak.

90 *Sanran*: 散乱 (*pin yin chinois: sàn luàn*) ; *Kontin*: 雷沈 (*pin yin chinois: léi shěn*)

91 His dates were 538-97 CE.

92 See: *Extension du Domaine de la Lutte* and *Platforme* for example.

93 From Samuel Beckett.

not good for the body or the brain, in the long run; for, as was already said, it creates mind deformation.

To recapitulate, *sanran* is the state of agitation and doubt. From the rising of doubt we come upon passion and anger. Doubting means not accepting and not understanding the world which is *mujo*: not realizing deeply enough (and here I'm no longer talking about Molloy or Malone) that all phenomena are impermanent. Through the deep grasping of *mujo*, the wise ones having truly developed an understanding that all things are impermanent, no longer fall into the snares of passion and anger. In fact, understanding this, they deepen their faith in the practice of going beyond the two types of mental deformations, and enter, as implied in this second line, into the world of satori.

So, *kontin* is the state of heaviness, darkness, sleepiness. Going from no-thought to no-thought, causing an individual both mental and physical fatigue (a state of mind most common amongst us human beings). *Kontin*, as Sheng-yen[94] says, is like "being on the dark side of the mountain in a cave inhabited by ghosts."[95]

So, to get rid of these debilitating deformations of mind, you must go between the two. Aim "for the horizon between earth and sky," or as Carlos Castaneda would say, aim for "the crack between the worlds."[96]

In the first line: doubt on the one hand and sluggishness on the other; and now, in the second line, how to free ourselves of this: by finding satori, that is by finding the place "between earth and sky," where in Sosan's words there is "neither love nor hate."[97] Indeed, don't dream. Don't have doubt and don't compare, all of which brings darkness to the mind.

With our own very personal outlook on the world, we only end up escaping from this same world which, ironically or perhaps for this very

---

94 Ch'an Master Sheng-yen, 1930-2009.

95 *Ch'an News Letter*, Feb. 1995.

96 You must learn "to get to the crack between the worlds and to enter the other world. There is a crack between the two worlds, the world of the *diableros* and the world of living men." *A Yaqui Way of Knowledge* (Penguin Books, 1970).

97 See the first verse of the *Shinjinmei*.

reason, intrigues us almost to obsession. This is how it is in one's everyday life. Either we get lost in this world and we suffocate to death, or we escape from it into ourselves. Even while in meditation it is so. But it must be said, with decreasing intensity in the early years of practice. During the first years, one usually finds oneself struggling away in *sanran* with one's own—with my own—little illusions, with my own little mind. I'm speaking from personal experience.

Why, we even write books about this kind of suffering—the suffering of the lost souls in the world—and we get them published and everybody reads them too, thinking that they express the truth about Buddha, Buddhism, meditation and the like. But it's all false. My books are false, and so are theirs. And that's because while I write from one point of view, the other writes from another.[98]

∽

So, as long as neither *sanran* nor *kontin* afflict you anymore, the next step is the realization that practice and daily life, as Sosan would say, are the same thing. And that's what he probably meant in this verse when he pointed to the place where neither love nor hate exists.

It's not easy to not hate somebody. It is much easier and much more common for people to live a life hating somebody than it is to live a life loving somebody. Nonetheless, the two are very connected. It is even said that the two are really one and the same.

In the state of doubt, sanran and kontin arise.
In the state of satori, neither love nor hate exists.[99]

---

[98] We see this, for instance, in H.W. Shumann's otherwise splendid 274-page book *The Historical Buddha* by his completely overlooking the importance meditation held in the life and teachings of the Buddha and his sangha. And not just overlooking it a little bit, but overlooking it entirely from the first page to the last (Penguin Books, 1982).

[99] Interesting to note that the most used translation in America is the Richard B. Clarke version that translates "neither love nor hate" with "no liking or

Either way, satori destroys all this—that's what it is said in this verse. "In the state of satori, neither love nor hate exists." It does so by bringing an end to living in a world of pronounced preferences and pronounced differences, that allows things like love and hate to be two completely exclusive entities.

Satori is defined as mind returned to the normal condition. It's very easy to do, to be normal. And very hard to do as well. Because, for this to happen, the merging of the brain and the cosmos is required. Only in this way can the "two" we are now talking about become "one." So, it's easy to say, but hard to do. In Buddhist poems and sutras, hundreds and thousands of us are becoming "one with the all"—and this is thus, say the sutras, so that we may understand all elements and all existences.

To explain this matter of elements and existences differently, Master Dogen used the word *genjo*, which means "the immediate manifestation of things as they are." It is the actualization of satori in our daily life, not so much through the mental process, but through the physical experience in which it is expressed. And how so is that? Through our words, through our awareness, through our bodies . . .

By cutting (that is, by going beyond) the states of *sanran* and *kon-tin*, which are at the root of illusion, we manifest things just as they are (*genjo*).

By expressing the Way in our daily lives, we can cut, as it is said, the ten-thousand illusions.

---

disliking." Sheng-yen translates it thus as well. With Deshimaru and Kodo Sawaki it's "love and hate." This is, I think, a little like conforming to the modes of the times rather than to exactness and depth of meaning.

44

You want to think too much
About the two sides of all things.

There are always two aspects: earth and heaven, subject and object, life and death, good and bad. Buddhism, however, teaches us not to fall into the suffering provoked by these two sides, and to find the Middle Way instead. This is a fundamental point. And this is why we're always talking about not chasing after or rejecting anything: not running after *shiki* (phenomena) or wanting to stay on *ku* (emptiness).

In the *Platform Sutra*, Eno the sixth Patriarch listed thirty-six pairs of opposites; today we could list thirty-six thousand.[100] Anyway, the most prominent opposites are of course love/hate, good/bad, true/false, subject/object; and finally, there are even more startling opposites such as sentient beings/buddhas and samsara/nirvana. Samsara is the Wheel of Life (and Death) and we never get off it; nirvana, however, is the Wheel we do get off, and we get off forever.

This makes sense. A non-buddha is always a non-buddha and a buddha is always a buddha. In Zen, however, we have satori or enlightenment and, seeing this for what it is—namely a concept—the Zen monk goes beyond.

∽

100 Eno listed thirty-six pairs of opposites while Sosan, who died thirty-two years before Eno was born, had only listed thirty-four. The Buddhist writer and scholar, Mu Soeng, says that Sosan mentioned these many opposites in the very poem in question, the *Shinjinmei*. Opposites such as: "Love and hate, like and dislike, lack and excess, right and wrong, object and subject, coarse and fine, easy and difficult, fast and slow, wise and foolish, movement and rest..." etc. See: *Trust in Mind, the Rebellion of Chinese Zen*, by Mu Soeng (Wisdom Books) for more.

It is said that if you reject ignorance in order to obtain wisdom, if you discard one thing in order to have another, then you are only living in illusion. And yet this happens all the time, like thinking that *we are wise* when really *we are just ordinary everyday ignoramuses*. Or again, like thinking that we are indeed ordinary everyday ignoramuses when all along we're only feeling sorry for ourselves.

Zen teaches us that if we don't fall prey to the suffering provoked by the two sides, we can have satori, and that, in fact, by being beyond the two sides we can find our original face.[101]

During zazen we become Buddha, beyond phenomena, beyond emptiness.

Master Sokei-an states that Buddhism is not in the writing, but in the mind—your mind. Buddha-mind. There is no other. And yet, as we have just shown, all kinds of minds exist in human beings: when you remove the lid you discover all the minds and spirits that lie in the earth, that dwell in the sky, the mind in the trees and the mind of invisible existences. Mind is just that, a multitude of invisible existences.

So, where are the distinctions to be made?

Distinctions and contradictions disturb. We're always confronted with them in life; we are being pulled towards our own personal ideal, for example, and we are in conflict with what is real, and we only see how someone is different from us, while completely overlooking what we have in common. This is what Master Sosan is referring to in this strophe: people tend to focus on the differences between things; they think too much about it, talk endlessly on the matter at hand, and do not act with their bodies. And this provokes suffering.

∽

101 Nietzsche writes in his *The Anti-Christ*: "...There are no more oppositions, the kingdom of Heaven belongs to children, and the faith which here finds utterance is not a faith which has been won by struggle—it is there, from the beginning, it is as it were a return to childishness in the spiritual domain." (Penguin Books, 1968).

Almost all philosophies demonstrate intellectually that one-is-all and/or that all-is-one (as Dogen would say, it is "to become one with the ten-thousand phenomena"); and likewise, in almost all spiritual practices, and particularly in Zen, this is not merely expressed verbally, but actually assumed through the correct posture and deep attitude. But for this to come about, whole body and whole mind are required.

Part of the cortex, our frontal brains, has undergone intensive development in the evolution of humanity, and one of its consequences is an over-developed frontal lobe with its resulting weak body—a body lacking in *ki*[102]—sickly and prematurely old. This is where and why our doubts germinate and grow into horrifying contradictions, horrifying in that they completely take over our frontal brains. At this point, one might be wise to watch out for the terrible specter of insanity. Once the fragile, threadlike mind-body connection has thus weakened, and our doubts, distinctions and disagreements take over, just watch out, that's all. This is why, as I've suggested earlier, it's most interesting to study all the pairs of opposites, the contradictions in fact, that are exposed, and most piteously at that, in this long Sosan poem the *Shinjinmei*.

∽

The word "buddha" means "awakened one," the person in the non-conscious state beyond the dual and contradictory world of things.[103] For this reason, we say that zazen itself is enlightenment or awakening. In zazen, as in the other great meditations, we are beyond the physio-

---

[102] In this context, *ki* means the energy of universal life from which we all come.

[103] "If, as the sutras say, all human beings are endowed with Buddha-nature," asked Dogen (this was the young man's great doubt), "why is it that one must train oneself so strenuously to realize Buddha-nature, that is, to attain enlightenment?" Master Eisai replied: "All the buddhas in the three stages of time are unaware that they are endowed with the Buddha-nature, but cats and oxen are well aware of it indeed!" This means that buddhas do not think of having-not-having the buddha-nature; only the animal-like (that is the deluded) think in such terms.

logical conditions of cortex and hypothalamus, or again of the so-called "left and right brain."

> Kyogen asked his master Isan the following question: "Please Master, explain to me what self existed before the birth of your parents." Isan refused to answer and Kyogen, feeling frustrated and unhappy by Kyogen's insipid non-answer, went off to practice elsewhere.
>
> Then, one day, while sweeping in the yard, he swept a stone against a bamboo stalk, and the sound of it, coming from the outside, caused him a great satori.
>
> Feeling most grateful to the master for *not* having answered his question earlier, he turned in the direction of Isan's dojo and did *sampai.*

Whatever answer one might wish to give the disciple, you just can't reply to this kind of question by approaching it from one side or the other, nor even from both sides together.

So, the message here is simple enough: don't fall into the trap of contradictions or that of distinctions. Live through the body and thank you very much.

This 44th strophe says, in a few poignant phrases, that all opposites are created by our own madness. And, for those who follow the Way, it suggests that instead of trying to do something through the practice, one should simply practice without "thinking so much."

45

Your life is like a dream, a ghost, a flower of emptiness.
Why should you suffer to grasp this illusion?

A good question, why do we suffer so much? And for what, finally? According to this strophe, we suffer for a ghost, or for a flower in the sky [see footnote 108]. . . for a mere dream—that is, for nothing much really. And this, says Sosan, is our life. We suffer for nothing.

Yet, when we think about it, we can understand that did we *not* suffer, and even if it were just for nothing, then we wouldn't even be here in the first place. We have often heard it said that this world is indeed suffering, and that's the case for everybody, even the most happy and privileged of us all. Buddha pointed this out in the first of his Four Noble Truths. Life is suffering.

Thanks to this suffering, however, we can come into direct contact with the world of religion, the Dharma, its practice and its teaching. This is the path of the bodhisattva, the path of wisdom.

Suffering is certainly the most important factor in bringing us to the practice, or at any rate to the teaching of the Buddha. Once we learn to use this suffering, we can use it as we might the sword of Monju.[104] The Bodhisattva Monju used it to defend himself and others from the demons of illusion and ignorance—whether they are the demons of doubt, of anger, of arrogance or some other thing, they are still demons. Likewise, we learn to defend ourselves and even to slaughter them, these demons, these *bonno*, these *klesa,* which are best executed in one blow, by sudden decapitation, as taught in the Southern School of Ch'an in the time of Eno the 6th Patriarch.[105] Later, in the time of Rinzai, it was the same; it was kill the Buddha.

---

104 For more on Monju see footnote 83, page 200.

105 ". . . the Ch'an of the Southern School represented an unorthodox approach to realization and transmission of the buddha-dharma. This school stresses the 'suddenness' of enlightenment." *The Shambhala Dictionary of Buddhism and Zen* (1991, 209).

However, the monk does not practice zazen because he's had enough with suffering and simply wants is to be done with it, as Nietzsche would say of the believing Buddhist in his book *The Anti-Christ*.[106] But, from my own experience as a monk, I don't think that we who practice the supreme Way are particularly interested in doing away with our sufferings. On the contrary, we know that suffering will never be done away with, not for the common man or woman on the street nor even for the monk or nun in the monastery, and that—whoever we are—it will be with us always, even unto our coffins. We also know that suffering (or not suffering) is *not* the primordial matter.

The Wheel of Life diagram, which I already alluded to in the previous verse, depicts just that: suffering. It divides suffering into six different world categories, and they represent the six worldly or unenlightened existences.[107] This is also referred to as the Wheel of *Samsara*, *samsara* being the repetition of suffering—of everyone's suffering—in one form or other, throughout the *kalpas*.

In the hub of the Wheel are the drawings of a cock, a snake and a pig. In Buddhism, these three animals represent the principal causes of suffering: the cock personifying passionate desire or attachment, the snake hate—or say for instance, repulsion, aversion and repugnance—and the pig personifying the multiple forms and shapes of what one calls "ignorance." In the drawings, we see all three of them running in a circle after each other's tails. This is the cycle of *samsara*, the turning of the Wheel forever and ever. And who's that running? That's just us.

---

106 "Buddhism," writes Nietzsche—who liked Buddhism very much but who had a particularly critical eye on all peoples and things (though not always exact)—when he writes that—Buddhism [opposed to Christianity] no longer speaks of struggle against 'sin' but in accordance with actuality, 'the struggle against suffering.'" And further on: "Buddhism is a religion for races who have grown kindly [....], and who feel pain too easily: it leads them back to [....] a certain physical hardening." Nietzsche, Friedrich, *The Anti-Christ* (Penguin Books, 1968).

107 The six are: 1) the Gods (Devas), 2) the Titans (Asuras), 3) the Pretas (Hungry Ghosts), 4) the Hells (Naraka), 5) the Animals (Ignorance), 6) the world of Humans.

In this *Shinjinmei,* Sosan alludes to all the different types of suffering found in humans. Here, lost in the perpetual struggle between opposites, we live in suffering, always suffering, and not only greatly, but *needlessly* as well. Indeed, all that suffering, and for what? For nothing.

Your life is like a dream, a ghost, a flower of emptiness.
Why should you suffer to grasp this illusion?

Like a dream, like a ghost, it shall evaporate into the air like so many flowers everywhere. "Flowers of emptiness," he calls it.

Yet, we suffer anyhow. There is no reason for it, it is like a flower in the sky,[108] a flower in the mind, but we do so anyhow. First, we grow a flower, watering it every day and taking good care of it, and slowly but surely, we begin to take it for something real; and from that point on, we end up believing in it too. It's for this reason alone we have all the wars in the world for all time.

Buddha pointed out in the first of his Four Noble Truths that all this is suffering. True as this may be, it is still nothing more than an observation, a simple fact, and not the crucial point. The crucial point is the Four Truths put all together, thereby demonstrating to all that there is, finally, no suffering at all. This too is what the *Hannya Shingyo,* the *Heart Sutra*, teaches. Here, the *Shinjinmei* does so as well.

The message is clear: all is not lost. For once we see the eternal unconscious mind behind it all, suffering is no longer.

---

108 The Japanese word for this flower is *kuge*—*ku* meaning both "emptiness" and also "sky"; and *ge* meaning "flower." Some important scholars who do not practice zazen, like Blyth, D.T. Suzuki and Clarke, but who are nonetheless the most prominent authorities on this question of the Sosan Zen of today, translate *kuge* as "flower of the air," "flower in the air," "flower of the sky," or even "space-flower." Master Deshimaru, however, remains with the word "*ku*," the emptiness of all things, saying that it is "like flowers in the air, flowers like bubbles on the water which appear and disappear." The flower of *ku*. Expressed less philosophically, one old master (whose name I can't remember) said that the problem was his eyesight. Because he couldn't see very well anymore, what he did see was just flowers (*ge*) in the sky, and this was why he no longer counted on his eyes to see things.

46

Gain, loss, true, false:
Please, abandon them.

Sosan suggests that we abandon everything, and by that we even abandon the idea of abandoning everything. And, though this may not be so difficult a feat to accomplish as one might think, it's still not easy by a long shot. Sosan says precisely this in the very first verse of this poem the *Shinjinmei*[109]; it's not a matter of easy or hard, that's not the problem, the problem is one of non-attachment ... Non-attachment to oneself. This is the basis of the Buddha's teaching. It's at the root of the practice of zazen and of Buddhism as a whole. It's also the foundation stone of all religions. Some of which use "God" to free men and women from their small selves, i.e., you don't work for yourself anymore but for God instead, and it is there that you find peace. Put another way, if you do not find peace within your own self, then you rest within Jesus, who himself is within God.

In Buddhism, it's more a matter of living on the earth, and by that it is about finding your own originality, your own original nature, as opposed to finding the originality of God. In Buddhism there is no duality; and its philosophy is utterly not-two. Neither *shiki* (phenomena) nor *ku* (emptiness), neither gain nor loss, neither true nor false, God nor not-God. Only continuous effort, with no goal: this is to be one with Buddha, one with the earth and sky. But this is only a feeling, a kind of prefabricated notion. Be it Christian, Buddhist or Taoist—it's the same—for this approach or understanding of religion is ephemeral and empty, which is why it (this feeling, this living experience) usually lasts for only a short while, one lifetime at the very best.

109 Entering the Way is not difficult / But you must not love or hate or choose or reject. (Verse 1 of the *Shinjinmei*.)

Don't run after anything, don't run away from anything either. That's the state of mind during zazen, too. In the beginning, you always practice for *something*; otherwise you would never make it into the dojo to begin with. Certainly, you come to the practice out of curiosity or because you want to rediscover the Christian religion through Zen meditation, or perhaps because you're writing a thesis on different meditation practices, or again because you've heard all the good things that Zen can bring a man or a woman; and since there are a lot of things you want in life, you might just try it out and see for yourself; or again, you might just want to learn how to concentrate and perhaps how to breathe better while you're at it. Some people come to Zen because they want to find a wife or a husband, it's the same "something" they are after[110]; others come for higher goals, though goals they still be: like coming to Zen to find oneness in life, or maybe in order to meet with Buddha and with eternity.

It doesn't matter what you come looking for—for a woman, for God, or for oneness . . . be it gross or subtle. These are not the same, and yet what they are is in fact the same.

Finally, though, making such distinctions in the Way is of little interest, I think.

The goal can be God or it can be another woman, it doesn't matter much what you *get*—God or the other woman. Actually, what matters is not what you *get*, but what you *give*, what you *bring*.

And, bringing something is no big deal. That's almost easy. Just bring *you yourself*; that will do. It is this way in both Hinayana and Mahayana; it's the gift of yourself that counts.

This bringing of yourself as a gift occurs without your even noticing a thing; a kind of *fuse,* a kind of offering that you do but don't see, and don't even suspect exists. An offering that is not only invisible, even to

110 Buddha, seeing that his cousin was interested in finding himself a beautiful woman, told him that if he visited the sangha he'd find one more beautiful than any other in the world. Buddha meant by that the Dharma. The cousin came and found just that, took the ordination and stayed on as a disciple.

the person in question, but without merit as well, in life as well as in death. This is what deep Buddhism teaches.

This offering is done without waiting for anything in return—not in life, not in death. This is the teaching: *fuse*. The boy who was born in Kapila in Northern India, and who subsequently became the living Buddha, had done just that, made a *fuse* of himself, body and mind for all of us, even until today.

∞

To practice in order to obtain something is much easier than to practice in order to lose. To want to lose something takes a stronger will and a stronger drive, and what's more it takes much longer to accomplish (as though there was something possible to "accomplish" in the first place). The difference between fulfilling your own desires and thereby gaining your own well-being, and that of losing, say, your hate or your fear, is great indeed. Be this as it may, neither gain nor lose is what Sosan says here in this verse: "please, abandon them both right away."

Gain, loss, true, false:
Please, abandon them.

To abandon both gain and loss together isn't so easy to do. Especially as we have never been taught how to see through the duality of things—to see its absurdity and even its illusory basis—not in school, nor at the university, how can we suddenly "abandon them" both, right now, today?

Not only are we taught to hold on to what we've already got—good family, good grades, good diplomas, good jobs and lots of money—but we are taught that these must be put to use in order that they yield a profit, and a substantial one at that. Apparently, going by what we learn in school this is what should bring us true happiness on earth. The teaching here clearly being that money and success is what gives a person meaning in life.

Sure . . . who hasn't wanted meaning in life? Who here has not wanted to make something out of their time on earth? But, the problem with this equation is that it gives you only one of two possibilities in life: that you win or that you lose. ("Lose" meaning, of course, that you be categorized and classified by society as one member of the mere multitude. Apart from being good at "bowing with the hat off" and for paying the bills, you are of no importance whatsoever on this earth.)

The miseries of the world, what people do to people, the killings and the suicides ... It's all terrible, and yet what can you do about it, *you* who are one of the nobodies? "All the nobodies like you are good for is cannon fodder," says one of the somebodies to one of the nobodies, "and good for nothing much else sir, I'm afraid."

Suicides, there's much to say about suicides, and nothing much to say either. For even within the perimeter of religion, even within the sangha, it's usually beyond comprehension; they practiced zazen, sitting still without object before a wall; and what's more, they had studied the teaching for so many years before finally taking the ordination of *shukke* (literally "out from home"), and what do they do? Kill themselves. And that's suicide, it can occur outside religion just as it can occur within.

Suicide can happen and happen it does. A disciple of the Buddha, or at least a child of the Buddha, and he goes and kills himself. What distress. It must've been awful, and especially when the despairing disciple of a true master kills himself.

In any case, the education we receive from early childhood until today, the education we—all of us—have been giving ourselves, always, has caused humankind irreparable brain damage, especially to the millions and millions of the frail or fragile-minded ones amongst us everywhere; and as was just said, this is so even within the holy sangha, the church and the mosque as well.[111]

---

111 However, education was not always so shallow and harmful, as for instance in the time of the Buddhist king Asoka, in India in the 3rd Century BCE. In Asoka's time, the school curriculum consisted mainly in the study of non-duality, and namely, that loss and gain were not separate entities but one and the same. This is how young people came to look and to understand the world around them in the Golden Age of King Asoka.

In other words, whatever one's early childhood and environment may have been, with our upper-class or lower-class parents, teachers, friends and all the rest, no one and no thing is responsible for what *we* decide, what *we* choose to listen to in order to understand and to follow, no-one but ourselves. What one gives importance to is, clearly, what one wishes to *be*, now and in the future, and if we are not responsible for that, then who is? In other words, we are responsible for our own cerebral functioning. It's not God who is responsible; it's not karma, not family, nor even the injustices that lurk over us like shadows in the dark. For after all, what can one do about the things one gives importance to? Stop them? Go through some kind of shock therapy?

Certainly, there is also a kind of psycho-medical approach to this question of responsibility. Take, for instance, a man who is being strapped into the electric chair for having committed a particularly heinous crime. He rotted away for seventeen years on Death Row waiting for this moment, and he thought a lot about it—about his close ones, his parents, his last moments—with the fear . . . the fear. He is fully aware that he is going to be electrocuted any minute. Now, at that time, what was going on in his mind? Probably he had no longer any notion of gain vs. loss. He has abandoned those notions, by the force of circumstances, or perhaps by sheer necessity. What a good day! (even if he's about to die). What a good education! This is so because such things as "right," "just" "good," "only justice"—these alone are of no concern to the man anymore. He's a healthy person in the prime of manhood and he's about to be executed. Nothing else means much of anything anymore. In this sense, the killer seems almost like an enlightened monk walking alone on a road. He has abandoned everything (except perhaps his own life).

. . . But has he really? Were this killer to live through an execution fiasco, as has happened many times already (and usually due to a mishap in the functioning of the current in the electric chair itself), would this man, now liberated, no longer feel the impulse to kill again? Had the convicted killer finally learned his lesson? Or was he simply adapting himself to the given circumstances? No one knows.

Now, imagine that this recently liberated criminal were to rejoin us here amongst all our law-abiding local laws and townships and whatnot. Will he be able to restrain himself? Or even better, will he have actually gone beyond the world of duality and self-interest (and remain beyond it)? In other words, has this man-killer actually freed himself of his past karma, including his present crimes committed in this one lifetime? And, has this newfound freedom come about due to the very tough conditions on Death Row for so many years? And now? Now, suddenly, the moment has arrived: he is standing naked before his destiny. Had the deep shock of what was unfolding before his eyes awakened the man to the illusion of it all? Or, as Takuan would say, to the dream? Or again, as someone else might say, to the nightmare?

This question cannot be answered by anyone but the individual himself. Certainly not by you or me.

We talk about "freedom," and yet where, one might ask, is this freedom located? In the act of living and *not* of dying? Or is it freedom, not so much from life and from death, as it is freedom *in-and-from* oneself, and nothing else?

Learning to free yourself of yourself is to follow the cosmic order, and not yourself. "To follow the fundamental cosmic power is best," said one master of the lineage.

> In the Meiji Era, five samurais were going to be decapitated. They had been in prison for fourteen days, waiting for their time to die. On the fifteenth day, just before the execution, the authorities announced that there had been a mistake: the samurais were free to go. Not in the least bit traumatized, all five of them burst out laughing...[112]

Such expression of body and mind—in this case laughter over one's own commuted death sentence—is to follow the fundamental cosmic power. This is what is called "being beyond one's own life and death."

---

112 For a more detailed rendition of this story see Sekida, Katsuki, *Zen Training* (Weatherhill, 1975).

∽

Gain, loss, true, false:
Please, abandon them.

To want to gain something, to want to become someone special, someone different, somewhere near the top if not on the top altogether: we have all wished for something like this. To gain position, power and wealth, and for the more subtle fellow specimens, to gain truth—and that, usually by ridding ourselves of the false. But this doesn't work, I don't think. I don't think anything "works."

Seekers of the truth, as for instance those who practice the koan method, always have a target in mind, even if it's the sky itself; they shoot their arrows straight into the sky, aiming like archers to pierce it in the middle. Then there are those who learn to shoot the sky without aiming to pierce it at all. It is said of these sorts of archers that it is not because they no longer want to touch or hit the center, rather they have simply and naturally transformed themselves, unconsciously and without knowing it. Like the person who throws a sword into the sky. It's the continuous effort of sword and body. The sword is thrown upwards and all that's left is the shimmering brilliance of the blade in the blue sky.

47

If the eye never sleeps,
All your dreams will vanish.

The eye that never sleeps is the eye that sees things as they are, while the eye that sleeps, or at least half-sleeps, is the eye of relativity and subjectivity; this eye sees things from a very limited viewpoint. The eye that sleeps is a metaphor for ignorance, while the word "dream" found in the second line is a metaphor for *samsara*, the Wheel of Life and Death. The cycle of longing, clinging and becoming is set into motion, and the individual in question is left advancing forever in a kind of sleepwalk. No one wants to advance like a sleepwalker, but sleepwalking or not, there are many who think that dreaming is a very effective way to analyze and study oneself. Indeed, according to Sigmund Freud and C.G. Jung, a dream is a direct manifestation of the unconscious mind, and therefore worthy of our full attention. The Zen master however is not so fascinated, let alone interested or even kindly inclined to the study of dreams. For him, it is simply more of the same old illusion. Might it occur while asleep in bed or even while out walking in the street, it is still a dream. "And to realize that your life is just that, a dream," to again cite Deshimaru, "is a big satori." So, even if you have a good karma and live a life full of love and other good things, this personal karma of yours will not carry you far, nor can you count on it to solve the situation. Any way you look at it, karma may be karma, but it is seen through a dream, and a dream is still only a dream. This is the little eye that sees life as something basically personal.

We dream and we dream, even when we are awake and walking in the street we dream. In the street, however, we no longer call it "dreaming," we call it "thinking." We call it "thought"; but either way, dreaming and thinking come from the same source: from longing, from clinging and from becoming. One must always become that *something*, as if one wasn't that something already. As for longing and clinging, it goes on all the time! Past, present or future it's all the same: we ruminate and we ruminate, we delve into our memories and rarely come out of them, except perhaps to make plans to go on vacation or something. Otherwise, we just go on analyzing, comparing and evaluating everything we can get hold of. In fact, were we to hear what the sages of the past, present and future have to say about all this, they'd say that any way you might wish to cut it, you are—believe it or not—still only dreaming. On the other hand, *were your eye never to sleep,* as Sosan says, *then all your dreams would vanish,* and here Sosan brings to our attention our third eye.

We have a third eye, everybody does. It's the eye of Buddha, that is, the not-dreaming eye-mind that sees all things as they are. In high Buddhism, this is called *inmo* or simply "suchness."

Inmo, or the concept *inmo*, or *tathata* in Sanskrit, means, in so many words, the eternal present. It also means reality. Practicing this deeply, we observe our illusions in all tranquility. Then we correct them; and by this means we return to *inmo*, the eternal present.

Through the practice of zazen—which is *not* a meditation, and this point can never be underlined strongly enough[113]—we can observe our illusions, correct them and come back to *inmo*, to the eternal present that we come from in the first place; so why wait for our own demise to rediscover the wonderful evidence.

∽

We are basically dualistic from the very beginning: we come into this world with two eyes, two ears, two nostrils, two hands, two feet, etc. Even the brain's in two pieces, the left and the right (also referred to as the intuitive and the analytical, the instinctive and the frontal, or again the cortex and the hypothalamus). Then you have the different species,

---

113 In zazen we do not meditate, neither on something tangible, like on a burning incense, nor intangible, like on love; for zazen is not sitting or leaning on anything at all. It is only, as master Dogen has said, "like the unmovable mountain," and nothing else.

genders, sexes. It doesn't really matter seeing that one doesn't really look at life, nor live it, except through one's own two eyes, own two nostrils, own two eardrums, and that's it. Now, there are many waves in our lives, sometimes even during zazen, but like all waves, during zazen and elsewhere, they come from the ocean and thus they return, all the time.

The same coming and returning occurs with the body and mind. The hands become one, the knees become one, the mind becomes one; and when you ask yourself: which is my left hand and which my right? Well, you don't know anymore . . . too complicated. All you know is that your hands are in the mudra *hokkai jo-in*—the single circle created by thumbs and fingers, representing the universe.

If the eye never sleeps,
All your dreams will vanish.

Let us not always analyze our thoughts—as suggested in this strophe—but instead, observe them with the objective eye that never sleeps.

48

If the mind makes no distinctions,
All beings in the cosmos become one.

This is what we have been saying. Here in this strophe, however, Sosan takes this notion even further. The mind during zazen . . . yes—but by this he means the mind in daily life, the mind here and everywhere as well. Zen mind, like Zen practice is not separate from anything. Zen mind is getting out of bed in the morning with your right foot, and not with your left. This of course is a metaphor, no need to take it literally, the left foot's at least better than no foot at all! Of course, people don't really *have to* get out of bed with the right foot, or even get out of bed at all. Just be aware of what's happening to them—and of where it's all taking them. The direction is very important, which is why a master or at least a guide up front is necessary.

The ancients, like their contemporaries today, always emphasize this aspect. "Even if you sit facing a wall until you die, if you do not practice this teaching I give you in daily life, it is not Zen, it is not *ku sokuze shiki* or emptiness-becomes-phenomena." Otherwise, all you are practicing is emptiness-which-remains-empty and phenomena-which-remain-phenomena, and nothing more than that . . . You're still stuck, they tell you. Stuck, in what? In something. Like the convict stuck in prison, or like the monk hermit stuck in the desert; that is, like those stuck in phenomena or otherwise stuck in emptiness.

When we think beyond our own little self-interests we understand that no one is actually imprisoning anyone. Whether you are behind bars or not, who finally is imprisoning whom? We ourselves obviously.[114]

---

114 In July 1846, Emerson was talking to Thoreau through the bars in a cellblock in the Concord, Mass. Jailhouse. He had been locked up for disobedience in the face of the law—something to do with the War of Aquisition then raging in Texas and California, which until that time belonged, in most part, to the

If the mind does not discriminate, as Sosan says in this present verse, then everything is as it is. "All beings in the cosmos become one." We could also say that they become *inmo—inmo* the Mahayana of "suchness," of the "here and now."[115]

If you don't get lost in differentiations, everything naturally and unconsciously becomes one single identity. And to be this way is to follow the universal law, which is change: *mujo*, impermanence. Indeed, everything is in perpetual change, even differences are in change. What's more, and as always, everyone is different. Everyone's thinking, everyone's posture, everyone's zazen is different.

But, go beyond personal thinking—go into *hishiryo*-consciousness—and sitting immediately becomes unity, and not only unity for those who practice, but for all peoples and all things.

Hishiryo-mind is the mind in perpetual motion, and as such, subject to the laws of desire. Even during zazen, which is always active, desire is present. We desire to go the way we want to go, and not some other way. Desire Number One. Little by little, however, unconsciously and unbeknownst to oneself, this desiring mind enters more and more into the state of *hishiryo*, into what we see as change itself. To a place where we are no longer disturbed or even taken in by our desires and our emotions, of attraction, of repulsion; and even if they too are present, it's because they too unwind themselves into the blue azure.[116]

∽

---

country of Mexico, and only after the war became part of the United States of America, with New Mexico becoming the 47th state of the Union. "What in hell are you doing behind those bars, Henry?"

Thoreau, who didn't agree with his own government's act of outright agression and thievery, looked back at Emerson standing on the other side of the prison bars, and replied, "Hey Waldo, what are you doing in front of them, tell me that?" In other words, it's all a matter of mind, as Sosan points out in this particular verse.

115 See *inmo* commenatry in previous strophe.

116 See: "...blue sky'" at end of strophe 46.

Sometimes the mind is as calm as the surface of a mountain lake, while at other times it becomes agitated like a mountain torrent. Still the water is always the same: sometimes mirror, sometimes wave, but always water. It's the same with all of us. Everybody gets angry, and to claim that there are certain bodhisattvas and saints who never get angry is very lightweight thinking. In fact, it's the opposite. If they never got angry, they would not be bodhisattvas, let alone saints.

> One day Master Nyojo was furious with a monk. The monk was sitting beside Dogen, sleeping. Nyojo grabbed his sandals, shouted loudly *Shin jin datsu raku*! ("Throw down body and mind!") and hit the monk squarely on his head and shoulders), and the shock of it acted as a catalyst to Dogen's own awakening.[117]

Later in life, when Dogen was a master in his own right, he got so angry with one of his own disciples that he threw him out of the temple and told him to never come back. Presenting himself as a disciple of Master Dogen's, this monk in question had paid a visit to a rich individual of the ruling class in Kyoto and returned to the temple with a gift—a package of money—a donation for Dogen's mission to spread the dharma of Buddha.

In fact, the only thing this poor fellow wanted was to help his master and the temple, and all he expected in return was a simple sign of recognition, a *gassho*, a thank you from the master. And perhaps a cup of tea. Why not? The master certainly had a little time for a tea break. After all, there was a lot of money involved.

The fellow didn't mean badly . . . it wasn't that. No, it was the monk's true inheritance, his inward potential that interested Dogen; it was this man, suddenly appearing with this money, that interested Dogen. Was this monk so utterly corruptible, and irreparably so, or not? This monk who stood before him, before the abbot of Eiheiji in his own private

---

117 See: Kodera, T.J. *Dogen's Formative Years in China* (Routledge & Kegan Paul).

quarters, with all this money in his hands . . . was this man ready to assume his role of monk of the Dharma, or not? Anyway, the master decided that he was thoroughly immoral and therefore thoroughly corruptible and threw him out.

One might ask the question right here, right now: Was Dogen in error himself, expelling this poor soul for seemingly such a trifle? It's possible, and I think so myself, but not having witnessed the scene, who knows. In any case, selection is necessary, and so too is the discriminating mind; a true master always selects his disciples, sorting out who is best and who is not for the journey.

Dogen was indeed very angry, and it's too easy to conclude that this was a teaching intended to educate his disciples, and that deep inside he wasn't really angry at all (as is said of this incident). I don't think so. I saw Deshimaru in a very bad temper with one of his own disciples. He broke the table with one blow of his hand and threw the young man down on top of the broken pieces. What the master emanated at that moment wasn't anything other than just plain old anger; it was no wonder, he was a 6th Dan in both Judo and Kendo in the pre-war Japanese grading system, and actually it was better to get out of range of the man . . . I mean, to leave the room quickly and to hell with the teaching, at least at that point.

Of course, the masters do care about the education of their disciples; however, had they no disciples at all to educate, would they have acted differently? Had Dogen no disciples but this one corruptible fellow, he would have acted the same way; for, to have disciples or no disciples, one still wishes to influence the world for the better, rather than for the worse, I should think.

"...For the Way, for the Dharma," writes Kodo Sawaki in his notebook, "strength is necessary—strength in the right proportion. When I was a younger, I would sometimes become so angry that it seemed to my disciples that my head had detached itself from my trunk. Just the sight of it all marked them for life." Their minds had been altered. However, it must be said that many of Kodo Sawaki's disciples left him from displeasure, particularly in reaction to these occasional fits of anger. But, Kodo wasn't the more disturbed by these occasional departures, no matter how much he felt or did not feel for these departing disciples. In fact, he observed once, "this way he could sort out the best for the journey."[118]

If the mind makes no distinctions,
All beings in the cosmos become one.

This 34th strophe was translated, as in all the other strophes herein as well, by Master Deshimaru. The same one translated by R.H. Blyth, whom I already talked about in my commentary on strophe 34, says: "If the mind creates no discrimination / All things are as they really are." Blyth did not do zazen, and he was even hostile to the practice or at least indifferent, but his vision and his translations were nevertheless true and profound.

As Blyth would have it, all things are fine just as they are, if only we can learn to leave them alone. When we don't make discriminations or differentiations—which is not easy to do—then we are as one. No difference between inside and out, or between body and mind. Even between the immaterial and the immaterial, like Buddha, Allah and God.

In this strophe, Sosan does not talk about awakening so much as about *rejecting* everything . . . Finally, even to *rejecting* the oneness of the cosmos, as he does here in the following strophes.

---

118 Taisen Deshimaru, *Zen et Vie Quotidienne* (Albin Michel, 1985).

49

If your body profoundly realizes the One,
You can instantly cut all relations.

Little by little, with a strong but calm posture, life loses its complications and its complicated relations. As Sosan says in the previous verse, "All your dreams will vanish."[119] So, you decide with your body, which means you use your intuition. "If your body realizes," says Master Deshimaru, "then during zazen intuition is very strong, and your understanding becomes that of the body, not of the mind."

When you do not discriminate, you see everything as one, with no difference between. Mind is unified. Sit in this fashion and your practice will become like that of the ancients.

The Wise do not speak of unity, they do not speak of samadhi either. "Samadhi is not Ch'an," said Eno the 6th Patriarch one day, for practitioners of Ch'an—unlike practitioners of samadhi—are really nothing special,[120] they don't show anything, not even samadhi, and they don't hide anything either. Such a one might appear to be insignificant and uninteresting, but this is not generally the case. Such a one does not pass by unseen; he or she is neither transparent nor invisible; the contrary in fact, because the enlightened one—the person without obstructions, or if you will without attachment in the mind—is *inmo.*

> "I have something that has no head or tail," said Eno one day to his monks. "It has no back or front, and no name to call it by. Does anyone among you know what it is?"
>
> One of the monks said, "Yes, it's the original nature of all Buddhas, and my own Buddha-nature as well."

---

119 If the eye never sleeps, All your dreams will vanish.

120 See: Sheng-yen, *Faith in Mind*, 120.

> "I said it has no name, yet immediately you call it 'Original Nature' and 'Buddha-nature.' Your understanding is only theoretical," continued Eno without mincing his words, "It is only names."

This *mondo* took place in the 700s, but it's exactly the same today. The only thing that is different is the way we express ourselves. We learn to express ourselves in school, we learn our lessons, each in their own given language, and then we repeat them to others, and all the while completely convinced that we know what we are talking about. This is one thing that is different. The other is that what we are repeating to others has nothing to do with our cosmic body, or more precisely our cosmic body/mind.

> "I have something that has no name," said the master.
> "Well what is it?" asked the monk.
> "It's the mystery of all things just as they are."

If we understand the mystery of the unity of all things, says the master, then we are free from hindrance, Dharmic hindrance included.

∽

In the world that master Sosan is alluding to, there exists no doubt about the Buddha-way, the path of normality. He lives like everyone else; he doesn't give off any particular feeling, nor emit any special odor. In short, there is nothing "spiritual" about the man of the Way, nothing at all.

Be this as it may, his comportment is different than that of the ordinary man, and for the discerning eye, this difference can be seen by the way he moves about in life, with ease and sensuality and precision. And too, inwardly his sole concern is the practice of the Way.[121]

---

121 This is not at all the same as Edward Conze's description of the true man of the Way: "A true spiritual man is known to be androgynous." *The Memoirs of a Modern Gnostic*, Privately Printed in 1979, by E. Conze.

As just pointed out, these similarities and differences can be seen and expressed in many ways. For instance, we can say that, when body and mind become one, when there are no more thoughts (meaning by this, no more thoughts connected one to the other), when all relationships in the dojo are cut away, we are indeed different from the ordinary person in the street. And yet, we are nonetheless like the person in the street, cut off from nothing and from no one.

Sosan, however, is not so much talking about similarities and differences, nor about the wayfarer and the ordinary streetwalker, but about one who awakes to reality. To the ultimate non-conditioned nature of all things.[122]

If your body profoundly realizes the One,
You can instantly cut all relations.

It is written in the *Fukanzazengi*: "Reject all commitment and abandon all business." In other words, cut off all relations. Also, stop mulling over personal affairs, love, family or whatever. Otherwise it is simply being elsewhere. Certainly not like being one with the cosmos, or as Master Dogen would say, being one with all things.

How to be with our body to such an extent that it is one with the cosmos, one with the ten-thousand things, that's the important matter. Dogen has a suggestion as to how this can be done: "By learning to direct your light inward to illuminate your true nature. Do this and body and mind will fall away, and your original face will appear. If you want to reach *inmo*," he continues, "then you must practice *immo* without delay."[123]

> Shortly before Ungan's passing away, his disciple Tozan asked him, "After your death, if I am asked what your true face was like, how should I reply?"
>
> Ungan answered, "Just this, just this."

[122] *Inmo*, which was discussed in the previous commentary (#48), is also called "suchness" or "thusness"; in Sanskrit it's *tathata*.

[123] See: Dogen's *Shobogenzo*, chapter: "*Inmo*."

What is reality, real reality? It is original nature, *inmo*. You cannot see *inmo*, you cannot smell it or taste it. You cannot prove its existence either, because you cannot conceive of it. Though there are no words to describe it and no thinking about it can possibly exist, *inmo* exists. Without knowing it, you are it. You exist.

50

If you consider all existences with equanimity
You will return to your original nature.

To "consider all existences with equanimity" means, as was just said, to face things calmly and without emotion. This is not so easy to do, for it involves looking at things other than from our usual personal perspective. If you and I look at a rose, the object is the same, yet the feelings it stirs up are different for you and for me. However, this strophe invites us to consider the flower from a higher viewpoint, one that is not obscured by personal emotions or concepts. Another example: when we look at other people, we tend to judge and measure, however unconsciously—the person is tall or short, smart or stupid, generous or mean, likable or unlikable. But Buddhism teaches us to look precisely beyond the next moment, and this naturally and without effort, and therefore beyond judgment itself. This is to look naturally and unconsciously at the Buddha-nature in all of us.

It is important to see the essential similarity of all things, and not just to see their differences. Unfortunately, these differences are what we look at all the time, particularly here in the West. What's more, such differences are usually equated with the positive idea of "individuality." The essence of Buddhism is equality and compassion. We don't have more compassion for a poor person than for a rich one, but *not* the opposite either. So, what then is individuality?

For most of us, the concept of individuality is seen through comparison, and this is a trap to avoid, especially so if you wish to grasp this teaching and to share in the wisdom of the ancients. Comparing people is making a judgment based on personal values. And finally, it is to compare them with us, with you, with me ... From this arises the mind of competition, followed by that of envy, jealousy, hate, and sometimes even the mind of murder—that is, if you see yourself as inferior in any way. However, if you see yourself as superior, then you will have the horrible stigma of self-pride (which too can lead you to murder). According to the Bible, the essential vice, the utmost evil is not hatred, it is pride. In fact, according to the story, it was through pride that the devil became the very Devil himself!

So, true individuality, as it is taught in Buddhism, is each person's original nature, and that's simply not realized through comparison.

> The "*mu*" koan, one of the best known koans of all times, comes from a *mondo* between Master Joshu and one of his many disciples. The disciple asked, "Does a dog have buddha-nature?"
>
> Joshu replied, "*Mu*!"[124] (i.e., something like: "no, nothing.")

Clear as Joshu's reply may appear to some, it has led to all kinds of interpretations, mainly philosophic in content. Does a dog have buddha-nature or does it not? Does Joshu's "no" really mean "yes"? Are the two, the "no" and the "yes," together and bound in nothing less than the teaching of Absolute Oneness? Or are they not?

So, the professor emeritus might say to the monk, by way of interrogation: "Yes, but what if this 'no, the dog has it not,' really means precisely that he has it indeed! Now what would you say to that, Mr. Monk?"

Or on the other hand, there is the person who sees everything as *mu* right from the beginning; they see this Joshu, this monk, this dog, all the existences and the universe all together as *mu*, the so-called formless form.

Well, the answer Joshu gives the monk is kind of prosaic. When one understands that the master is *not addressing himself to the question being asked of him, but simply to the monk who was asking it*—see that and

---

124 The word *mu* is generally understood to mean "no," though not in the sense of "something" vs. "nothing," but rather in the sense of "no," of "nothing." So if this "no" is anything, it is still not a negation.

it changes everything. Because now you understand that it's not at all the question itself that counts. It's the monk who counts. Nothing else.

Thus we understand that the problem for most people is that, here in this exchange, there is no philosophy, not even religion. Indeed, there isn't anything to repeat to anyone here in Joshu's reply. I mean there's nothing, no message to pass on.

In other words, it's the monk's mind and not the theory behind it, whatever the theory may be worth, that counts. "Hey, Mr. *mu*-monk man, tell me about your own Buddha-nature, and forget about nothingness, and forget about the dog as well, please."

∽

Considering all things with equanimity doesn't mean that you ignore the differences between things, of course not. We're all different from one another, we are all made up of different cells and molecules, each have different parents, different names, a different karma and a different vision of the world and ourselves.

Similarity *and* difference is necessary in order for harmony to exist. In this practice, as in life itself, opposites make the whole; making it that similarity and difference exist all the time, in all things profoundly.

Be this as it may, during zazen there is neither difference *nor* similarity. Your hands are not holding anything, your eyes don't look at anything, your nose identifies no odors, your feet are not touching the ground, your legs are not trying to keep you standing, and your sexual organs are, at that moment, non-existent. Most importantly, your head's not running after or away from anything at all. In the end, there is only *shin jin datsu raku*: throwing down body and mind. This is the essence of Zen as hammered into our own brains by the master.

In this life we are always confronted by others and by ourselves. When you have really absorbed this teaching, when you manage to see both similarity and difference together, then you can harmonize with those around you—man, woman, animal, insect, everything. When you are in a relationship with another, you have to be able to distinguish, not so much between the sex, weight, height, hair coloring of the other, as between you and yourself and what is ego and what is not. I think that when you do this, compassion is immediately present. For then we see all things with an equal eye. With vast mind, vast enough to embrace everything. So we are equals, and yet we are different. And this is not deduced by comparison.

∽

If you consider all existences with equanimity
You will return to your original nature.

Do this and, to use Sosan's words, "You will return to your original nature."

If you consider all existences *exactly as they are*—and as evident as this may be, it is also impossible, alas, to carry it out—then you return to authentic freedom.

There are many ways of expressing "freedom," and here Sosan expresses it as "original nature." But he could just as readily have said, "Buddha-nature." Or again "*inmo.*"

What is authentic freedom? According to Marx and Hegel, it is to understand "necessity"; but this is still, as far as I can see, belief in the mere material, and has little to do with the way Zen sees things. Freedom, at least according to this verse in question, is being able to move without obstruction between affirmation and negation; not with "necessity," but rather with "neither one existence nor another." It is, I believe, to be unattached to existence-non-existence, the material-immaterial.

When Sosan says that "you return to your original nature," he is talking about satori, about returning naturally and unconsciously to your very own nature from before your very birth, after your very death, in all existences, all phenomena, all dharmas. Or more simply, you come back to yourself, no longer disturbed by illusions, emotions or concepts.

To obtain satori is to lose. To lose what? To lose all one's preconceived ideas and attitudes, all one's heavyweight baggage. It's to lose everything that prevents this great thing we are talking about from happening.

∽

This strophe reminds me of the first verse of the *Shodoka*, written about a hundred years after the *Shinjinmei*. It is obvious from this verse that its author, Master Yoka Daishi, had been very much influenced by Sosan:

Dear friend, do you see this true man of satori?
He has forgotten all intellectual understanding—and everything he has learned,
And everything he was supposed to learn.
And so he practices everything he learned or hopes to learn, easily and freely.
He lives in equanimity, calmly and happily.
Being free of all worry he acts naturally and reasonably.
He makes no effort to avoid illusions and does not seek satori:
He knows that illusions are without foundation.[125]

The "he" here is not the small "he"; otherwise "the satori of himself' would have no meaning at all. Shakyamuni Buddha spent six days under the bodhi tree. When he obtained satori, he didn't obtain it "himself"; it was not his own consciousness he became one with, but with the universal consciousness. When he saw the morning star he was able to consider both sides of all things. He became truly free, and everything around him became free and pacified as well.

The nature of our minds is so deep, so unfathomable, and so full of mystery.

---

[125] Rough translation by T. Deshimaru along with myself in the re-writing. See: *Le Chant de l'immediat Satori*, by Taisen Deshimaru (Retz, 1978).

51

Once you have examined it,
Nothing can be compared anymore.

This strophe refers to the previous one. The "it" to be examined is the causes and reasons of existence. Sosan is saying that if you examine existence—phenomena, the dharmas—what is there, in the end? Look closely at an atom and what do you see? You see nothing. Every time you think you see something, you see nothing. Nothing, not philosophy, not religion, not even God or Buddha. You hear no explanations and you see nothing. Except one thing: you see the finger pointing to the moon, and that actually says everything. From then on, you never again lose your direction. You know where to go. "Nothing" is not, as people say, a negation, and Buddhism is not nihilism.

"Nothing" in Buddhism is not a philosophy, not a religion, not even a negation. It is not "no thing" any more than it is "no non-thing." Rather, it is *ku,* or *sunyata* in Sanskrit.

The Buddhist word, "*ku*" is that "nothing" from which all notions and all things come. And this, I think, is very different than anything we have here in the West.

∽

There are many who attach excessive importance to the idea that the five *skandha*—or the five causally-conditioned elements—are empty and have no nature of their own. The problem with putting so much emphasis on the "emptiness" of all things is that it can lead the person into seeking for a way out of samsara and into nirvana; that is, a way out of the world we live in, and a way into something else, something better. Those who have succeeded in moving from this world into the other one are the saints of Hinayana Buddhism, called *arhats.*

Though the true bodhisattva, like the true monk, knows well that the five skandha are completely empty, he or she also knows that all five exist, or at least they should know this; that is, that the five skandha or aggregates, like all sentient beings, are ku and shiki (emptiness and form) together, simultaneously empty and existing. The result of this realization—though unconscious as it may be—is that the bodhisattva, the monk or nun, is not attached to phenomena, nor have they any desire to escape from it; and the same is true for ku, nirvana or the Dharma. This monk or nun, therefore, has neither repulsion because it exists; nor attachment, because it is empty; and thus, unlike the saints of the so-called Hinayana, the bodhisattva of Mahayana remains without hindrance in the material world of samsara, and at the same time not separate from the world of life and death until, as the chanted vow of the bodhisattva would have it: "all sentient beings have been saved."

Here is a poem by the Chinese monk Jo Hoshi.[126] It impressed me greatly and I can never forget it. Jo Hoshi was about to be decapitated by the emperor,[127] and he composed it shortly before the execution took place. It was to be Jo's farewell poem. He had refused the emperor an order. This was in the year 414:

The four elements have originally no master;
the five skandha are essentially empty.
Now I confront the sword with my head;
let's do it like reaping the spring breeze.

Unlike the monk in the hut earlier, Jo Hoshi took phenomena not only for being empty but for not existing at all. Naturally and unconsciously. This is perhaps why he could be so free in mind, even then. Even in the act of dying by execution, Jo Hoshi could still help others.

---

126 Jo Hoshi, Seng-chao in Chinese. (384-414 CE). Disciple of Kumarajiva. He traveled from Central Asia to China in 401, translated many Buddhist scriptures and was a great influence in the development of Buddhism in China. Sekida, Katsuki, *Zen Training* (Weatherhill, 1975).

127 Emperor Yo Ko.

Master Unmon once said, on another occasion: "Every day is a good day."

Yes, and as for the great spiritual dimension of Jo Hoshi, we can perhaps gather that for him every day is not just a good day, but in fact a good day to die.

Because everything comes from *ku* (or emptiness), all existences are One. This is what Buddha teaches in the sutras. The first paragraph of the *Hannya Shingyo (Heart Sutra)* says *shiki sokuze ku, ku sokuze shiki*: form becomes emptiness, emptiness becomes form. Form here does not become form; it becomes *ku*, emptiness. All phenomena are distinct; we are all different. But, as we saw in strophe 50, all phenomena are also alike and, in fact, they're already the other anyhow. This is so, according to essential Buddhism, because everything is, from the beginning, without noumenon or substance.

Once you have examined it,
Nothing can be compared anymore.

To compare emptiness with emptiness is like comparing abstract thought with itself, or like comparing phenomena with phenomena, or if you will, people with people, blacks with whites, blondes with brunettes, small-sized people to large-sized ones, and even animals with animals, flowers with flowers and so on.

Don't get stuck on *shiki* the visible, don't get stuck on *ku* the invisible; that's the teaching; and this is just another way of saying: don't follow your thoughts.

Everybody compares. We compare ourselves to others, "She's more talented than I am," we compare ourselves to ourselves, "I was better at this when I was younger." If we habitually make comparisons, we'll always be seeing just that, the differences among the phenomena; we'll always be creating categories and concepts, and finally, we'll always be looking for explanations to it all. When we criticize, compare and judge, we're just seeing one small part of things—the differences, the surface, and only some of that as well. We're looking down at the foam while calling it the ocean depths.

By this means, we learn to believe that the foam is the bottom. In fact, it is madness.

If you study and examine all this and think about it deeply, you come to understand that causes and existences are indeed One. Those who understand in this way are beyond their eyes and their ears—being themselves in a condition in which comparing becomes impossible. ("No eyes, no nose, no ears" as it is said in the *Hannya Shingyo*, the Heart Sutra.)

This doesn't mean that you suddenly become a blind and speechless ascetic, or worse, a zombie or the walking dead. It just means that you're no one's fool anymore. By no longer seeing yourself as the primary cause (i.e., through the senses), you are no longer trapped by the elements of your own mind (i.e., by say the emotions). You have just stopped fooling yourself.

It is necessary to follow a master; otherwise through the investigation and analysis of the "reasons and causes of existence," this so-called "self-observation," can drive you into madness. This is why a master sometimes advises people to practice less. For people who are frail in mind structure, it is better that they practice body movements, preferably yoga that rests the mind; but for someone in the normal condition, this immobile investigation of the self leads to the limitless.

Once you have examined it,
Nothing can be compared anymore.

It is said that the disciple must understand and believe in an invisible world. Its existence, as has already been said, is real; even though we cannot provide any explanation of it. Yet this is a fact. For instance, one can't see one's own face with one's own eyes. So, if you cannot even see your own face, you might as well conclude that indeed all true existences are invisible anyway. Right up until the day you die, other people can see you well enough, but not you—you alone cannot see, and can only go by what others say of you; that is, until your reflection in the mirror becomes apparent to you. But even then, that's not enough. Your reflection on a flat piece of glass? "I've got nothing against that face reflected in the mirror," you ponder to yourself, "but it's simply not me!"[128]

Some people always do things in the visible world. You can see this even in the dojo. They enter the dojo and take up the posture and sit down in zazen, and all this quite visibly. They get up for *kinhin* "visibly" and during *kinhin*, when they get to a corner, they stop, turn to the right, and wait for a fraction of a second, as it is written in the *Eiheiji Shingi* (Dogen's pure standards for the Zen Community), before continuing. This is going from *shiki* to *shiki*, from visible to visible, from concentration to concentration. But practice, like life, is not only concentration.

What is life? What is existence? I think it's better to understand what the invisible world is made of, to be open to this existence (or non-existence) rather than wanting to explain or to answer this question of life.

This existence and this non-existence is real; however, as it is said, we cannot furnish any explanations for them. People who can explain everything are very tiring because, in the end, they don't explain much of anything, except for just explaining the explainable, if not just explaining what everybody else knows and explains already.

> When Nangaku arrived at Eno's, Eno asked him, "Why have you come here?" (Or in some translations, "What comes?" or again, "How does it come?")

---

[128] This comes from story of Tozan looking at his reflection in the river. "That face is mine, but it's not me."

"What is being admonished here," writes Dogen in his *Zuimonki*, "is an attitude in which one feels no shame before unseen beings, and covets the esteem of worldly people." See also: newspaper article in *Courrier International* (#428, 36 du Jan. 1999) about the inhabitants of that lost Scottish island… i.e., about the woman who sees a woman in the mirror—she's never seen a mirror before and didn't know that she was looking at her own reflection; didn't even recognize the face as her very own because until then she'd never yet seen herself in a mirror, and consequently she takes the reflection for a picture of her husband's lover, as in fact her rival and accuses her husband of infidelity.

> Nangaku didn't know what to say to that. He stayed to practice with Eno for several years, and he often thought back to the question that Eno asked him at the very beginning. He thought about it for three years. Then one day, Eno saw him going by and asked him, "Hey monk, you understand my question now?"
>
> Nangaku turned to the master: "Even if I reply, master, my reply cannot approach the truth."
>
> Eno was very happy with this answer. There was no error in it. It's as though, after three years, Nangaku had dropped the question, just as we should drop our own questions; anyway, this is what is called "dropping mind and body."

The *Shinjinmei* was written for people who do Zen; to help them with their practice and their unconscious understanding. Not just in the dojo but in life. If we intuitively understand the true nature of things, then this is the "dropping off of mind and body." It is said that if we truly and deeply examine ourselves, without continued outside interferences, we open ourselves to others; we drop our small self.

52

If you stop movement, there is no more movement.
If you set stillness into motion, there is no more stillness.

In other words, as mentioned in the previous verse, when you really embrace the contradictions (first by not grasping at things, and secondly by not chasing them away either), like for instance your thoughts, all of which flow from phenomena-to-emptiness-to-phenomena again, then you can have stillness.

Just like stopping the movement of a wave, when its movement stops, the wave is nothing, just water. But when it moves again it is again the wave.

Spin a top on its pointed base and it becomes still. And what's more, the quicker it spins, the more it loses its shape, and its visibility as well. The spinning top becomes invisible. The opposite is also true. The slower it turns the more visible it becomes. So, it is possible, after all, to become invisible—at least invisible to the naked eye. Apply the right energy in the right place, effortlessly and automatically, and lo and behold if you haven't become utterly invisible! It's a matter of applying the right energy in the right place, effortlessly and automatically.

Here too, when you, the adept of the School of Magical Powers, begin the practice, you do the same thing we do in zen, you take up the right posture and maintain it. Or, as the Tibetan saint Milarepa,[129] who once practiced black magic, said, "the Black Art for Producing Death."

Then, in China and later in Japan there was the Fuke Sect[130] also based on this art of invisibility, though in a different way.

---

129 See: Evans-Wentz, *Tibet's Great Yogi Milarepa* (Oxford Univ. Press, 1928, reprint 1971).

130 The so-called monks of this sect played the *shakuhachi*. Due to their talent for becoming invisible to the naked eye, these "monks" often worked for the government in the capacity of spies. The Fuke Sect was officially prohibited during the Meiji period and has remained so ever since. See: *Sit, the Zen Teachings of Master Taisen Deshimaru* (Prescott, Arizona: Hohm Press, 1996).

When it comes to energy, be it visible or invisible, magical or not magical, evil or good and even blessed, what's important is that this deep energy or *ki* circulates freely, with the breathing, slow and deep. For it is then that one becomes truly invisible. Through the living posture one becomes completely transparent, empty—the non-posture of no shape and no form.

It is said in the *Sandokai*:

Darkness exists in light: do not see only the bright side.
Light exists in darkness: do not see only the dark side.

Likewise, don't grab onto movement; don't hold onto non-movement either. And why? Because there is already non-movement in movement, and movement in non-movement. So, one might say, don't hang on to anything. Hanging onto life is only grasping at death, because that's where such movement takes us, directly there, into a box in a grave in the ground.

If you stop movement, there is no more movement.
If you set stillness into motion, there is no more stillness.

In zazen, if you stop your consciousness, there is no more consciousness, and this is called "samadhi." It's a bit like the rider who forgets himself on his horse. He forgets the horse too, even while it's galloping. On the horse, no rider; under the rider, no horse. And this is so, it is said, because the horse's mind and the rider's mind have become one and the same. In other words, movement doesn't become stillness, it is *already* stillness. While at the same moment, stillness is already movement. This, however, doesn't mean that they are the same.

The same with stillness: stillness too is the same as movement. *Or almost.* I say "almost" because nothing really stays the same, even for the horse and the rider; they are not the same before the ride as after it. It's the same too with phenomena and emptiness. When one becomes the other, there is always change. For that matter, so it goes with samadhi as well—samadhi is not something changeless. Like stillness, samadhi is nothing but change itself.

When you do something, you are no longer what you were before you did it. At least not completely; you're no longer quite the same. This is so because phenomenon and emptiness are not two equal entities; rather, they are unequal and always have been. Imagine a world without the chance of change—that is, the chance for transformation—at any moment of the day or night!

So, stillness and movement are different, and this is why there is change, and for the better or for the worse we change. We can readily see this in the dojo. Our state of mind before we sit in the posture is different than what it is after we sit in it.

Things change all the time, but this continual change never leads to exhaustion; it's sunny, it's rainy; it's winter, it's summer; it's daytime, it's nighttime; mind moves, and yet it is always still.

There is no judgment involved in these changes. There is no moral order to it all, just action of mind and body that is like the eternal, flowing river.

Change is your original consciousness. It is no-mind translated as "reality." And zazen is the quest for that reality. What is real? Your original nature, your body, your breathing. Yours and others," and other. As the Sixth Patriarch[131] once said: "I teach nothing which is incompatible with the reality of my own nature. If anyone teaches some truth that distances him from the body, it is nothing but an abstract theory."

Your breathing is real because it is here and now, and not yesterday or tomorrow. When you're aware of your body and your breathing, you are not somewhere else; all your energy is in the moment, like the spinning top. This is *muso*, transparent posture, and *mushin*, transparent mind.

131 Eno the Sixth Patriarch 638-713. See: *The Platform Sutra.*

53

Since two is impossible,
One is as well.

After a while this teaching becomes almost redundant. And besides, many of us have heard it before; maybe not before the author's own time in the 600s, but certainly in this last century as Hinduism and the Buddhisms of all schools from India and China, and Budo from Japan, have saturated the landscape in both Europe and the United States. Perhaps this is why we know it all by now, in this 21st Century; namely, we know that opposites come about through making comparisons, and confrontation occurs when there is comparison. This is clear, and the message too is clear: do not let the mind fall into comparison. Opposites are okay, in fact without opposites we wouldn't even exist in the first place. Imagine if everybody suddenly looked and talked and thought just like you, with no differences to note at all! Of course, we'd all go mad on the spot.

Just be aware, this is Sosan's message here.

In reading closely the *Shinjinmei* we discover how much our thoughts are self-centered. Therefore, the question still remains: how to get out of this bind?

By practicing self-transformation—this is one fine way of getting out of it. But if we opt to go about freeing ourselves in this fashion (in the one taken by all Buddhist practitioners everywhere), does this then mean we must destroy the "One" as well? Well, according to this verse the answer is, "Yes."

∽

Sosan, in fact, goes further than ever in his socio-spiritual quest for truth, for here he is saying that where there is no duality there is no real unity. Imagine that! No unity—unless it includes disagreement and confusion! If this doesn't sound like the world we already live in here-and-now, then I don't know what does.

Most religious people (except certain Zen masters like Sosan) teach the unity of God and humanity, and of human with human. Yet, these same people couldn't even imagine it in their worst nightmares: that the deep teaching clearly points out, finally, that there is really *"no unity" at all*, and by that you can forget about a one-to-one relationship with God, Buddha or anyone or anything else, for that matter.[132]

∽

Master Sekito who lived in China in the 700s, expressed it this way:

> When one of his disciples asked him what was "*the essence of Buddhism,*" Sekito replied: "It can neither be obtained nor learned. You cannot learn to drop one and two."
>
> "Master, please explain yourself in different words."
>
> "The vast sky is not disturbed by the flight of the white clouds," Sekito answered.[133]

When you become one with what you're doing, one with what or who you are, then there is nothing. Nothing or no self. People are afraid of this "no self" because they're looking at it from the point of view of their own personal self, and therefore imagine that this teaching, or say this mental process, might very well lead them directly into self-annihilation; and no one in their right mind wants to annihilate themselves, I don't think.

From the point of view of the "non-self," however, this "nothing" is exactly the opposite of what one might think it is. In fact, this nothingness is exactly what self-searching people are looking for: mountains,

---

132 One day someone asked Master Deshimaru if God existed. He was not interested in this question of the existence of God, and he just shrugged and replied, "C'est comme vous voulez."

133 For a slightly different version of this same exchange between Tenno Dogo and Sekito (-790), see commentaries of verse # 59 herein.

trees, rocks and stars. It's the vast sky undisturbed by the passing clouds. It is you and me, it is us.

But to be thus, or to be "us," we must first do *something* with it (or with "ourselves" as you like).

∽

In Buddha's time, that is 500 years before Jesus Christ, the full lotus posture was called the invincible and unshakeable "diamond posture"; and the half-lotus was called "the hero's attitude." Nevertheless, this defines the same seated posture that existed even before the time of the Buddha. Centuries earlier, in the Upanishads,[134] it was called "the Mystical Triangle" and "the Body of Fire," because this triangular posture that one takes destroys duality forever.

[134] The Upanishads is a collection of speculative Hindu treatises or secret teachings, composed and compiled around 800 to 600 BCE. "The Upanishads had a profound influence upon Gautama Buddha and consequently in the doctrine which was later developed in Mahayana Buddhism. But against this, one must also consider the horror with which many Brahmins [even today] hold the Buddha," writes Edward Rice in *Eastern Definitions* (Doubleday & Co., Inc. 1978).

54

Finally in the end,
There is neither rule nor measure.

Insofar as obeying or not obeying the local laws in your community, the masters don't say, "You must obey those laws!" Rather, they pretty much say, "Do as you like."

One who practices the Way of Buddha is not obliged to follow any of the laws of society, small ones on the local scale, nor even large ones on the international level—it's all the same.[135]

Meanwhile, we know that temporal laws (local, state and government or whatever they are, so long as they are "laws") hold a lot of power over their citizens, and actually run their lives from morning to night, all the time . . . and with good reason. When confronted with the temporal law, the Universal law stands no chance whatever, at least not in a courtroom or tribunal. What can the Universal law do for a person who is caught by a temporal law and thrown behind bars? Not much. Whatever the Universal law can do, it's not going to free you

---

135 On the other hand, Soto Master Shosan, who died in 1655, and considered to be one of the most prominent of popularizers of Zen in Japan, taught a Zen Buddhism quite different than the one herein described. In fact his teaching emphasized nothing less than bringing the secular world into Buddhism. "The worldly law is none other than the Buddhist law," he said, and moreover, "If you fail to follow the principle of realizing the Buddhist law through the worldly law, you fail to grasp the meaning of all the buddhas." For more on Shosan see: *Zen Notes Review* (Winter 2014).

This understanding is very reminiscent of what many contemporary Japanese Zen masters claimed when their Emperor took them to war, first in Manchuria, then in the South Pacific. It was a war in glory of the Emperor who was seen and proclaimed as none other than the Buddha himself. For more on this matter, see: Victoria, Brian, *Zen at War* (Weatherhill, 1997).

from the waterboard treatment in Guantanamo, nor from the electric chair in Texas, nor from the guillotine at the Bastille, nor from being stoned to death in Saudi Arabia, nor from being garroted by the Spanish neck-collar in Madrid, nor from being decapitated with a butcher's knife by a Jihadist somewhere. It's like this everywhere; even in the invisible world it's this way. If the law sentences God's son Jesus to die on the cross, what can his Father do about that?

"My God," Jesus cried out to his Father in the ninth hour of his crucifixion, "My God, why hast thou forsaken me?" To which God replied something that was not really worth noting down. In any case, once the sentence had been pronounced, and Jesus was already nailed to the cross, the Father could do nothing more to save his Son. Indeed, God met his match at the tribunal on that bloody red day in Jerusalem.

∽

So, do as you like, monk and wayfarer of the Way, but beware that if you break the local laws of the land, if you proselytize and preach an outlawed doctrine, if you lie and steal and even worse kill somebody, you will pay the price somehow.

This happened to a man I had met on several occasions in Formentera, Spain. Ira Einhorn was his name, and as far as I know he had never broken the law, local, international or universal. Then, one day, he goes and kills his girlfriend.[136] This happened while he was a top student at the prestigious University of Pennsylvania . . . or perhaps shortly thereafter. Today, he pays for it in a state prison in the same state. Born and raised in a normal Jewish-American family, Ira went straight from the university to celebrity (he created the first Earth Day in 1970[137]) to the penitentiary, all in one quick sweep of the whisk-broom, or like the decisive movement of the shadow of the moon sweeping the front

[136] Which Ira has always denied. It really wasn't "me who killed her, it was all a conspiracy against me from higher up," he claimed.

[137] Well-known in France as "Journée de la Terre."

steps.[138] And why? Perhaps because of the illusion of self-and-others—when taken to its extreme. He was a brilliant student, first in his class, open, friendly, and according to the newspapers at the time, he was "a living legend" for his good works. And in France, where he was hiding out, he could count on the complete support of many influential people in politics today.[139]

Yet, despite all this impressive outside help, he now finds himself in the state penitentiary, where he will vegetate until he dies. The rest of his life spent locked up behind bars, alone with just himself.

However one sees Ira, as guilty, innocent or whatever, it is still a one-and-only-life wasted away, flushed right down the drain—and for what? Such a waste of life, and not just one life . . . but two.[140]

Laws are here to promote harmony and interdependence among people. But these laws, as necessary as they may be, don't really work unless imposed through fear, like the fear of finding yourself in the penitentiary, in Guantanamo or elsewhere; and yet not even *that* worked for Ira. He at least wasn't very scared of the law, and perhaps he even felt above it (were one to believe the courtroom psychiatrist on this matter) as though he were God himself. But, as we just noted, God can't do much for you in such cases.

In any event, truth can only work when it lies outside or beyond the laws—when it resides there where there are no more laws. Only from there (where there are no more laws) can it (the truth) really work.[141]

---

138 The shadow of the bamboo in the moonlight / is sweeping the dust from the stairs...Anonym.

139 Noel Mamere, Jack Lang, Robert Hue, Daniel Cohn-Bendit, José Bové, Roselyne Bachelot, etc.

140 I met Ira Einhorn in Spain in the early1990s, before he was sentenced to life in the State Penitentiary of Houtzdale, Pennsylvania for having murdered his girlfriend in 1977. Ira was arrested in 2001 at his home in a small town in Charente in south-western France, from where the government extradited him back to the States.

141 Gurdjieff is quoted in *In Search of the Miraculous* by Ouspensky (Harvest, 2001)."The first step in this direction is to escape from general laws . . . The man who wishes to establish his individuality must first free himself from general

When you arrive at supreme truth, supreme activity, says Sosan in this verse, there are no more rules. When he says that "in the end there are no rules," he is talking about (or is it to?) the wise man who doesn't need any of this, rules included. Why? Because the wise person—man or woman, it's the same—personifies all the rules, laws and measures of the universe, naturally, automatically and unconsciously.

Be that as it may, for this truth to exist—truth and freedom being the same here—it simply needs these laws, little and big alike, and not only that but it needs the rules and regulations which inevitably come about automatically with the laws themselves. So, despite the pre-eminence of the Supreme Law over all other laws, without them, without the other laws, Universal Law would not even exist, at least not for us sentient beings. For living bipeds like ourselves, the Universal Law is completely dependent on these *other* laws. In fact, from this point of view, human-made laws are its essential ingredient.

Finally in the end,
There is neither rule nor measure.

Sosan is *not* saying that we should ignore the rules and laws of country and society. Rather, he is talking about the Dharmic or Cosmic law of the universe. To follow such a law means to follow a master, which in turn means to follow the Buddha, which means to follow all the buddhas in-and-beyond time and space. Or again, it means to follow the rules and regulations set down by the sangha or community in which we practice.

This said, it still holds true: to follow the laws laid down by humans, or not, "do as you like."

---

laws. Such a man is not obligated to follow all general laws; he can dispense with a great number of them if he can manage to free himself from obstacles and imagination."

∽

We know that there exist many paths to attaining the Way, and that depending on the path you take, you must learn to follow the rules of that particular school, sangha or community in which you belong. Otherwise, the Way cannot be attained. (I am not talking about the "other" Way, the way of the self-illuminated—the Way through reading the teaching, or in Sanskrit, the *pratyeka* way, where one is awakened by and consequently for oneself, and all alone as well.[142]

Rules should always be subject to close scrutiny, modification and sometimes even outright abolition. Here is an example of one rule that should have been abolished long ago:

> During the evening zazen in a certain temple in Japan, the cat who lived in the monastery made so much noise that it distracted the master and the sangha. So, the master ordered that the cat be tied up. Years later, after the master died, the cat continued to be tied up during zazen. And when the cat eventually died, another cat was brought to the monastery, and was also tied up. Almost a century later, descendants of the master, believing that they were transmitting their ancestor's teaching, even went so far as to write articles on the religious significance of tying up a cat (any cat would do) during meditation time.

It should be noted that this "tying-up-the-cat rule" was finally abolished; but it certainly took the monks of this tradition a long time to do it, for it wasn't until almost two centuries later that, by overruling this injunction, they managed to free themselves of such a worthless and even harmful ruling.

---

[142] It can also be said that the *pratyeka* is the awakened one who lives in a time when there are no buddhas.

Clearly, it is necessary to understand rules in a larger context, a wider perspective. Understand them through the practice and through oneself and through all the tied-up cats in the world as well. Anyway, laws, rules, and regulations—at least within the sangha—are not used to dominate others, but rather to promote harmony and interdependence among all peoples, animals and things included.

∽

All the different schools of Buddhism—Hinayana, Mahayana, Tibetan, Tendai, Zen etc.—have their own distinctive rules. Likewise, within them are many subdivisions, as in Zen for instance: Rinzai, Soto, Obaku, and derivations thereof such as the School of Direct Pointing, the Unborn Zen School, the Mind Only School, just to name a few. On top of that, we have the different family traditions, as in Soto. Today, in this particular school, there are the family traditions of Suzuki, Maezumi, Jiyu Kennett, Kodo Sawaki, Uchiyama, Yasutani, Deshimaru, and others. Similarly within the Rinzai line, and the other lines as well. What's more, each has its own lineage traditions, rules and regulations: Rules concerning how to sit and how to move about in a dojo; rules concerning how and when to wear the *kesa/rakusu*; and those concerning use of the *kyosaku*—some sanghas in the States are now forbidding its use altogether, in the name of "peace and love."[143] The recitation of the sutras—some lineages insist on the recitation being done in translation, others not. And then there are rules concerning the ceremony, and those concerning the ordination of monks and nuns, as well as the rules of the transmission.

Each school has its own rules and if for some reason you decide to change schools, then you must forget what you've learned in the old school and learn the rules all over again in the new one.[144]

---

143 "We have finally succeeded in getting rid of the stick for good, as a gesture in favor of peace and love," writes Norman Fischer, one-time Abbot in the Suzuki lineage in San Francisco. *Tricycle Review* (7/1999).

144 It should be said, however, that many masters disapprove of practitioners who change schools, let alone masters, if not entire lineages. "There is such a thing

So, the disciple must learn to follow and to commit to the tradition and rules of whichever sangha or community to which he or she belongs. And to follow this, is to follow one's own master, and thereby to follow in the line of all the buddhas before and after. Thus it is said.

∽

Finally in the end, there is neither rule nor measure.

This is certainly true, and yet it's essential in life to have a direction, and in Buddhism to have a master who gives this direction. Buddhism is in fact just that, a direction. Hotei,[145] pointing to the moon, shows that direction; he's pointing out where to go to get to the moon, and how to do so as well—that is, by going straight ahead without looking sideways or backwards.

It's a long and arduous trip with pitfalls everywhere, and to set out along the Way you will be needing not just a guide but companions as well to accompany you along the path, which Walt Whitman evokes so well in his *Song to the Open Road*, his *Salut au Monde*, and his *Song of the Broad-Axe*: "the house-builder . . . the six framing-men . . . the crowded line of masons . . . the flexible rise and fall of backs . . . ." The Buddha too needed the same companionship. "Shakyamuni wanted to have a spiritual companion. To express himself, to express his satori, to go together to the other shore . . . to the shore of satori."[146]

---

as ethics," says Kennett Roshi, expressing her own personal opinion on the matter, "and a really good Zen teacher or master will not accept someone who has given allegiance to another teacher." *Roar of the Tigress* (Shasta Abbey Press, 2000).

145 or Pu-tai in Chinese. Chinese monk who lived during the first Sung Dynasty in the 900s. Often depicted in statues and *sumi-e* pointing a finger upwards to the sky. *Shigetsu* means "finger pointing to the moon"; the study of books and sutras being just that: Hotei's finger pointing to the moon—the finger itself not being the real thing.

146 See under: "Companions in Satori" in the book *Sit, the Zen Teachings of Master Taisen Deshimaru* (Prescott, Arizona: Hohm Press, 1996, 173).

Some popular writers on Buddhism put this master/disciple relationship into question. Not only the fact of practicing under a master, but also of practicing in a sangha, along with others, all under the same master. For many specialists this is a pure waste of time, "for the real master is here." They point to themselves—always to themselves—and say: "It's inside here!"[147] On one level of consciousness they're right, and what's more, every master of the transmission says the same thing. Yet, those who doubt and question point not to the moon, but only to themselves.

To practice without a master, and to continue this way, you will end up at best like a pratyekabuddha with only yourself in mind—at least this is what is said.[148]

"If you do not have the desire to truly see into your own nature, arguing thereby that all things are the Buddha dharma, you will be like a band of children that rushes to board a large boat which has no captain," Hakuin writes in a letter in 1747.[149] "They do not know where they wish to go nor what the harbor of their destination really is, and they cry out, "Let's row over here!" or "Let's row over there!" And so, they pull the oars merely in accordance with their own whims—yesterday they followed the tide to the east, today the tide to the west—and in the end they find themselves hopelessly lost at sea. But then, an actual ship's captain who knows the way suddenly appears in a small lifeboat and, climbing aboard, he sets the compass right on line, takes the rudder and in less than two days, he heads the ship into the harbor."

"The captain is like the Buddha master," Hakuin tells us. "He is the great aspiration to see into one's own nature. The compass is the

---

147 The journalist and Buddhist writer Hervé Clerc writes that he himself never followed a master and he doesn't think it is necessary to follow one, because as he puts it, "the best master is in ourselves . . ." *Les Choses Comme Elles Sont* (Editions Gallimard, 2011).

148 *Pratyekabuddha* is a term that also refers to one who is enlightened but does not share their understanding with others.

149 Master Hakuin in a letter to a Nichiren nun. See: *The Embossed Tea Kettle* (George Allen & Unwin, 1963).

teaching of the True Law. The rudder is the direction, determination and conduct throughout one's life." Hakuin then explains how exactly "one is to row the boat into the harbor of the Wondrous Law," and that means, not to row in the wrong direction! "Ordinary practitioners are accustomed to always rowing to the outside," says he, "seeking the Buddha, seeking the patriarchs, seeking nirvana or seeking the pure land, and so the more they row the further they find themselves from their goal."

Master Hakuin is hereby pointing out that to practice *without* a master is no different than to find yourself in the hands of a bunch of children, on a captain-less ship, and all of them just as lost as you yourself.

∽

To reach the "wondrous harbor" is not so much a matter of rowing the boat as it is one of faith, and that faith does not come about by simply following all the rules in a given sangha, or by following the sutras as exemplified through the line of the patriarchs. Faith is not in any way the imitation of a tradition.

However, it cannot be denied that, in the long run, we are our own leaders, and indeed our very own captain . . . For this reason, one can well understand one's outlook on this matter of *not* following a master other than oneself, and as one might say: "Why bother looking for it elsewhere (than within ourselves)?"

But to do this—to be able to steer the ship into the "wondrous harbor," without a captain and with a crew made up of mere children—is pretty near impossible. We are only human beings, and too limited for such a grandiose exploit.[150]

Since, according to this story, it's impossible to arrive at or even to approach the harbor of the Wondrous Law without a captain, a master

150 "Human beings have been limited," says Master Deshimaru. "The karma of civilization creates limits that just add to the personal limits of our spirit."

or a guide, who in their right mind would wish to go about it otherwise? Well, it seems that not everybody is of the same mind, right or wrong as it may be. As, for instance those writers of Buddhism whom we were just now referring to, those who never themselves had a master, and never wanted one either.

Whatever the worth of the written work or the spoken word, when speaking with someone about the Dharma, always ask them early in the exchange (before they sit down to write their article or book about Zen, the Dharma and the Buddha) what exactly their religion and their lineage are, and of course under whom have they practiced; and this only so you can know with whom you are talking.

∽

Sosan points out that "there is no rule, no measurement," but this does not mean we need *not* follow a master, as some would have it. Rather, it means don't be imprisoned by ideas or categories—not even by those of the Zen teaching of our own Soto School. The same goes for the Buddha's teaching as well. All in all, this teaching is very simple; once you are set in the right direction, it works, and it works naturally, automatically and unconsciously at that.

Finally in the end,
There is neither rule nor measure.

55

If mind coincides with mind,
The seeds and traces of actions vanish.

This strophe is particularly subtle and nuanced. To explain it I must refer to the *kanjis*, the ideograms by which it was composed.

The *kanji "kei,"* located in the first line or verse, means "to coincide": mind coincides with mind, with the idea of two detached halves that match. This brings us immediately to *I shin den shin,* mind-to-mind, my-heart-mind-to-your-heart-mind. Two minds coinciding like the *zagu* (cloth rectangle) of the master and the *zagu* of the disciple that touch during *sanpai* (bowing), with no space between. And in this sense, *kei* implies a vow or promise.

Here's what the 4th Century monk Seng-chao[151] says:

The sky and I come from the same root,
Wherever I go, there is no dharma but mine.[152]

Dogen's added comment to this profound observation by Seng-chao reads: "Even though it abounds in each of us, we cannot actualize it without practice, nor experience it without realization." This is the *kanji "kei"*: to work together as one, to coincide—as with practice and awakening. This is one of the leitmotifs in Dogen's teaching, which he expresses in many different and original ways, time and again.

Another ideogram in this first verse is *shin*, mind. Master Deshimaru defines it here as the "completely harmonious mind which becomes One."

---

151 378-414 CE. Brilliant scholar/monk who studied under Kumarajiva. His work and thought represents a synthesis of Indian and Chinese Buddhism.

152 Again: ". . . there is no difference between the Dharma and myself." Or more exactly, ". . . between myself and the Dharma."

Kanjis are more than interesting. They have many meanings and they all differ according to the context. Chinese and Japanese ideograms are much more fluid and flexible than are our own word equivalents. But this doesn't mean that our own Western ways of verbal communication are more limited than theirs, the multifarious Asiatic ways.[153] They are just different.

Another important *kanji* in the second line is *byodo. Byodo* means equality, sameness. Sameness, yes—yet not in the sense of oneness, but, in the sense of grade, degree, stage, level or ranking; in other words, something quite fixed, something that doesn't change much. What's more—as far as this *kanji* is concerned—it refers to a place where a kind of rhythmical harmony exists, a balance between the different energies. Master Deshimaru says of *byodo:* "The mountain is high, the sea is wide, the bamboo is straight, the eyes horizontal and the nose vertical." That's *byodo,* balance, that which is nothing other than the normal condition.

Again, the *kanji syosa* in the second line means "gesture" or "action." But in what direction? In the direction of mind that returns to its original purity. Here we come to the notion of immobility, which is *not* the opposite of action or gesture. Likewise, the meaning of "monk" is not the opposite to that of movement. So "monk" means he-or-she who does not produce karma-creating seeds of *bonno* or passion. Indeed, this word "monk" means that even though there is action, there is no trace.[154] If the monk practices exactly, his or her brain is motionless; that is, it has no *bonno* seeds.

...And every trace of action vanishes.

We all want to leave our mark somewhere, and some of us even want to leave it everywhere. On Sunset Boulevard in Hollywood,

---

153 Japanese Zen master Sokei-an said, "I believe that in 500 years everyone will read Chinese characters... I prophesy that at this time Americans will read the sutras in Chinese characters." (See: *Zen Notes Review,* Fall 2012 for this talk given in New York City in 1939, shortly before his internment near Washington D.C. for being a member of the Asiatic race.)

154 That is, movement which is non-karmic-producing.

celebrities leave their footprints in the sidewalk for everybody in the world to see,[155] and being cast in cement they hope for more than just being seen by everybody in this world today, but hopefully in the next one as well.

But for those who sit in a dojo, it is already entering another world, and within this very lifetime at that. Action here leaves no traces, and no particular karma either.

If mind coincides with mind,
The seeds and traces of actions vanish.

Another *kanji* found in this last line is *yamu*, which means "to finish." Like all the other *kanjis*, it means more than what first comes to mind—"to finish" yes, but "to finish in itself" only. Though the trace may well be finished, this is not so with the action. Its traces, and even its seeds disappear, but the action continues.[156]

Like for a bird: you may think the bird is flying about because she likes to fly; or perhaps because she likes to gaze at the scenery from on high; or again, perhaps, that the bird flies about because she has nothing else to do. But actually, the bird is flying about looking for food. She's hunting. And yet, even if she's a bird of prey ready for the kill, even then she leaves no traces, at least no karmic traces.

---

155 "Memory Lane" it's called, and it contains the traces of many footprints—such as those of James Dean, Marlon Brando, Paul Newman, Marilyn Monroe and hundreds of others.

156 In one sense, karma means "thought." So we can change our karma, but we cannot erase it. Our actions, our conscience, influence it constantly. This is why it is so important in zazen to "let go of thoughts." When one truly achieves this letting go of thoughts, one leaves no trace—at least during zazen. Then, where is karma to be found?

56

Since the fox's doubt does not exist,
Passions completely disappear, and suddenly true faith appears.

Having freed oneself from the illusion of I, me and mine, as Sosan demonstrates throughout these poems, doubt simply is no longer; it simply doesn't exist. Still, the masters of the Zen lineage often speak of doubt, which they refer to as the great affliction of humanity, and here in this verse Sosan refers to it as the "doubting fox."[157]

The fox doubts all the time, even when it's running. It looks left, right and even behind itself while still running forward. This is why the fox is a perfect symbol for doubt.

Animals are often used in Zen: foxes, oxen, even cows, as for instance the cow of Isan.[158] There are many others, too. The elephant is the symbol of the holy. Also, in moving forward it brushes aside all obstacles in its path carefully with its trunk, without doing any harm. Anyway, the elephant cannot be stopped, which is why it is used as one of the several symbols for the great disciple.[159]

---

157 In this strophe, Master Deshimaru translates the *kanji* "*ko*" by the word "fox." Of all the translations I know, this is the only one that talks about a fox, *ko*. I studied the translations of a number of scholars and others, but none of them say fox, and yet the *kanji* is indeed "fox." They leave the word "fox" out altogether. See the translations done by Seng-Ts'an, Blyth, D.T. Suzuki, Kennett Roshi, Sheng-yen, Rommeluere, and even R.B.Clarke whose translation is the most referred to and renowned of them all.

158 As the story goes, master Isan of the 9th Century, along with the cow out front, were considered as one. And it was pointed out by Isan that when he, Isan, died he would still be present, in the cow out front. Therefore, it was debated, should this particular cow wear a sign on his left flank stating to the effect that "I am Isan," or should it not?

159 The lion and tiger are also images of great disciples, as well as the dragon.

The snail is another popular symbol as well. Legend has it that while the Buddha was doing zazen under the Bodhi tree, it was very hot, and the snails, sensing his difficulty, crawled up onto his head to cool him with their cool and humid bodies. The cobra too: on ancient Buddha-thrones we often see the sculpture of a king cobra figuring as a backrest, with its hood spread open to protect the Buddha from the sun. We don't see anything else of the cobra, just its hood, spread out on either side of Shakyamuni's own head. The turtle, too, is another symbol. In zazen we cut through the six senses, as the turtle does when you go near it, pulling itself back into its shell, head, tail, legs and all. Then there are the mythical animals such as the phoenix, and the Kirin, a kind of giraffe, and Benryu, the seated dragon that symbolizes meditation. Garuda, an enormous bird that feeds on dragons, is the symbol of Buddhism and the Buddha's teaching. The salmon is another symbol—swimming upriver to lay its eggs and die. (Note: the further the salmon heads up the river, the less water there is to swim in, as the river is becoming consecutively a stream, a creek, rapids and, depending on the weather conditions, nothing but a mere trickle. At that point the going becomes very difficult indeed.)[160] Few fish actually make it back up to the headwaters.

It's the same with the practice of zazen—few take it all the way.

In any case, whether these creatures make it to the headwaters or not, they are in complete harmony with the cosmic order, and this is their faith. It's being one with their own true nature.

∽

In Mahayana, if you have faith in some one thing, then this is not true faith. Faith is faith in everything. If life brings you to birth, you have

160 "The students' practice is kind of like the salmon when they go up river. The river gets narrower and narrower and there's less and less water. They have to jump over high rocks and waterfalls [....] As they continue up, their energy gets more and more concentrated, until body, mind and circumstances are all one thing..." Sojun Weitsman (*Windbell*, Spring 1991).

faith in birth; and likewise, when life brings you death, you have faith in death. If life gives, take it; if life takes it back, give it back.

It is said that most human beings are incapable of the slightest bit of faith, carrying within themselves feelings of doubt, fear and selection. They cannot decide, they simply hesitate. "And intellectuals more than anyone else," says Deshimaru, "are possessed of this mind of the fox."[161] He points out that this illness in modern people is more and more widespread. Compared with our ancestors the Cro-Magnons, who acted not through their frontal brains, nor even out of wisdom, but through faith, moderns have little wisdom and no faith left at all. And that's because, as he puts it, "In those times religion, manners, faith and morality were simple. The great wisdom of those ancient times was in the act of doing *sanpai*. Humans were not complicated." Today, I shouldn't think you would find many intellectuals, academics, let alone simple ordinary cerebrals busy doing *sanpai* for very long.[162]

Faith is essential in Buddhist practice. It is the essence of the *Shobogenzo*. In fact, the entire *Shobogenzo* is a testament to faith. Wisdom is

---

[161] Master Deshimaru in his *Shin Jin Mei* (Cesare Rancilio, Editeur, 167). The fox is an animal in constant doubt. When it moved forward it is always looking left and right, and even behind. It's the same with people these days. They appear to be incapable of walking straight ahead. Their behavior and state of mind is plagued by suspicion, incapable of the least modicum of faith, they are troubled by feelings of fear, by doubt and by choice. They are unable to decide, and spend their lives in hesitation. Intellectuals more than others have this mind of the fox.

[162] The psychoanalyst C.G Jung said in his book *Memories, Dreams, Reflections* that he'd had a very perturbing dream in which he was trying to do a prostration (one single prostration or a *pai*), but couldn't manage to do it. For some reason he could not get his forehead to touch the ground—something prevented him from going down that far. He would drop to his knees, and with his elbows, forearms and hands resting firmly on the ground, as they should be, he would try again and again to get his forehead to touch the ground. But it never happened. Jung never quite touched his forehead to the earth, but stopped short each time, though only by a mere hair-width. (Vintage Books, 1963.)

necessary, but it's not enough: faith is even more necessary, perhaps, than wisdom. Anyway, without faith, it is very hard to continue practicing year after year. The Way is full of traps and pitfalls, and no one can take it easily.

Faith is not an element that we add to our universe. Faith is the spirit of true Buddha-nature, and it is faith that discovers this nature. This faith is also the same one that the Buddhas teach. Otherwise, the Way is impossible... or so it is said.

...And suddenly true faith appears.

57

All elements being impermanent,
They leave no trace in the memory.

Yes, all is impermanent, including that which is beyond before and beyond after. When you are dead, you don't come back. And yet, if here and now is complete and each instant becomes eternity (as it is said), then where do you stand, where do you go?

At the beginning of the *Shobogenzo Genjokoan*, Master Dogen talks about the relationship that exists between firewood and ash, or say, to take the image further, between the living body and the dead corpse. In this famous passage, he explains that wood cannot see its own ashes and that likewise that the ashes cannot look at the wood.[163]

Ashes do not think about the past, when they were big trees in the forest because the ash is completely unaware of the tree that it once was, and so with the tree whose ashes it will soon become. In other words, our life cannot see our death. Our karma is unique and it can only be our own. In other words, we ourselves are in our own Dharmic position in life: man, woman, tree or ashes. Yet, each Dharmic position (state, aspect, condition, appearance or Suchness)[164] is different from that of every other thing or person.

Dogen says, in so many words (as does Sosan here in this second line), that nothing remains, and that when one dies it is forever . . . and that is so even in the memory.

There is nothing left. Or said differently, all our thoughts, memories and desires simply become unimportant and even inconsequential. But

---

163 "...We should not think of ashes as the potential state of firewood or vice-versa. Ash is completely ash and firewood is firewood. They have their own past, future, and independent existence." Master Dogen in *Genjokoan*.

164 "Suchness" is the quality we see in things once we understand emptiness, or so it is understood.

then one might ask, what *is* important really? *Letting your thoughts pass, letting go of what is impermanent*—I think that is what's important.

If we are able to realize the extent to which everything is *mujo* (impermanent), then no more thoughts exist; and this has nothing dark or negative about it. Simply meaning, no more anxiety, no more fear, no more doubt, and consequently no trace thereof. In fact, "impermanence," *mujo,* also means "not remaining" or "not dwelling."

People who have spent any time in concentration camps, or even in prison, certainly retain a trace of these experiences in their minds forever. If we dwell on the past (or the future—it's the same, one being a projection of the other); if we dwell in time and space while we are physically here in the present we are divided; and for people who have undergone severe trauma it is normal, even necessary, to maintain such memories in the mind. But perhaps it is not necessary to maintain them as traumatic. For, "in *whose* mind?" might just be the right question to ask oneself; that is, "Who am I?" These events were true, perhaps, for then . . . at that time, in the dark pit of horror; but are they still true now, in the relative joy of living in the world?[165]

In any case, the brain is already divided: right and left, frontal or cerebral, hypothalamus or instinctive brain. But, through the practice of meditation (zazen), we become less and less divided and more and more centered in the present, the here and now beyond time—without even knowing it. So, although we may, right now, be living totally in the *now*, if this "now" is not beyond time and space, then presently living in the *now* is no guarantee that it will continue into the next *now*, and in the next one after that.

Nothing is guaranteed, not even wisdom. This is true for everybody, even for the wisest of the wise. Nothing is guaranteed, not even wisdom. Perhaps this is why we so often hear talk in Zen about the continued practice, or *gyoji*. Practice is continual, and effort is constant. At first, when we begin the practice of Zen, it's for the future, that is, for

---

165 I am here thinking of Primo Levi, of his book *Survival in Auschwitz*, and of his eventual suicide.

our own well-being and maybe even for that of our own children. This can also be understood as being done *for* the past (our own personal past), for our own foundations and maybe even for our own parents, all of that being of the same importance or significance in this world of cause and effect.

Mind you, this does not mean that past practice can be counted on today. While today is today, the past is the past, and as Rudyard Kipling would have it, "East is East, and West is West, and never the twain shall meet."[166] And as master Dogen would put it, "Ashes cannot look at firewood."[167]

All elements being impermanent,
They leave no trace in the memory

The successes (and the failures) of past and future exist only in the mind—in the grey matter where we find all those exhaustive traces and memories that Sosan refers to in this second line. In other words, only mind knows success and failure, gain and loss.

The thinking brain doesn't know what's happening when nothing is happening—and this too is a way of explaining mind in zazen. The mind cannot know *hishiryo*, the "now" which is *hishiryo,* the cosmos. "The now includes the whole cosmos," said the master one day, this "now" that is pure change, pure *mujo.* So, according to the masters, we would do better to live in *mujo,* in impermanence. Living this way is true well-being.

This strophe is talking about a person who is totally free and without any baggage; it is talking about Buddha, and about the buddha within all of us.

---

166 From *The Ballad of East and West.*

167 From the *Shobogenzo, Genjokoan.*

58

Illuminating your inner self with the light of emptiness
Does not require the power of the mind.

Here in these lines we find the notion of "illumination," which comes not from the outside, but from within. Sosan says in this second line that illumination does not require the usual mind process to which we are all attached, and sometimes even blindly so.

We are talking here about the inner light of emptiness; that which is the essence of Soto Zen; and which is also the universal truth: that which comes from within yourself, which came before your birth and will continue after your death.

This universal truth comes from within; and one who has it is the bodhisattva who lives in all beings—since all beings live in that one. The bodhisattva has no need, therefore, as the saying goes, to go into hell to help others; rather, by illuminating his or her own interiority, the bodhisattva helps all, in hell and elsewhere.

This strophe contains the kanjis *ko, mei, ji* and *sho. Ko* has several meanings, one of them being: do not block mind and body with thoughts, with the intention of projecting them in one direction or another. Instead, do as Sosan instructs us in this poem: be like a channel in which the current flows freely between the personal and the universal, without obstruction ... *Mei* means clarity or light... *Ji* is possessive, the self. And s*ho,* to illuminate. This mantra, *ko mei ji sho,* means "to shine from one's own inner self, naturally, unconsciously and automatically."

In China in Sosan's time these ideograms became a mantra, like many others in the Zen of the times that capture the same image. For example:

The moon shines on the lake,
The wind blows in the pines.

This passage from the *Shodoka*[168] by Yoka Daichi became a mantra used specifically to ward off ghosts. Today, it's no longer to ward off ghosts but fears and anxieties. So, if you're feeling anxious about something, think of the moon on the lake and the wind blowing in the pines, pronounce it in mantra form and it might just have the great calming effect so needed.

"The light of emptiness": nothing hinders the mind, it is empty and without obstruction. Empty and yet fluid. As for the light itself, all religions talk about this light. It's an important symbol. It is the light that shines on the world, without object. Master Wanshi, who died in 1157, expresses this in a poem, *The Chant of Silent Illumination,*[169] as a silent light that does not depend on any object. And this statement of Wanshi's refers to a light that shines without any object to shine upon, or so I understand it. Or again, the light that doesn't depend upon any object in order to be the light itself. In any case, master Dogen says that he was influenced every day by this particular poem by Wanshi, composed more than fifty years before he was born.

∽

We always want to create the object: the object "him," or even the object "me." This is how things function in the world we live in: It's either me, him, her, them or us. It is said in the ancient writings that this way of seeing the world comes from the use of mind power. This strophe, however, teaches us that there's no need to use your head or your brain, at least not when it comes to being awakened. In zazen, we shine by ourselves, unconsciously, and this has nothing to do with cutting off our thoughts; nor with falling into darkness; nor has it to do with *kontin*. In fact, *kontin*[170] has more to do with the dark side, while awakening is, so I have been told, utterly illuminating.

---

168 Yoka Daishi, *Le Chant de l'Eveil,* commented on by Kodo Sawaki (Albin Michel, 1999).

169 Master Wanshi, *Le Chant de l'Illumination Silencieuse*, commented on by Etienne Zeisler (Daruma AZI, 1991).

170 *Kontin*: when the mind falls into obscurity or simply into plain dullness.

Illuminating your inner self with the light of emptiness
Does not require the power of the mind.

This miracle is not apprehended "by" the self any more than it is "through" the self. It is not so much a matter of apprehending or attaining as it is to "illuminate the self with the self," as Wanshi would say. For, as has been pointed out above, the truth does not come from the outside. But then, if it doesn't come from the outside, how could it come from the inside? This light that does not come from the outside is nevertheless certified by all external things; that is, all external things bear it witness. Master Wanshi once said of this: "Everything in the universe shines and preaches the Dharma." We all know those Zen stories where someone is awakened by the morning star, the sound of a stone hitting bamboo, the sound of the river in the valley or the sight of a peach blossom falling. If this isn't proof that the stimulus comes from the outside (i.e., and not from inside, not even from zazen), then I don't know what is.

This light or illumination is the letting go of all things; of letting them pass. It is the true practice of *shikantaza*: precisely that zazen which is without goal and without end, which is the very spiritual action of stillness of the posture. Yet the ceremony—with the chanting and the prostrations, very simple and almost primitive (that is, like the religion before all religions)—is also stillness, but stillness in action; it is concentration and observation while doing *sampai* and chanting the *Hannya Shingyo*.

In Wanshi's time, Soto Zen was called "silent illumination," as opposed to Rinzai Zen, which pursues satori, and was called "koan Zen." Soto Zen, however, points out that if we continue to pursue satori, which is the idea behind koan solving, then we will never obtain it—and this because we are still dwelling in the constricting domain of what Sosan here calls "the power of the mind."

In the beginning, it's inevitable that we use mind power to practice. This is why many people who practice Zen (in other schools than our own) have techniques for focusing the mind, for example, on resolving koans or on counting the breaths. Many of these methods are very effective in the beginning. Later on, however, they are of no use at all, or so it would seem, except to further develop themselves, over and over again, thus becoming little else than mind-directing robots. Anyway, this is not how they practiced in Buddha Shakyamuni's time, nor in Sosan's, nor in our own times.

It's always the same, one shines because of inner mind.

59

As far as hishiryo is concerned,
It is very difficult to think about.

The 59th strophe of the *Shinjinmei* is a classic of its genre. It talks about *hishiryo* for the first time in the history of Zen. This poem was composed at the end of the 500s, so it was during this period that the word first appeared in the language, and it was coined or created by Sosan himself.[171]

The word *shiryo* means "thinking," and *fushiryo*, "non-thinking." Sosan went further: to *shiryo* he added *hi,* which means "beyond," which is not a negation. *Hishiryo* is not thinking, and it is not not-thinking; it is beyond thinking.

Virtually all the masters of this lineage (i.e., the Kodo Sawaki line) consider *hishiryo* (that is, *hishiryo* consciousness) to be the substance of zazen.[172] Since Sosan's time, this word has become a key point of both body and mind during the practice. Anyone who has practiced in the Kodo Sawaki line, with any of his very diverse modern descendants such as Uchiyama, Narita, Kishigami, Okumura or Deshimaru, knows well the meaning of this term.

However, from the time in which the word came into being to the time it came into wider use took a very long time. About six or seven hundred years later, masters Nyojo and Dogen turned their attention to the word *hishiryo*, and its great importance. And, the first text Dogen

---

171 Yet, even today, most of the translations of the *Shinjinmei* do not use the word *hishiryo* at all. *Hishiryo* becomes for instance, "the place where thinking is useless." *Zen and Zen Classics* by R.H. Blyth (Hokuseido Press 1982, 91).

172 See: *Sit, Zen Teachings of Taisen Deshimaru* (Prescott, Arizona: Hohm Press 1996, 203, 207. etc.) And Coupey, Philippe, *Zen Simply Sitting*, a commentary on the *Fukanzazengi* (Prescott, Arizona: Hohm Press, 2006).

wrote on his return from China[173] was the *Fukanzazengi*, which deals specifically with *hishiryo* consciousness as we understand it today.

"Think about non-thinking"—this is the standard translation and we find it everywhere.[174] But this expression isn't precise enough because it's too passive and too abstract to really penetrate through to the hypothalamus. To facilitate the penetration, we place the expression in the present, and so "non" becomes "not." And the "about" of "about non-thinking" disappears completely. This way we simply have: thinking/not-thinking, or even better: think/not-think.

There are other ways of translating this word this as well. Ch'an master Sheng-yen says: "It is not the place of thinking."[175] Or again, Clarke's: "Here, thinking is of no value,"[176] though never once mentioning the word *hishiryo* itself. It was lost in the translation.

So, asks the master, how do you think/not-think? And he replies to his own question: *Hishiryo.* This is the essential art of zazen. *Hishiryo* (or *hishiryo*-consciousness): when mind is not stuck on anything, when it is "beyond."

∽

Hishiryo is not a state of intellectual awareness. Intellectual thoughts—and even the one that excludes thought all together, such as the intellectual thought of "non-thinking"—are born to die just as we do ourselves. Such however is not the case with *hishiryo*-consciousness. For the *hi* of *hishiryo* does not mean "no" as it is sometimes translated; rather it means "beyond." Beyond everything, and without any hint of negation: that's our practice. "Beyond," not meaning excluding anything either, but embracing everything.

∽

---

173 In 1227.

174 ...while the single root word "*hishiryo*" can hardly be found anywhere in the published works of our times.

175 Sheng-yen, *Faith in Mind* (Dharma Drum Publications, 1987).

176 Genpo Merzel, *The Eye That Never Sleeps* (Shambhala, 1991).

One can translate any foreign term imaginable: *ku, mu*, and even words like *mushotoku* and *hishiryo*. You can put the term into perfect French, English or German, depending of course on what language you prefer, and that being no one else's but your own, of course.

Be this as it may, it's important *not* to translate everything.

Take for instance, the meaning of a sutra, a mantra or a text. What most people take to be the crux of the matter is the "meaning"—when in fact it's not that at all. It's the sound, not the thinking, that is the essential element. The sound comes from the earth, your body. In this way you can forget the meaning and so feel it in your gut and in your hypothalamus. So, why insist on translating everything, as most scholars are wont to do? In fact, why must one *understand* everything anyway? What's necessary, or so it seems to myself, is just *that*, as it is.

I wonder what the *Daihishin Dharani*[177] would sound like in modern translation. How, for instance, would you translate the "*hula hula mala*!"[178] of the *Daishishin Darani* into English or French?. . . Anyway, to return to the words, or variations of the words, such as *ku, mushotoku* and *hishiryo*, in translation: now, good translations are necessary certainly, but are they really all that *effective*?

Imagine what it would be like to recite and to chant the *Hannya Shingyo* (the "Heart Sutra" in translation), not to mention the *Daihishin Dharani* in its modern rendition, and at the same time to forget about the sound of it in Kambun, the sound from the root. To forget from where the sound of the sutra comes and, since we defeated the Japanese in the Second World War, to replace it with the new-world version as we have it today, in French, in English, etc., in most all the dojos

---

177 *Daihishin Dharani, Mantra to the Great Compassionate One*, is a sutra, or more exactly a mantra, which is often recited in Zen temples.

178 Here's part of the passage in an "attempted" English translation: "Come, come! Listen! Listen! / A great joy rises in me! / Speak! Speak! / Show the direction! / Hulu hulu mala hulu hulu hilé!" Etc. This in *Kambun* is, I believe, "*Ku ryo ku ryo, mo ra ku ryo ku ryo, ki ri sha ro sha ro, shi ri shi ri, su ryo su ryo, fuji ya, fudo ya, fudo ya...*" etc. And it ends thus: "Hello! Salut! Salut and hear my prayer!"

everywhere, from coast to coast and from continent to continent, while the essence of it is forever lost in translation.

What happens then? Chant the sutras in the language you were taught as a child and your practice will no longer be one of the body, of sounds, vibrations, and resonances from the hara; what you do will no longer be a practice of the body, as it has been for all these past centuries, but sounds right from the mind, and from a very personal mind at that.

As far as hishiryo is concerned
It is very difficult to think about.

> One day after zazen a monk asked Yakusan, "What exactly are you doing when you are unmoving like a mountain?"
>
> Yakusan replied, "I am practicing *shiryo* concerning *fu-shiryo*."
>
> The monk continued to question him: "And how, master, can we obtain *fu-shiryo*?"
>
> Yakusan simply replied, "*hi-shiryo*."[179]

Hishiryo is not a philosophy. It is action, both physical and mental action—as are these stories, the one above and the following:

> "What is the essence of Buddhism?" a monk asked Sekito. To which he replied, "That which cannot be understood nor obtained."

This is pretty much what Sosan says here in the second line: "*Hishiryo*? It is very difficult to even think about that."

[179] For instance, one could say: *shiki*=thinking, *fushiryo*=non-thinking, and *hishiryo*=beyond thinking.

This *mondo* with Sekito and the monk could very well have ended there. But it continued, and became famous as a result.

> "If it cannot be grasped or understood," the monk continued his questioning, "then where is it?"
>
> "The vast sky is not disturbed by the flight of white clouds," answered the master.[180]

Of course, sky and white clouds are symbols, but one doesn't have to "understand" symbols in order to experience the depth of *hishiryo*-consciousness as expressed here in this particular exchange.

∽

"Thinking about *hishiryo* is very difficult." For instance, when we are sitting in zazen-without-object we are in the action of the here and now, action and experience being exactly the same thing—and how can you think about that? How can our senses and our awareness conceive of impersonal, cosmic thinking? The master may *talk about* "hishiryo," but his words will penetrate no deeper than that of a mosquito trying to bite through the hide of a bull. In other words, the only way to understand it is through *personal experience*, which is not only beyond verbal expression, but beyond mind as well.

Anyway, master Deshimaru said, "*Hishiryo* is the unity of the objective and the subjective. As soon as we classify it in a category, limits immediately appear. We can only experience it and understand it for ourselves."

In the condition of *hishiryo*, we come to a place where "thinking" is no longer the right word. And to discover this place, where thinking is no longer the question, to be in harmony with the cosmic system, is the essential condition.

---

[180] For a different version of this same exchange, see herein commentaries under strophe # 53.

"*Hishiryo* is a most excellent, global and universal consciousness," says the master, "beyond all things."

In terms of the practice itself, by concentrating your awareness on your posture and your breathing, you not only learn to think with your hypothalamus—the primitive, instinctive, intuitive brain—but you thereby learn to forget yourself entirely.

60

In the dharmic world of reality as it is,
There is no ego, no difference.[181]

The word for "reality as it is" is *tathata* in Sanskrit. The term is often used in Mahayana and can be translated as "suchness" or "thusness" or "reality," or more exactly as "*inmo*"[182] in Japanese. At least *inmo* means that all forms which are free of intention and non-created (i.e., all things that do not arise from the small ego-mind) are true forms.[183] Dogen either used the Sanskrit *tathata* or the Japanese *inmo* to explain the meaning. Here Deshimaru, like Sokei-an before him, simply translates *tathata* with the word "reality."

Tathata or *inmo*, the reality of the Buddha in each of us. Master Deshimaru talked about *shinnyo*, the set of laws that constitute the truth of the cosmos; Dogen talked about *inmo*, about "it," about "this," about "things as they are." *This* exists as *that*.

---

181 Another version of poem # 60 : In the world of *Tathata* / There is neither being, nor ego nor any other difference.

182 The Sanskrit word "*tathata*" translated respectively by D.T. Suzuki, C. Humphreys, Sokei-an and Dogen. In any case, English translations of this strophe do not talk about "one" but about "suchness." *Tathata* is better than "suchness": in the world of *tathata* exists not-two, *funi*.

183 *Shobogenzo-Hotsumujoshin*. Translated by Nishiyama, Kosen and John Stevens (Tokyo, Nakayama Shobo, 1977, 123). All forms that are free of intention and non-created are true forms. True form is the true form of suchness is the body and mind of the eternal present. This body and mind emergeces with *hosshin*, resolve; do not stop pumping the water wheel [of Tozan] or pushing the grindstone [of Eno]. Hold up a blade of grass to make a six foot golden image of Buddha. This is *hotsubodaishin*, the Buddha-seeking mind: seeing Buddha, hearing Buddha, seeing the Dharma, hearing the Dharma, becoming the Buddha and practicing Buddha.

"In the dharmic world of reality as it is," says Sosan in this poem, "there is neither ego nor difference." This means that from the highest point of view, from the point of view of *tathata*, existences have no differences. Of course, differences exist, but where are they, these differences, when thinking comes from the body, from the whole being?

> One day Master Hotetsu[184] was sitting in front of the dojo fanning himself. A clever monk appeared and asked him, "Master, since wind blows everywhere, and its nature never changes, there is no reason to use a fan. So why do you use one?"
>
> "Although you know that the nature of wind never changes," Hotetsu replied, "you do not know what 'blowing everywhere' means."
>
> The monk nodded, "Then what does it mean?"
>
> The master continued to fan himself and did not reply.

That's all.

The monk is saying that the nature of wind is everywhere, that air is everywhere, and he doesn't grasp the master's reply, which could simply be a demonstration of *gyoji*, the continuous practice. Or, it could be a demonstration of energy that is everywhere, the wind alone being inconsequential. Or again, it could be a demonstration of mind that is nowhere; that is, mind does not appear.

In any case, if you don't practice it with and through your own body, you cannot receive it. So Hotetsu continues to fan himself, without replying.[185]

∽

[184] Disciple of Baso (-788) and master in his own right.

[185] For more on the story of Hotetsu fanning himself, see strophe 24 , pages 110-111 in Part I.

First, we learn that the world is full of differences, then we learn—at least in Zen and in certain other spiritual practices—that even though we are all different and separate from the world, we are completely alike and in harmony with it as well. *San do kai*: *san* means "difference"; *do* means "similarity"; and *kai* means "harmony."

Sosan says, "no difference" and even "no personal differences."[186] This is the cosmic world of *tathata*, which is non-dualism. No opposition: this is the meaning of the second line. Whether it's our body, our senses, a house, something that moves—it's life, it's existence without personal differences; this is *hishiryo* consciousness.[187]

There are other stories pertaining to wind and mind as well, such as the one called, "Not the Wind, not the Flag, not the Mind."

> Three monks were arguing about a flag. One said, "The flag is moving." The other said, "No, the wind is moving." The third said, "No, it's the mind which is moving."
>
> At that point a nun showed up and put them all to shame. "You are all wrong," she said. "It's not the flag, not the wind, nor even the mind which is moving; everything is moving!"

Hotetsu and the nun were in fact saying the same thing.

∽

186 "The difference amongst men is only nominal," so it is said in the *Sutta-nipata*. See also: Coomaraswamy, Ananda, *The Buddha and the Gospel of Buddhism* (Harper & Row, 1964, 282).

187 Again, another version of this poem translated by the scholar Richard B. Clarke, and a little different from the one used above, goes as follows : To come directly into harmony with this reality / Just simply say when doubt arises: "Not two."

In the dharmic world of reality as it is,
There is no ego, no difference

This strophe is talking about cosmic consciousness—also referred to as "transcendental" or "universal" consciousness (i.e., as opposed to phenomenal or to subject-object consciousness). In cosmic consciousness there is no difference between subject and object, and from this insight into things, one may infer that there are no differences among any existences at all.

"In the dharmic world"—the cosmic world, the world of *tathata*—"of reality as it is," says Sosan, "there is neither ego-entity nor other differences." Neither one nor the other.

Zazen should lead us beyond subject and object; if we practice correctly, it should lead us into the cosmic world beyond all differentiation. The master used to say that, through zazen we can become aware of the totality of the cosmos, there where creation springs up automatically, unconsciously and naturally.

61

If you want to realize One,
It is only possible in funi, not-two.

The mythical bodhisattva Manjusri[188] asked the real flesh-and-blood bodhisattva Vimalakirti, a lay disciple of Buddha, "What is your principle of *funi*, not two?" Vimalakirti responded with a silence—a silence that has incited many a learned scholar to prolonged analysis and study of what it means exactly to be "silent." It is true that all kinds of "silences" exist. This one, however, was a very special and very powerful silence; more powerful, it is said, than the sound of "a hundred thousand thunderbolts." The idea here, I believe, is to convey the transcendence of all categories, even this category here, of silence itself. Vimalakirti's answer to Manjusri on this matter of *funi*, not two, was of this quality.

> "All but you have spoken," Manjusri addressed Vimalakirti, "Now tell us please what is the bodhisattva's initiation into the Dharma of *funi?*"[189]
>
> Vimalakirti kept his lips sealed and did not utter a word. At that, Manjusri exclaimed: "Excellent, excellent; can there be true initiation into the Dharma of *funi* until words and speech are no longer written or spoken?"[190]

---

188 In most statues of Manjusri, we see him brandishing in one hand the sword of wisdom, and in the other the book of the *Prajnaparamita* sutras, containing shorter sutras dealing with the emptiness of things (*ku* or *sunyata*), such as the *Hannya Shingyo* (the Heart Sutra) Sutra) and the Diamond Sutra.

189 The "Dharma of funi" also translated as "non-dual Dharma."

190 *The Vimalakirti Nirdesa Sutra*, translated and edited by Charles Luk (Shambhala, 1972, 100).

Funi is the principal *kanji* in this strophe. *Fu*, negation, *ni*, the number two. *Fu-ni*: not-two. However, no one says *funi* anymore—perhaps because the word is considered too Japanese or simply too foreign for contemporary readers to appreciate.

However, *funi* means much more than "not two"—for it not only means "not-separated," but it also means "actualization."[191] The Indian scholar Coomaraswamy,[192] famous for his fine works on Buddhism, wrote that "all Buddhist meditation was contained in '*funi*.'"

One could also say: *funi* is the ego and the cosmos as they *should* be, the ego and Buddha, the ego and God. And to say it more simply, not-two.

∽

The *Shinjinmei* is the primary source from which many later texts come, in both the Rinzai and Soto lineages. As a result, when we hear or read such expressions as *funi*, we find ourselves at the source, at the origin of this teaching.

All the masters before and since Sosan have talked this way. In the ancient sutras and the Ch'an and Zen texts, we come across *funi* almost in the opening lines. For example, Yoka Daishi begins his poem the *Shodoka* with these words:

> See this man of satori who has ceased to study and remains inactive
> And does not seek to push away illusions, nor to find the truth?

The first line of Hakuin's *Zazen-wasan* (*In Praise of Zazen*), also mentions *funi*: "All sentient beings are in essence buddhas."

---

191 Or as Master Katagiri puts it in his book, *You Have to Say Something*: "What is truly actualized is beyond the dualistic world," or again, "With actualization we don't see life as opposed to death." (Shambhala, 2000, 102).

192 Coomaraswamy, *The Buddha and the Gospel of Buddhism*. See footnote # 186.

Keizan, in the *Denkoroku*, begins with: "When Shakyamuni saw the morning star, he was awakened." He was not-two.[193]

Tozan in his *Hokyozanmai* writes in the first line: "The teaching of thusness (*funi*) has been intimately communicated by the buddhas and the patriarchs . . ." In fact. all the masters of the Dharma immersed themselves in the teaching of *funi*.

This is not abstract talk, nor is it ancient philosophy; rather, it is an expression of our own lives as we are living them today, right now. The *Shinjinmei* presents even "the two"—even man and woman—as *funi*, or at least in their essence. As much as the "one" can be "two"—the double personality, the two-faced individual—the two can also be one. Even the married couple can be *funi*, that is, in total fusion.

Being One does not mean that one loses one's identity, let alone one's personality or individuality.[194] On the contrary, one's individuality is enhanced thereby, most certainly due to the fact that, at that moment, they no longer see it, the world, through their own personal selves, but through the moon.

∽

Master Dogen has often said, in one way or another, that most people who come to the true Dharma want to escape this very same Dharma. They wish to seek an erroneous one, and that was true even in olden times. Therefore, one might deduce that the majority of those who came to the practice were as "ordinary minded" as they are today, and not *funi* at all.

Of course, in society we deal all the time with duality. There's no way around that. But at the same time, so it is said, monks must have a deep understanding of *funi*, and for them this is possible. Deshimaru, speaking simply says: "*funi* is other people's egos *and* our own." He also

---

193 And Buddha himself said of this moment related here by Keizan, "I awakened simultaneously, instantaneously with the universe."

194 See strophe 54, footnote on Gurdjieff.

says, "*Funi* is practice *and* satori." And again, "*funi* is earth-*and*-god, body-*and*-mind."[195]

∽

Some say that only deep-thinking men and women, who have developed the third eye, can understand Zen and the Dharma without ever having practiced it (except maybe once or twice) in their entire lives! Master Dogen, of course, says the opposite and points out that even Vimalakirti, who, though a close disciple of the Buddha Shakyamuni, was still only a layman who had never taken the monk's ordination and therefore could not really understand the Dharma as taught by the Buddha. For only *a monk* ordained in the true lineage going back to the Buddha on Vulture Peak—Dogen would argue—could have access to this understanding, or say, experience this great awakening. So how can someone who is not a monk and does not practice at all, how can such an impostor, so to speak, possibly possess the same understanding, the same awakening, as someone who is a bona fide monk and on top of that, who practices daily all the time for everybody and forever?

This said (and everyone says it), to whom does the Dharma belong, finally? Only to the practitioners, to those who practice zazen in their own proper lineages . . . and not to the others, who don't? What's more, to which faith does the Dharma belong? Well, we know the answer to that: the Dharma belongs to Buddhism more than to any other faith, certainly.

Yes, but is this really so? The Dharma, as I understand it, belongs, not just to Buddhism, but to all religions, sects, faiths, and even to all non-faiths; and by deduction, to all of us as well; and this is what *funi* means. It belongs to the universal and therefore to all of us.

If you want to realize One,
It is only possible in funi, not-two.

---

195 All my italics.

In most religions we admire the angel and repudiate the devil. But to do that we must first create them: angels here and devils there, and we do so through the imagination, through the frontal lobes. Then we proceed to believe in what we've created. That is, in heaven and hell, and all of these beliefs get confirmed, sanctioned and endorsed by the holy priests in all the churches, synagogues, temples and mosques the world over. Beliefs, namely, that God and the devil really exist, the one in heaven and the other in hell. Some of the more tragic souls who think in this manner, and thus have gone off to hell themselves, have actually come back to tell us all about it! Otherwise, how would living humans ever know of hell, in the first place?

> Rabelais, through his character Epistémon,[196] pays a visit to hell. He finds hell not so bad as all that, though indeed there were some little surprises awaiting him there. For instance, it bemused him to note that the heroes and leaders of old, the ones who'd been so important and, in many cases, glorified here on earth, had changed, at least socially and economically speaking, down there in the *bas-fonds* of hell. For instance, he runs into Hector who has become a mole-catcher, and into Nero now none other than a fiddler; he gets to meet Cleopatra who has become an onion seller, Trajan a mere frog-fisher, Julius Caesar and Pompeii both of them tar workers, and so on with such names filling the pages. In any case, everybody has their turn at the treadmill in this book: Caesar, the Pope, even God…
>
> Anyway, Epistémon who has examined hell for himself, actually comes back to testify to its existence, pointing out that hell is finally not something imagined

196 Rabelais, François, *Gargantua* and *Pantagruel*, translated and introduced by J.M. Cohen (Penguin Classics, London, 1955, 265).

> by mankind, not at all! This he knows for a fact, because he has seen hell with his very own eyes!

By the same token, the heavens above are also the "real thing." Real, yes, but then again real only in relation to hell below. Therefore, it follows that the embezzlers, rapists and killers in the hells of yesteryear are now happily running honest governments up in the clouds, controlling the banks, the conglomerates and the churches. And as for the more wicked and hateful specimens of the bunch, like for instance the worldly perpetrators of genocide of yesteryear, we see them flying about like angels with halos over their heads, administering the everlasting merits of loving kindness to all peoples. In other words, not not-two. Not here in this world, not yet at any rate.[197]

So, for all these reasons, one might venture to say that it's not necessary to actually avoid duality, nor is it necessary to make "One" a lifelong principle. In a word, there's no need to run away from anything, or to run after it. Even *funi*, not-two, should be rejected.

[197] And perhaps, in order to break the ice separating the two, that Kodo Sawaki at one point extols the virtues of "begging money from the poor in order to give it to the rich."

62

In not-two
All things are alike,
beyond contradictions.[198]

"I always repeat: neither object nor subject. Everything is included in the reality of One," says the master, Deshimaru, when commenting on this verse. It's true, he was always repeating such statements, much as do all the other masters, past and present.

Zen teaching is not in the least bit complicated: neither object nor subject. Of course, our personal thoughts and our individual actions still exist despite what has just been said; and to know this means to feel it, practice it and live it.

> Do you know the story of the monk Tanka,[199] who found himself alone in the outskirts of Peking late one evening about a thousand years ago? It was extremely cold and he took refuge in the local temple. There was no one about, and seeing three wooden Buddha statues in the Buddha hall, Tanka took one of them and burned it to warm himself. Smelling the smoke, the Abbot of the temple came running. He had a long white beard and bushy eyebrows and he was dressed for bed. He saw the burning Buddha statue in the fireplace, and he gaped at it, then over at Tanka. As you can imagine the Abbot was altogether stunned, shocked and horrified. "What-what have you done?" he stuttered. "Do you realize, young monk, that you have just burned the Buddha!?"

---

198 Another version of the same verse: Within this "not-two" all are alike / and nothing is not included. (Kennett Roshi).

199 Tanka (739-824). For another account of the same incident see strophe 41, page 198.

This said, Tanka picked up a broom handle and started to poke around in the ashes, searching for something. The Abbot, in a state between rage and bewilderment, exclaimed in a loud voice: "Why, may I ask, are you so intently poking about in those ashes? Yes? Well, I will have you know that those are the ashes," he pointed emphatically at the ashes, "*of the Buddha!*"

"Yes, your reverend," replied Tanka, "and that is precisely why I am poking them about. I am looking for the *sarira!*" (*Sarira* are the remains of a saint's cremation).

"Ohhhh," the Abbot moaned and shook his head. It had suddenly occurred to him that he wasn't dealing with a man in the normal condition of mind, and that maybe this fellow in a black monk's robe before him was one of those monks from that Zen school he'd heard about. Mad.

He addressed Tanka again in a loud voice: "Now listen here, young monk, you cannot find *sarira* in a wooden statue no matter how much you poke around in those ashes!"

"Yes, your reverend, I understand you perfectly well," Tanka nodded and put down the broom and looked over at the other wooden statues in the room. "So perhaps, your most honored reverend, since there is no *sarira* to be found in these ashes, what do you say if we burn the other two?"

"You, a monk? Ha! You're a demon! You're Mara! You're mad! Get out! Get out!" The Abbot pointed to the door, and Tanka, without another word, went out into the freezing night.

Epilogue: Shortly after this incident, the Abbot lost his beard and eyebrows, which in Buddhism is a sign of spiritual retribution. While Tanka, becoming a true master in his own right, went on to enlighten many people in the north of China.[200]

In not-two
All things are alike,
beyond contradictions.

Since we can say "neither object nor subject," we can also say, "neither similar nor different." That is, the similarity of the not-two. Even though both birth and death indeed exist (i.e., differences indeed exist), similarity is eternal and beyond words: *tathata.* It's our face before the birth of our parents, before Adam and Eve. And seeing it in this light, based on "similarity" being everywhere, then what exactly is the difference between Adam and Eve anyway, besides their sexes?

Even though we are all totally different, one from the other, at the same time, we are all even more deeply identical than we can possibly know.

∽

This thinking process does not merely entail the notion of "embracing the contradictions." It obliges us to go beyond the contradictions themselves, beyond sides, beyond self-motivated judgment. To go to that place where there is no "beginning or end." This means the cosmos.

∽

200 Master Dogen in *Zuimonki*, speaks of Tanka as a man who practiced "in accord and conformity with the rules of the dojo, as well as with the Buddha-Law. Tanka was always courteous. When he was talking or listening he held his hands against his chest in *shashu*, like other monks of the time, as a sign of respect for others." And perhaps it's from this perspective that one should regard the story of Tanka burning a statue of Buddha to keep warm. *Shobogenzo-Zuimonki, The Sayings of Eihei Dogen Zenji*, recorded by Koun Ejo, translated by Shoku Okumura. Kyoto Soto-Zen Center, 1987, 125-127.

"At the moment of our death, our consciousness can unconsciously reach the depths of the cosmos," said the master. And this is not accomplished through one practice or another; there is no practice in the face of death. In the Zen school they are *hishiryo*, meaning they leave death alone—that is, in the hands of the elements. This is another way of saying that those dying in Zen know where to go, anyhow.

So, don't follow your thoughts—not now and not at the moment of your death—and this way, by not being bound and gagged by your karma, you will be able to go to wherever you want.[201]

That is the great awakening, something not prefabricated by humans nor conditioned by man-made methods, and I believe this is what Sosan is expressing when he writes: *In not-two all things are identical, alike, beyond contradictions.*

---

201 This is different than in ancient Buddhism where, according to master Sokei-an, the Arhat took a long time to prepare himself for death. And different from the Tibetan approach to death whereby, according to Lama Govinda in his book *The Foundations of Tibetan Mysticism*, one must carefully prepare oneself for the end of one's life, and for the dangers of death and of the after-death, otherwise there will be no "better rebirth," let alone "final liberation." Govinda, Lama Anagarika, *Foundations of Tibetan Mysticism* (Rider and Company, London, 1960, 122-123).

63

Sages and all of humanity
Go towards the original source.

Wisdom is not attained through having a high IQ, nor through learning, through knowledge,[202] nor through the great talents of our own times—the Honoré de Balzacs, the Louis-Ferdinand Célines, the Pablo Picassos, and so many others, great artists for a fact, but not such great human beings. "The great sages of all humanity," as Sosan calls them, are not the learned, the intelligent or the talented ones; rather they are *all* the buddhas and *all* the patriarchs in *all* the ten directions. This strophe is addressed to them, to those human beings who "go to the original source" as Sosan says, with *all* the others.

So, how do you get to this source he is talking about? By reading books, memorizing passages by heart? Well, certainly by reading books on the matter, at least nowadays. Who didn't come to Buddhism through the works of Coomaraswamy and Lama Govinda, and to Zen through Alan Watts, D.T. Suzuki, Herrigel, Kerouac, and maybe even Castaneda?

In other words, youa man can come to the supreme way of the Buddha and the patriarchs from books or from anything else; and to approach the matter with books, or through them, is a very effective way to go about it, e. And especially in our own time when books on spirituality are found everywhere. So, if you come to the practice through books, then books are good.[203]

---

202 A study was recently conducted to find out why certain men and women became important people in our society, people who have had great influence on this earth. And the conclusion: it was never thanks to the education they had received in school, nor thanks to the diplomas and other grades they had acquired in society. It was due to their character, which blossomed during their lifetime.

203 For more on the huge importance of books, see Manguel, Alberto, *A History of Reading* (Penguin, 1996).

In fact, however, one doesn't have to take it that far, as would a famous poet with worldwide circulation, stating that the written word, “the Haiku, offers a method for reaching ultimate truth.”[204] Here with Sosan and all the others in the Zen lineages, we're not talking about getting enlightened through books and/or through Zen poetry, nor are we talking about Roland Barthes' observation concerning both the haiku and the koan, “their purpose being to stop language in order to obtain satori.”[205] observation concerning both the haiku and the koan, “their purpose being to stop language in order to obtain satori.” This is not understanding much of anything about Buddhism, let alone Zen. In fact, one Zen master says that “the haiku is not at all a deep teaching; it is simply a vulgarization of the Zen koan.”[206]

Then, there's the other extreme, usually associated with the Rinzai line, and what they call *kyoge betsuden* (i.e., the teaching outside the scriptures, outside the writings). Indeed, this position is reminiscent of Socrates who argues that books are useless tools, since they can only repeat the same words over and over again.[207]

> Tokusan was a scholar of ancient China, later to become one of the great patriarchs of Zen. “I have completely mastered the *Diamond Sutra*,” Tokusan was prone to saying, when he was still a scholar—indeed, he had already written 12 volumes of commentaries on this one particular sutra, and “the incomparable depth of his discourse” was widely praised.

---

204 Ginsburg, Allen, *World Fellowship of Buddhists Review* (April 2004, 24).

205 Roland Barthes (-1980), writer, critic and Chairman of Semiology at the College de France.

206 Master Deshimaru, Vol. II, *Poemes de Daichi* # 212.

207 Manguel, ibid.

Within the scholarly circles, and among the Palace pundits of the time, Tokusan was considered the greatest scholar in the whole of China. And he too saw himself as such. Anyway, it was clear that he put enormous importance on the written word; what's more, he proclaimed the supremacy of the sutras above all practices.

Meanwhile, Tokusan had heard talk about the celebrated Zen master named Ryutan. He was intrigued and wondered what was so special about this Zen master, or any other Zen master at that. "Why is he so famous? What does *he* know about the sutras? *I* know them! Yes, we must meet right away!"

Shortly thereafter he set off with all his books and commentaries. He was intent on testing Ryutan on the sutras.

On his long trek to Ryutan's place, Tokusan had a disturbing encounter with an old lady he encountered along the way. She sold rice cakes in a tavern by the roadside. Tokusan was very hungry and he ordered one.

"Certainly, honorable monk, but first tell me what are you carrying in that big bag?" (Scholars were often called "monks" in those days).

"In this bag I have my commentaries on the *Diamond Sutra*. My name is Tokusan, I wrote these commentaries. Have you not heard about me and of my work on the *Diamond Sutra?*"

"No, I have not heard about you, but I once heard that very sutra being recited. May I ask you a question on this subject?"

All Tokusan wanted was to eat a rice cake, not to be confronted by this old woman who didn't know anything. But she asked her question anyway. "Here is my question, and if you can answer it, I will sell you a rice cake; if not, then no rice cake." He nodded his head in agreement. The woman continued: "It is said in this

> sutra that "the past mind cannot be grasped, the present mind cannot be grasped, and the future mind cannot be grasped." You wish to buy a rice cake. Which mind do you propose to eat it with?" Tokusan[208] was struck dumb and could not answer the old woman.[209] And he left for Ryutan's place, bewildered and hungrier than ever.

Master Dogen says in his *Shobogenzo*[210] concerning this story: "It is truly regrettable that such a great Buddhist scholar, who studied thousands of volumes of commentary and for many years explained their theories, could not answer an old woman's simple question. There is a big difference between acquiring knowledge through books and acquiring knowledge through experience. For the first time, Tokusan learned, much to his chagrin, that a painting of a rice cake cannot satisfy hunger."

∽

---

208 Tokusan (782-865) was quite evidently uninfluenced and even unaware of the arrival and the teaching of Bodhidharma in China, already 300 years earlier. Others however were influenced, and little by little Bodhidarma's teaching swept away all the "superiorities" of the sutra scholars, even Tokusan himself.

209 There exist many more stories depicting the path taken by the great scholars from the study of the sutras and the reading of books, to the actual experiencing of the awakened mind of the great sages. Like Eka, who before becoming the 2nd Patriarch of Zen, was a highly esteemed connoisseur of Indian Buddhism, and yet who finished by cutting off his left arm in order to prove his faith in front of Bodhidharma. And Kyogen, who was a specialist on the spoken words of the old masters—that is, until he had his *mondo* with master Isan, after which he burned all his writings and declared: "I will never again study Zen." [see strophe 44]. And of course Tokusan himself, who after meeting with master Ryutan, burned his own books and commentaries on the *Diamond Sutra* in order to follow the master and to practice and transmit only zazen. (See strophe 17 for more.)

210 *Shobogenzo* chapter entitled, "Mind cannot be grasped," translated by Nishiyama, Vol. 1, 28.

Books on Buddhism and Zen may not satisfy your hunger for the true teaching, yet they can still make you wish to taste it for yourself; and this is indeed how the majority of disciples today discovered the practice of Zen in the first place. "Ah, what a sutra! Vimalakirti, Manjusri! What I've just read is grandiose! Unfathomable." Then you come to the great masters, Huang-Po in China, Milarepa in Tibet, and you say, "More than great, it's pure living freedom!"

You are so moved by what you have read that tears come to your eyes. And sometimes with feelings so strong that you can't even breathe anymore. You almost die from auto-asphyxiation. That's what words written in books can do to you in the beginning.

Such emotion can carry you to great heights: first the Christians: Eckhart and Kierkegaard; then the Asians: Buddha, Bodhidharma and Dogen.

But, sooner or later, books don't work anymore, especially if you have already read them all. Certainly, one reads the great books over and over again, but the first encounter is gone, and slowly the truths you read and re-read about, cosmic though they may be, have lost their freshness, their teeth in fact, and become kind of boring.[211]

Eventually, one will need something more . . . more than the written word. One will need human exchange, contact and comradeship, which is what is called "taking the Way."

In a word, books are good because they can direct you straight to the original source (that is, if you don't become misled by all kinds of contradictory thoughts along the way). This is what is called the condition of *Sotapanna*, "the man who has entered the stream."[212] Enter

---

211 Socrates once more said, concerning the written word: "They seem to talk to you as though they were intelligent, but if you ask them anything about what they say, from a wish to know more, they go on telling you the same thing over and over again forever." Manguel, Alberto, *A History of Reading* (Penguin, 1996).

212 *Sotapanna* literally, "the stream-enterer." The first of the Four Noble Truths. "It is said to be a guarantee of attainment of enlightenment, in this life or in the next," writes Christian Humphreys. "One who has had vision of Nirvana."

the stream, it is said, and the Way will open unto you, like a flower in bloom.[213]

Sages and all of humanity
Go towards the original source.

[213] "Your treasure house will open of itself, and you can use it as you please," go the last words of Dogen's *Fukenzazengi.*

64

The original source being beyond space and time
One instant becomes ten thousand years.

This is why, when you teach, you speak of earth and sky. Of the cosmic truth without human interference.[214] In any case, this is what Sosan himself expresses in the *Shinjinmei,* the first part with "not-running-after" nor "running-away" undertone, the second part concerning *funi* or not-two—which together is precisely that: "without human interference." This can be seen and heard when reading these poems in the order they were composed.

Now, in this third and final part, Sosan's vision becomes more global and cosmic. What's more, the way Sosan uses his metaphors changes. Here in the poem he uses the *kanji* "s*hu,*" "source," "origin" or "source-origin." That which is beyond thinking, *hishiryo.*[215]

There's nothing mysterious about all of this. It's simply a way of recognizing the original source when you see it. *Funi,* that which lies somewhere beyond the human conception of space and of time as well.

∽

Time is the measure, and space is the place in which things are measured, but otherwise there is no measurement anywhere at all.

---

[214] "It's for this that, in order to teach, you must speak of sky and earth. Explain the cosmic truth." Deshimaru in *Daichi* (Editions Integrale, Vol. 13, 260).

[215] In fact, the word/expression *hishiryo* was first used by Sosan in around 600, and that was here in this very poem. *Hi* is the negation, though in Japanese it means "beyond." *Shi* means "thinking." And *ryo* means "measure." Considered by Dogen to mean *anuttara samyak sambodhi,* or the highest awakening, ultimate awareness.

Many Zen stories try to capture this need of man to always measure things, as in the case of the following story where we see Bodhidharma recognizing the different attainments among his four disciples. But is it a question of "measure of attainment" or not? In other words, does the understanding of truth grow and deepen as it enters through the skin and makes its way into the marrow, or doesn't it? And did the Second Patriarch, Eka, advance the others in attainment, or not? Or again, what exactly is the measurement of attainment?

> One day, Bodhidharma took his four disciples aside and asked them point-blank what they had, each of them, attained by this teaching. None had any difficulty in answering him, and the first one, Dofu, said, "Neither be 'attached' nor 'unattached' to words and letters. Utilize this condition freely..." (That is, use it as a tool along the Way).
>
> "You possess my skin," replied the master.
>
> The second disciple, Doiku, took over from the next and said, "This is how I understand it: After Ananda had seen the Buddha land of Akshobhya only once, he never looked at it again."
>
> "And you possess my flesh," replied the master.
>
> His only female disciple, Soji, got up and said, "The four elements are empty and the five *skandhas* are non-existent. In my view there is not one thing to be gained."
>
> "You possess my bones," replied the master much as before.
>
> The last disciple to reply was Eka. He prostrated himself, hitting his head on the earth, and without speaking returned to his seat.
>
> "And you, Eka, possess my marrow."[216]

[216] See Dogen's *Shobogenzo*, chapter entitled "Katto."

This story has not to do with relative depth, like that of thinking only vertically: "skin" being more on the surface and therefore on a lower level in the spiritual hierarchy than the marrow, or the essence, which is deeper down within the bones and therefore more invisible to the naked eye. For this simple reason, Eka finds himself on a higher level in the spiritual hierarchy than the others . . . or does he?

This typical type of interrogation has nothing to do with the story at hand. Bodhidharma was not measuring his disciples one against the other, as in a sports competition or other, but just saying, "You possess my—" and nothing more.

You possess my *what?* My body, my robe, my awakening, my Dharma, my original face, or briefly my entire being…? You mean you possess everything? Come now, since to possess anything at all is already impossible, wisdom included, so it goes without saying that you "just possess—" this is all.

So, this strophe, like this story, tells us that "transmission" (Bodhidharma's, Eka's or your own) only occurs "beyond space and time," and not within it.[217]

∽

The same story occurred with Isan and Kyogen: the original source, where is it? In what space, in what time is it?

> "It is said that you are an exceptionally bright young monk," said master Isan,[218] addressing his disciple Kyogen, another of the sutra specialists of the times. "And that your frontal brain is twice the normal size. It is said that when you were teaching in the dojo of master

---

217 Space/time is a human concept, creation or invention. The original source is not only beyond human invention, as it is said, but beyond human beings.

218 Isan (771-853), disciple of Hyakujo and master of Kyogen (-898). In the line of the Igyo school of Zen. In the tenth century this school was assimilated into the Rinzai school.

Hyakujo, you could give ten different replies to one single question; and to ten questions you would give a hundred replies..." (We don't know how Kyogen responded to this or how he reacted, but anyhow Isan continued): "Now what I want from you is a simple phrase that comes from a time prior to your birth."

"Utterly flummoxed and in despair," writes R.H. Blyth, "the disciple went back to his study of the sutras." But he could not find the answer there, and so took all his books and threw them into the fire. Someone asked him, "Why are you doing that, burning the sutras!?"

"You can't satisfy hunger with a painted rice cake," he replied, speaking of himself. "At least now I understand that much!"

But "that much" still wasn't enough, and one day he told Isan, "I am completely stupid! Please, give me a word that will show me the Way and open my mind!"[219]

"Certainly, I could tell you something; but if I do, later you would curse me to your dying day." (That is, whatever I may say would only be mine, it would have nothing to do with you.)

Kyogen was very disappointed with this answer and went off alone to live in the mountains where he built a hut and he grew bamboo for a living.

However, later, while sweeping away some brush, he swept a pebble against a stalk of bamboo. And "click"! The sharp report, which occurred at exactly that moment awakened his mind.[220]

---

219 Note the old saying that where there is measurement, there is life and death; there is space and time.

220 The same, perhaps, as with a chick when it is about to hatch. Its mother pecks the shell at just that moment, there's a "clack," and the chick is born!

> Isan's dojo was located at the foot of the mountain, across the valley, and Kyogen turned in that direction and bowed deeply and said, "If you had given a reply to my question when I asked it, today would never have happened."[221]

And this is what Sosan points out in the first line, that "the original source is beyond time and space."

The original source being beyond space and time,
One instant becomes ten thousand years.

Then, in the second line, Sosan points out that, "One instant becomes ten thousand years." Now, this is perhaps so for some, but for most of us who function within space and time, "one single instant becomes ten thousand years" is pure gibberish.

Where is the proof in all this, you might ask? Well, you can always point out that it has been proven, scientifically, that the earth turns on its axis at 70,000 kilometers per second; and that light moves through space at 300,000 kilometers per second. But that's about as far as you can go with proving things . . . at least the speed of things. For instance, you can't even time the speed of a thought. Because it goes too fast. And faster than thought is non-thought; and faster than non-thought is thought-non-thought, thought. Or what is called *hishiryo* consciousness.

No chronometer, not even a metal-plated one, could stand the jolt. Anyway, *hishiryo*-consciousness goes so fast that, as a fellow monk once confided to me while sitting on a bench at the temple, "it will never be possible to time *hishiryo*. No number large enough can express its speed."

∞

When we function within space and time, we always have a point of view about the time we live in and about the space we occupy. But as we

[221] See strophe # 9, page 46 and strophe # 27, page 127.

travel through the starry expanses, this way of seeing life and death can slow us down greatly, if not stop us dead in our tracks.

∽

For the old man, time accelerates gradually year after year. They say it's due to the slowing down of the brain and heart. A four-year-old child, however, finds time very slow, but for different reasons, or perhaps for no reason at all. One day I asked a four- or five-year-old boy who was sitting beside me on yet another bench, "Tell me pal, do you know when you were born?" I wanted to know his age, but his mind too while I was at it, and he answered, without even looking at me: "A very, very long time ago."

∽

The *Hannya Shingyo,* the Heart Sutra we recite every morning, is basically about *beyond* time and space: In *ku* (*sunyata,* emptiness, the void) there is neither knowledge nor ignorance, neither illusion nor the ceasing of illusion, suffering nor decline, nor death, nor the end of decline, nor even the ceasing of suffering. It's the same with the Four Vows: However innumerable are sentient beings, I vow to save them all. And with the passions, to conquer them all; and with the *dharmas,* to acquire them all; and as for the Buddha-Way, to attain that too. This sutra of the Four Vows advises us to accomplish such a miraculous feat but knows full well that this cannot be accomplished or attained—not in the world of space and time, at any rate.

The original source being beyond space and time
One instant becomes ten thousand years.

It has already been seen here in this long poem, the *Shinjinmei,* that in the beginning (as well as at the beginning of this very verse, and here at the end of it as well), Sosan places his emphasis on not being attached to this or that; then, on not running away from anything either; and in the end, one thought is worth ten-thousand years.

65

Neither existence nor non-existence,
Everywhere, right before your eyes.

As we progress verse after verse towards the end of this unending poem—great as it is—we notice in particular, and as has already been said though differently, Sosan's tone and even his audience has been metamorphosed into another one. Now, he is no longer addressing himself to the un-awakened person. He or she being addressed is no longer the un-awakened one who becomes awakened, because now, and for a long time, they are, as it is said, the "already long-ago awakened." Sosan is no longer talking existence, nor non-existence, as I think we see in this present verse. He is neither here nor there, but "everywhere right before our eyes." In any case, the "here and now" is the essential point, whether we may find ourselves at the beginning, middle or end of this poem, the *Shinjinmei*. Like right *now*, here, before our own eyes.

In the previous verse, Sosan *does not* show us that space and time, despite the limitations of language, are unlimited, and that one instant is no different than ten thousand years. On the contrary, he shows us that "space and time" are in fact quite limited. Now, in this verse, he shows how the Buddha's teaching is not in any way limited.

This notion is well expressed in the opening verse of master Wanshi's poem, *Song of Silent Illumination*:

When in the silence all words are forgotten,
It appears before you with clarity.
When you realize it, time has no more limits.[222]

∽

[222] Master Wanshi, *Le Chant de l'Illumination Silencieuse*, edited by Etienne Zeisler (AZI, 1991).

If we're not stuck on our personal problems, our bad luck and our injustices, on our God or the devil, then we can indeed be here now, we are ready for the practice. Such a "ready person" is told right off that, "if he or she does this (i.e., zazen), they will get that." They don't completely believe what they hear, but they do it anyway, zazen every day all the time. Then, after some years have gone by, and they still haven't gotten anything, they begin to hear another voice talking to them, saying things like, "All those years and you got nothing from it! You fool, nothing!"

Perhaps. And master Dogen could say the same as the monk who was stuck on some notion or other, and yet was nobody's fool. As in the year 1227, when Dogen returned to Japan.

In reply to the question put to him on his arrival by the high emissary of the emperor: *What had he, Dogen, gained from his stay in a Buddhist temple in China?* To which Dogen answered, *that he had brought back no Buddhism, not even any sutras to show, that in fact he had returned to Japan empty-handed.*

"My good monk," replied the emissary, taken aback. "You spent three years in a Buddhist monastery in China, and now you say you have brought nothing back with you about Buddhism?"

Dogen consented: "Only this, *Gen no bi choku,*[223] eyes horizontal, nose vertical."

∽

"In one glance, one thought, one breath, one sound, with our own bodies, we should see, feel, taste and touch the entire cosmos."[224]

To touch the cosmos—the present moment—with the five *skandha* (the five essentials) which make up our personality, our self; and also, with the four elements, with our body . . . It is this that Sosan is talking about when he says, "everywhere." "Existent or non-existent, everywhere right before our eyes."

---

223 *Gen*: eyes, *no*: horizontal, *bi*: nose, *choku*: straight, vertical.

224 See Deshimaru's own *Shinjinmei* commentary (Cesare Rancilio Editeur), concerning verse 64.

∽

Throw down, renounce, abandon. Abandon body and mind and you will have neither existence nor non-existence, *shin jin datsu raku.*[225] Kodo Sawaki defines it this way: "renouncing our egocentricity and believing in Buddha and being led by Buddha."

Here is a well-known *mondo* between Master Sekito and his disciple Tenno Dogo:[226]

> "Master, what is the essence of Buddhism?"
>
> "It cannot be understood or obtained."
>
> "But if it cannot be understood or obtained, then where is it?"
>
> Sekito's reply was simply this: "The vast sky is not disturbed by the flight of the white clouds."

Or to put it differently:

> "Master, what is the essence of Buddhism?"
>
> "It has neither existence nor non-existence."
>
> "And if it has neither existence nor non-existence, where can it be found?"
>
> "Everywhere, right before your eyes."

And again:

> An admirer of the famous artist, Pablo Picasso, said to him one day, "Pablo, please tell me, what do you do when you run out of red?"
>
> "Not complicated," replied Picasso, "When I run out of red I use blue."

225 *Shin*: mind. *Jin*: body. *Datsu raku*: throw down.

226 Both in the 700s.

> "And when you run out of blue?"
> "When out of blue I use red."

And here is the most modern *mondo* of them all:

> The writer Jack Kerouac was in a Chinese restaurant and at one point he went into the kitchen and saw the old cook behind his pots and pans, and asked him: "Why did Bodhidharma come from the West?"
>
> And the old cook answered, "I don't care."[227]

Neither existence nor non-existence,
Everywhere, right before your eyes.

This verse demonstrates the state of mind of *hishiryo* consciousness in zazen. Also, it talks about awakening. But what is awakening? Is it the state of mind that's called "total understanding," the state in which everything suddenly appears to you as clear as crystal? Or the state that, like a spark, suddenly goes off and lights up the brain? Maybe, but more likely, it's neither one nor the other; for if it's really a "light" caused by a spark, then it will dim with time and finally go out, just as it once came on. So too is it with "total understanding," for at some point you will forget this state and then you will no longer understand it. And alas, you'll have to wait until the next time it arises, god willing.

In this verse, however, as in so many of the others, Sosan talks about something that is never forgotten. Not even in death.

---

[227] "I don't care,' said the old cook, with lidded eyes, and I told Japhy and he said, 'Perfect answer, absolutely perfect. Now you know what I mean by Zen.'" *The Dharma Bums* (New York: Penguin Classics, 1971). Though this may simply be pleasant chit-chat in a hip place at a hip time, it does nonetheless make for fine reading, which was Kerouac's ultimate goal.

66

The smallest is identical to the largest;
The borders between places must be erased.

This verse means we can embrace the whole world with our body. You often hear, "I can't practice for other people." But that's not true. The small and the big are the same. So too is a little and a lot.

Small is the same as big. A little and a lot is the same too. So small, in fact, that nothing more can be included in it. And, something that cannot include anything is certainly unlimited. Likewise, it's so big that nothing can fill it up. This too is unlimited.

The same with the practice of Zen. Its practice does not depend on whether time is long or short. There is no measure, there are no grades, no titles, as has been alluded to already. When we are present in the moment, as we are, if we practice exactly this moment has no beginning, no end. This is why Sosan says in this verse, "Borders between places must be erased." Or more simply said: entering the realm where *bonno* (illusions) are cut.

That "borders between places must be erased" can be understood to mean that it would do us well to cut off everything that is pre-fabricated by humankind, even that of dimensions like size. The microcosm is the universe; it's so tiny that one can't imagine how tiny that really is. And yet so large (and just with one single letter changed, from the "i" in microcosm to the "a" in macrocosm), as to include the great earth and all the millions of worlds everywhere.

Here in this place, or more exactly here "between these places," we don't hesitate to "erase the borders." Buddha is everywhere, in everything, every gesture. As Sosan pointed out in the previous verse: the teaching is everywhere "before one's very eyes."

> One morning after *genmai*, a monk came up and asked master Joshu to teach him about Buddhism and the Way.

"Master, what is Buddhism?"
Joshu asked him, "Have you eaten your *genmai*?"
"Yes, I have."
"Then wash your bowl."

There's nothing strange or hidden in this teaching. It does not stray from the body. This is why we can say that "the smallest is identical to the biggest." Minimum and maximum are our original nature, here and now. This is to be free from preconceived notions. Not letting yourself get tied up or attached in any other way; not to be fooled, either by yourself, by anybody else, or by anything at all.

ᔕ

Remember the story of Gutei, the master who held up his thumb whenever anyone would ask him about Buddhism? He did this all the time, right up to the moment of his death. Without introductions, without explanations, Gutei just held up his thumb for the last thirty years of his life.

Gutei's thumb held up before his face is phenomena, *shiki*. Gutei holds up his thumb is non-phenomena, it is *ku*.

A scholar once asked a master, "Once we've become a buddha, where is the person?" And he never replied. Perhaps because he saw no use in replying to such a question—too clever to mess with. However, had he lifted his thumb in the fashion of Gutei, would that have awakened the scholar more than no answer at all? Probably not. And probably the scholar would have departed alone with his question, and as confused as ever.

Anyway, for such a method to have efficacy, you do not use the frontal brain, the one that calculates and figures things out, and which always falls into definitions which that lead quickly into cliché and imitation, especially when dealing with matters such as the universe and the cosmos. And so, we have the thumb of Gutei.

It is written in the *Mumonkan* that whenever master Gutei was questioned about Buddhism, he would

> simply stick up one finger. At one time he had a young attendant, to whom a visitor asked, "What is the Zen your master is teaching?" The boy, imitating his master, also stuck up one finger. Hearing of this, Gutei cut off the boy's finger with a knife. As the boy went out screaming with pain, Gutei called to him. When the boy turned his head, Gutei stuck up his finger. The boy, goes on the Mumonkan, was suddenly enlightened . . . And further on in the *Mumonkan* it is written that when Gutei was about to die, he said to the assembled monks, "I attained Tenryu's Zen of One Finger. I used it all through my life, but could not exhaust it." When he had finished saying this, he died.[228]

To use Gutei's thumb-up reply yourself would be an utter waste of time, for imitation is only that, like finding yourself in a pre-staged lightshow.

∽

The expression "ten-thousand dharmas" means infinity, limitlessness or the world without borders. And yet, as it is said, the ten thousand dharmas (i.e., infinity) can be realized on a single fingertip. This is the teaching. An instant, described in the *Shodoka* as a snapping of fingers, is not even an instant, not even a finger, a thumb. This is so, as it is pointed out in the following verse, because "boundaries are invisible" if not completely nonexistent. In fact, here in the next poem, #67, the boundaries are so small that they have no self, no noumenon anymore.

---

[228] From the *Mumonkan*, Case # 3, compiled by Master Shibayama, (New American Library, 1974). For another version of this same story see Coupey, Philippe, *Zen Simply Sitting* (Prescott, Arizona: Hohm Press, 2006, 62).

67

The largest is identical to the smallest;
Boundaries are invisible.

Boundaries between places are invisible, because they are too small or too big to be seen. They are smaller than we can imagine, because they have no self; they are bigger than we can imagine, also because they have no self.

When the United States bought Alaska, it became much bigger, but nothing really changed, except perhaps in the human mind of man. The manmade boundaries changed but the size of the earth did not change at all. When the Soviet Union found itself divided up into thirteen pieces, nothing became smaller. Yet it is said now that the United States suddenly became much bigger while Russia just as suddenly became much smaller.

If we can transcend not only places and sizes, can we also transcend ideas and concepts, such as that of nirvana and samsara, satori and illusion? Can we transcend concepts of calm and chaos, and in the end even those of places and no places? That's the practice: No limit to the state of zazen, to good or bad, nor even the feeling of good or bad. (We are talking here not of annihilation of course, but of freedom).

∽

How do we enunciate it, the Way? With words? With the body? With both, with neither? Keizan said, in his own commentary to this particular verse, that even if all the buddhas everywhere tirelessly repeated this very same point with words, they would still fall short of space and *ku.* "...To define infinite space," is how Keizan expresses it. And again, "Even if all the buddhas in the world wished to explain it, they couldn't, they just couldn't do it either."[229]

---

[229] Keizan in the *Shin Jin Mei, Poemes Sur La Foi En L'esprit*, commentary by Maitre T. Deshimaru (Cesare Rancilio Editeur). This edition appeared in

No master, not even Buddha, can provide explanations, let alone an answer, to that which is unlimited.[230] This is why *doshu* is so important: how we express the Way, with words or without, even in its smallest, most finite details. *Doshu* is the way one expresses the Dharma, through mind, mouth, body and posture, with all of it not moving.

∽

"In the world of the infinitely large, and in that of the infinitely small, the stars and tiny particles are just movement,"[231] phenomena and emptiness being completely interdependent.

∽

Water in a river, always flowing, never stops, not for a second. Sit quietly somewhere and you can hear the river, you can hear change . . . once the wind stops blowing. Just then, the waves of the mind are calm, and you hear the voice of the valley. RAnd right here, in this place, too, you can hear everything. Even the ticking of the clock. You hear *mujo*.

At first you don't hear the clock. But then you hear it, and more and more clearly too. But at other times, in other circumstances, you no longer hear anything. You don't hear the clock ticking nor even the master speaking, and no matter what your present inner pandemonium, there is nothing you can do about it. Then again, when the time is right, one hears the sounds of time, the sounds of cause and effect, the sound of karma: these are the sounds you hear at that time. If you practice zazen in a forest, you can hear the trees flowing; in a city dojo you hear the houses and the city flowing—even though they're flowing more slowly than the river.

1981, the year of the master's death. Also see Bendowa, the first chapter of the *Shobogenzo*.

230 Not only are we unlimited, we are the karma of life, and the actions of life are unlimited. What is more, we or it continues forever.

231 This phrase comes from Deshimaru.

It is said that you can hear change. If you don't follow your thoughts, then you can hear everything. If you don't follow your thoughts, you can see everything too. What you hear and see is *mujo*, impermanence … What is a monk? Well, it's someone who unconsciously and naturally practices *bodaishin*, observing *mujo*. This is a monk.

∽

To reiterate: The world of matter and actions is limited when we imprison them within one of the million categories which exist, as in matters of size, as in matters of mind. So, the world of reason is obviously limited by its own categories. Master Keizan said that "life itself is just one position of this realization; so is death."

Speaking practically: It's here and there, in the biggest and the smallest where we find the Way, and where we practice it, and not just one hour a day, but all the time, automatically and unconsciously. Without getting lost in limits. Without observing or analyzing. Without comparing or judging.

68

Existence is nonexistence.
Nonexistence is existence.

Concerning this particular strophe, master Keizan says: "Buddha-nature is composed of two aspects, *u* and *mu.*" *U* being existence, our life, phenomena, or sometimes form; and *mu* being nonexistence, nothing. So, an awakened mind understands existence through nonexistence.

If mind has no obstacles, no stains, no divisions and no separation between inside and outside, you look at yourself through nonexistence, and then, so it is said, you see all existences as equal to yourself, as having the same nature as you, in fact possessing the same root called *kano doko*, which means mutual sympathy and respect for everything that exists.

This state of mind does not come to us through understanding, at least not through frontal brain understanding. It is *kikai tanden* thinking, the heart-body thinking. Long practitioners of Buddhism consider this teaching to be that of the heart par excellence. Sitting without wearing street clothes—sitting in black robes, without distinction, without obstacles between self and others. "Heart-compassion" is the expression used by some, though not myself. Anyway, stillness is already that, compassion.

∽

It does well to be aware of some of the major themes of the *Shinjinmei*. Like the theme here: of not taking one side as opposed to another, and this because existence is not made up only of one side. The same with non-existence. Together, this is the whole.

As it is expressed in the *Sandokai:*[232] "darkness also exists in light." And in the *Hokyozanmai:*[233] "midnight is the true light, dawn is not bright."

[232] By master Sekito (700-790).

[233] By master Tozan (807-867).

∽

Here again is Keizan concerning "existence / nonexistence":

> It possesses a reason that neither comes nor goes, that does not progress and does not accept any other thing. But if it is concealed, then it becomes completely secret and mysterious. At that very moment, realization will cause it to become more and more hidden, secret and mysterious.[234]

". . . to become more hidden, secret and mysterious," does not mean that awakening makes us more hidden, secret or mysterious, neither does awakening make one less hidden and mysterious then he or she already was. This has not so much to do with "this" or "that" mental construction; rather it means manifestation of things as they are. As with the word "*gensho*" which means: the truth of our daily lives . . . this which exists and acts here and now . . . this truth which visits us, and which is indeed mysterious and secret.

Of course, it's better to talk about the Universal Law or the Dharma than to not talk at all about it. Yet equally, a man or woman can also remain silent on the matter. It's important to remain silent—not in order to hide something, but rather to be able to create an enclosure that contains and protects it.

And this brings us directly to the following verse.

---

[234] See footnote # 229.

69

If this is not so,
You must not protect it.

If this is not so (that "existence is non-existence and non-existence is existence"*)*, then in that case, "do not protect it." Do not protect even the One, whether it's written with a capital 'O' or not. Professor Wang says of this verse that as long as you haven't understood it, your situation will remain unbearable and even untenable.

Master Keizan says: "Please, study *u* (existence) with exactness, and deeply understand *mu* (non-existence). Do not become the eccentric companion who only preserves and protects one side. [....] If this is not so (concerning *u* and *mu*), do not protect it and do not preserve it."

These words—"do not protect just one side"—are also a message for our life. If we take one position, we must take the other position as well. (However, tell this to a fundamentalist, a fanatic or a terrorist ... and good luck.)

Keizan continues on the subject of this verse and the preceding one. He writes:

> If you preserve this teaching, you will be able to become a true and accomplished person, a Zen monk who understands existence...If you wish to deeply understand what that means, ask the columns of the *hondo*[235]; they will be able to explain it to you amply enough.

To ask the walls is sometimes more effective and the answer deeper, and this is especially so when asking questions relating to existence and non-existence.

---

235 *Hondo*: Main hall in a monastery, used for gatherings and meals.

∽

"If this is not so," refers to the previous strophe (68) which is about existence and non-existence, but also applies to the three remaining strophes to come.

As we approach the end of the *Shinjinmei,* not only does the point of view widen in scope, but the rhythm accelerates as well... Do not escape from anything, even if it becomes too painful to bear—we've already had this. Be wary of having preferences—we've had that too. Now it's about dropping our concepts, our viewpoints, and our attachments: to ourselves, to the smallest, the biggest (minimum-maximum), to existence and/or non-existence, to truth and illusion. Now it's not even a matter of escaping from the heat or the cold; but simply a matter of remaining intimate with the heat and the cold.

> The disciple asks, "When the cold and heat come, how can we escape them?"
>
> And the master replies: "Why don't you go where it is neither cold nor hot?"
>
> "Where is this place?"
>
> "In winter, let the cold kill you; in summer, let the heat kill you."

When it's cold, don't seek the heat, don't imagine it, and don't wish for it. Same when it's hot. Don't seek it (no more than escape it) but rather, become intimate with it, with this pain. (Or *any* pain for that matter). This is being intimate with the heat and the cold without looking for anything else. "If it was not thus," says Sosan, "to protect it would be useless..." So, do not protect the extremes, like borders, limits and nor even measurements, but make of them the so-called Middle Way, or more exactly the way of "Mahayana," where there is no more existence or non-existence.[236]

---

236 "Nonexistence" in the sense of "emptiness" and not of "nothing."

For this to become fact, it is necessary to practice zazen and to study. Keizan says as much in his commentary on strophe 69. And to *listen* to a *kusen* is study through the *kikai tanden*. Study and practice are, in the end, one and the same, and "If this is not so, you must not protect it."

∽

Do we exist or not? This is a question often asked. We study, we read, we write and finally, like so many other student-thinkers, spiritual, philosophic or otherwise, we come to ask ourselves, "Does my existence have any meaning or doesn't it?" We read the books on philosophy, on Existentialism and science and they tell us that our lives, precious to us as they may be, have no real meaning.

This is not what Sosan says. In the *Shinjinmei*, composed in the early 600s and considered to be one of the most profound poems ever written, it is said, in so many words, that emptiness is *not* void of meaning, and therefore nor neither is life.

To return to the verse at hand, Sosan suggests that we do not protect one side (existence) or the other side (nonexistence). Which means not protecting your own concepts and viewpoints, which also means not protecting your small self. In a word, do not be attached to it, the small self, in any way.

∽

Kodo Sawaki spoke about "making the seam disappear." Do I exist or not? That's the junction, the seam. Sew them together and make the "yes" and the "no" disappear; don't protect them. No junction between life and death, you and me, the modern man person and the ancient monk. And finally, no seam at all. Mind, with a big "m" is all that exists.

∽

> It was the time for the young monk Tozan to leave his master, Ungan. Ungan was dying, and Tozan didn't stay

> on to look after him. But they did have this departing *mondo*: "After your death, if I am asked 'What was your true face?' what should I answer?"
>
> "*Tada kore kore,*" said the master, "only this is this."
>
> Tozan went away not understanding. He was alone, walking through the mountains, day after day, when he came upon a bridge. He glanced at the water flowing below and he saw his face, and at that moment he understood. "Only this is this."[237] He composed a poem on the occasion: "In the mirror of the water, my image and its reflection face each other: My body, my shape, is not my reflection, but the reflection is me."

Look at yourself in the mirror and you know right away that you are *not* that reflection. You know your face well enough, you know the difference between imagery and reality, and you can formally declare that the reflection you see in the water below the bridge is clearly *not* you; and that it's simply a mirage, a reflection, and in moving waters as well—that it can only be a flagrantly distorted view of reality.

Besides, since we all know that a person's face cannot be located in front of their face, it can therefore be "only this."

Whatever this may mean to you, live with it for a while. Little by little it becomes your life, and your vision of the world is forever changed by it, in all your relationships, in all your thoughts and your non-thoughts. So, it is said: study what you are doing, study what you are becoming.

---

237 Or, as it is recorded in some texts: "Just this, just this."

70

One is all things,
All things are One.

In this poem, as in answer to his previous one about "*not protecting it,*"[238] Sosan goes one step further by reminding the reader that in any case "*all things are one.*" This is Kodo Sawaki's "seam that does not exist." If the seam does not exist, then by deduction, nor do I. No junction, no nothing. Just mind.[239]

Yet this does not mean that we should then go and "wrap up everything with one thing,"[240] as some will do. Like wrapping up a package with a pretty red ribbon. No, it's about not attaining one thing, nor is it about attaining everything. This is what Sosan is saying, isn't he?

When asked, "Why did Bodhidharma come from India?"[241] Master Joshu replied: "The oak tree in the garden." And Keizan writing on this particular verse: "Between two and one, between all existences, we do not have dualistic aspects."

It's like when you first look at a flower, you see it for what it is; and this is because at that first moment there exists no object and no subject. And if you are attentive, you will understand that you see this one flower as you would all flowers.

However, don't fall into the trap of thinking that likewise, once one person has satori, all beings have it. For then why not say that as long as all beings do not have satori, no one has it, myself included. For this would be like saying that since we ourselves are *not* awakened, the

---

238 Previous strophe 69: *If this is not so, / You must not protect it.*

239 Things which are separate burst at the seam, and no matter how well sewn iis; that's exactly where things come undone, at the seam.

240 A Keizan expression.

241 See Kerouac footnote, end of strophe 65.

master is *not* awakened either.[242] So, if some monk or other with equivocal intentions, asks the master or the *shuso*, about "everything being one" or about "everything not being one," you must ask him in turn to show you his own original nature, "Hey you there, show it to me!" you shout and slap him at the same time... Now, whatever happened to the monk thereafter is unimportant. What's important in this story, and even primordial I think, is that it demonstrates what it is to be in the present moment, and nowhere else.

"If you want to obtain my head," says Keizan, "then please, bring it to me after you cut it off."[243] And again, "If you state that all things exist without [the] One, how can you look at a few flowers of *ku* (emptiness) with your inner eye? Now tell me, if the master asks to receive your eyeballs, would you give them to him? In the past I gave you very precious eyeballs, better than pearls, but now you must give them back!" And then talking perhaps to himself, Keizan adds: "But then again do not say that I have finished explaining fully to— you—for this is only the half of all things"—that is, only half of the teaching, half the total.

∽

In the previous verse the question was one of duality; in the present verse, it's no longer about duality. There is no longer any dualistic aspect between one and two, and none between one and all existences either. No seam between "one" and "two," and nowhere can the thread break, no weak spot in the whole.

There is no more seam at all. This means that, since there is no trace left of any seam at all, *there never was one* in the first place.

---

242 This shows no grasp of master Dogen's teaching, such as when he says that "zazen itself is satori," or that "when one flower blossoms spring is everywhere." Nor when Buddha, upon his awakening under the Bodhi Tree, said that "With me all beings are awakened."

243 Note the merry-making tone surrounding such sometimes bloody imagery as this one: like saying: who is this so-called 'me' anyhow, now that this head and this body are no longer together, but in two different places, ha-ha! please tell me that?

∽

In the previous verse the question was one of duality; in the present verse, it's no longer about duality. There is no longer any dualistic aspect between one and two, and none between one and all existences either. No seam between "one" and "two," and nowhere can the thread break; no weak spot in the whole.

Since there is no more seam at all, this means therefore, that there is no trace left of any seam either, hence *there never was one* in the first place.

71

This being so,
It is not necessary to consider the not finished.

Knowing that one is everything and everything is one,[251] is also knowing that this has nothing to do with things thus finished. "Not finished" is that which has no end. That, or "he/she," which is "not finished" is what one might call the true man being of "perfect wisdom." Contrary to what is usually expressed concerning this matter of wisdom, according to Sosan perfection is never finished, never perfect.

> One day Tokujo the ferryman and Kassan the monk were having an exchange on Tokujo's ferryboat—in fact the word "*tokujo*" itself means "boatman."
>
> Neither had ever met before and knew nothing of one another, though Tokujo recognized his passenger as a monk from his appearance—shaved head, monk robe, etc.; and also as one of the Soto school to which he (Kassan), was affiliated; he (Tokujo) being a monk himself of that same school, though not so easily recognizable. For though Tokujo had long ago received the transmission from his own master, the much admired Yakusan (-828), he never wore the monk robe, never shaved his head, never recited the sutras, never gave ordination, and never had a single disciple. That is, until now. Kassan, on his side, had not yet realized that this "tokujo" boatman was really the long-lost monk,[252] the co-disciple of Ungan and first disciple of master Yaku-

---

251 This is a paraphrase of previous verse (# 70): One is all things, / All things are One.

252 Only later to be called "Tokujo-the-boatman monk."

> san. And now he, Kassan, was being ferried across the river by Tokujo himself.[253]
>
> The two men had an exchange and Tokujo right away realized the deep dimension of the man sitting before him in his boat. He asked him a question and Kassan answered, and at that Tokujo shoved him overboard with his oar. Kassan, bewildered and angry, climbed back into the boat. Tokujo asked him another question.
>
> We do not know at what moment Kassan realized that he wasn't dealing with any ordinary boatman but actually with another monk—the monk and dharma heir Tokujo—but we do know that Kassan was a learned monk and knew well the Buddhist doctrine; and what's more that he spoke clearly and well with words which sounded true enough, at least to the ear. But Tokujo wasn't content and once again he threw him overboard. This happened three times and the last time when Kassan came up for air, Tokujo hit him right on the head with the oar and shouted down at him: "and even if your answers are exact, they are not enough!" [254]...
>
> In fact, whatever one says or thinks, it's just not enough, it's not complete, it's not perfect; this is the message.

Anyway, Kassan did not drown but went on to become a master in his own right, and all this thanks to a perhaps chance encounter on a ferryboat.

---

253 Buddhist symbolism here is clear enough, the boat being zazen or meditation and crossing over being crossing over the river of *bonno*. *Bon*: troublesome, *no*: suffering.

254 We also find this observation in verse 15 herein: *Even if your words are correct and your thoughts exact, it is not in accordance with the truth.*

∽

This verse is clearly not about arriving at the top of the mountain. Nor about attaining satori. It is about the "not finished." This is all very good news, because it means that we needn't worry about not being perfect. We need not worry about becoming somebody important, nor about anything at all. Indeed, the source does not spring from a living tree, and not from a dead one either, but from eternity.[255]

∽

"This we do not find," said Deshimaru, "and so we do not and cannot assess its true meaning. This is so because non-existence is without real existence." And he goes on: "Now please, do not worry about getting things finished. Nor about being perfect or not perfect. And too, as far as failure or success is concerned, forget about that as well." This being so, it is not necessary to consider the not-finished.

This being so,
It is not necessary to consider the not finished.

The best way to rebuild the world, said Kodo Sawaki, is to "not try to be first in anything, nor to out-do anybody else." Though this is diametrically opposed to the basic concept of the Olympic Games, along with almost everything else in our modern-day society—games, studies or careers—this is the master's message: not to be first, or at least that's part of the message.

The *Shinjinmei* is full of messages, and this verse in particular expresses the unfinished one. What is unfinished? The teaching is unfinished. Unfinished teaching, unfinished answers—for instance, what does it mean to live and to die? Question and answer unfinished.

---

255 Master Tozan said, "A flower blooms on a dead tree" (meaning, not so much that we are born from a dead tree, but that we are born in the first place, born from *ku*).

The *Shinjinmei* in general, and this verse in particular, can be taken lightly and quite at one's leisure, and that shows clearly the great poetic talent and vision of this ancient Zen master. In fact, what Sosan is saying is just the opposite of what it sounds like, and not to be taken lightly at all, but very seriously. indeed.

Some masters even go further than Sosan. While Sosan says it should not even be "considered" at all, this matter of life and death, Master Keizan says it shouldn't even be "discussed" in the first place. Not with anybody. "Do not discuss the subject of the teaching of transmitted Zen or Buddhism. You seeker of the Way," he goes on a little later, "please do not confuse the dead rat with the precious stone."[256] The last verse (to come shortly) in this long poem talks of not falling into the trap of language. So, don't become attached to language. Don't fall into the error of opposing ideas. That's the "dead rat" Keizan is talking about.

∽

This being so,
It is not necessary to consider the not-finished.

"This being so"—that is, if this is so, if the truth is simply thus, then it is simply this, it is *inmo*. Being *inmo* is being identical to all phenomena, and since this is so, there's no point worrying about satori or about attaining or not attaining the Way. There is no need to *be* better nor *do* better than anyone else, to *have* satori and/or to *not have* satori. When one thinks about it, one can seriously ask oneself why should *I* have it at all, if my neighbor doesn't have it himself?

In any case, "this being so," there is no point writing or even discussing it, this truth, with anyone at all, and certainly not with a man of faith. *Jakujo*.[257]

---

256 That is, "We should not imitate and sustain illusions with words," as Keizan points out elsewhere concerning the dead rat.

257 *Jakujo: jaku* means no one to discuss with, and *jo* means the serenity or imperturbability that there is no one to discuss with.

∽

When defining the word "zazen," Deshimaru explained it as meaning "to be seated." But he goes on to point out that if you look more closely at the *kanjis*, the ideograms, you don't see *one* person seated on the ground, but *two*. Two different people seated on one single zafu!

So, true sitting is not done all alone after all. For even when you thinks you are alone, you are not alone at all! And that is because you alone are already two. And maybe even more. Sitting alone you are an entire crowd sitting all together, in a dojo or anywhere.

It was said somewhere that "two beings co-exist in our minds, sometimes at the same time, and there's no one to deny that, because in the first place there is no one else."

Buddha means becoming only one. Yet, in our minds, two people are seated; say the ordinary one and the universal one. Two opposing entities. The human being is not perfect. But at that moment, says master Deshimaru, "When these two characters return to the earth, that is nirvana. We return to the earth. We have Buddha, and we have faith."

∽

This is the teaching. In verse 63 we saw how grandly humiliated was the scholar Tokusan by an old lady selling rice-cakes along the roadside.

> Tokusan was very hungry—he was on his way to visit master Ryutan—and all he could think of was to eat a rice-cake. But the lady, seeing him with a sack full of books over his shoulder, started to interrogate him. And in the brief exchange, today celebrated in the ancient texts, the lady finally refused to sell him a cake, and the great scholar went off like an idiot, hungry and ashamed of himself.[258]

---

[258] See verse 63 for more.

> Anyway, when Tokusan finally arrived at Ryutan's dojo, he was no longer so sure of himself and his knowledge, which seemed not so vast at all finally. But now it was time to meet with the master.
>
> He and Ryutan spoke late into the night, about the sutras and the teaching, when finally the master said, "It's very late. Why don't you go to bed?"
>
> When Tokusan stepped out of Ryutan's room, it was pitch dark outside and he could see nothing.
>
> "Here take this." Ryutan offered him a lantern. But just as he handed it to him, he blew out the flame. Without the light cast by the flame they both found themselves plunged into total darkness. It is said that at this instant Tokusan had a great satori.

This story, certified historically, depicts the moment of transmission: At that precise moment when *nothing* is transmitted, and yet, at that moment when compassion and wisdom grow and spread throughout the Ten Directions.

Now, if the truth is thus, then what more need is there to consider the not-finished, any more than the infinite?

72

Faith in mind is Not-Two.
Not-Two is faith in mind.

In this next-to-last strophe of the *Shinjinmei*, Sosan takes up the subject of *shin jin funi*, faith in not-two mind. *Shin jin* means "faith in mind" (and in fact the title of this long poem in translation), and "*funi*" means "not two." Faith not-two mind.

But then again, faith in what? In God, in Buddha, in yourself? Of course, in yourself. But then again, the question is posed, "who really is this self you call yours?"

Wu, the Emperor of China in the early 500s, asked Bodhidharma who was just then standing before him, "Who is this man in front of me?" Bodhidharma replied spontaneously and without doubt, "I do not know, Sire."

For the author of this poem, and particularly of this penultimate verse, it's not so much a matter of placing faith in anything in particular. For Sosan, faith has no outside object; for him it simply means *funi*, not-two: Buddha and me, no object, no subject, no separation.

∽

"Do you understand Buddhism?" one of Eno's disciples asked him point blank. "No," he too replied, in the same vein as did Bodhidharma before him, and yet very differently, "I do not understand Buddhism."

Bodhidharma is expressing his oneness with all things, while Eno is simply stating that he does not understand the true nature of things. And this makes perfect sense, for how could anybody, even Eno, understand the workings of the cosmos?

∽

"The person who trains in the Buddhist Way must first have faith in it," Master Dogen said one day in his *Gakudoyojin-shu*,[259] "Having faith in the Buddhist Way means having faith in the fact that you yourself are the Way and always have been; that you are not prey to going astray; that you are not in the grip of false ideas; that you do not have backwards notions; that the phenomena of increase and decrease do not exist [….] And at that moment you strip away body and mind and completely abandon ideas of error and awakening."

∽

This faith is lived and experienced in zazen, when we let go of everything personal, of everything not universal. We let zazen take its place, naturally.

∽

The first words of the *Hokyozanmai*[260] are "*Nyoze noho*": "No error, no doubt, thus the Dharma." *Nyo* is lack of skepticism which means the same as "faith"; *ze* means "to certify"; *no* means "such is"; and *ho* is "Dharma." It's as though the end of the *Shinjinmei* were leading us to the beginning of the *Hokyozanmai*, the famous poem composed by Master Tozan 260 years later, concerning no error, no doubt.

∽

Master Sosan composed his *Shinjinmei*, his Faith in Mind, like any great artist, through his unconscious mind; and with Sosan, through the juncture of Buddha and himself.

There is no idea of measurement in any of this. There is no geometrical calculation. Nothing between small and big; no borders here. This

259 Translated and commentated by T. Deshimaru (l'Edition Integrale).

260 By Master Tozan (-867), translated by T. Deshimaru (l'Edition Integrale).

is the Middle Way, without extremes. Or again, the Middle Way which does not lie between the two, it being mind not-two.

ꕥ

A human being must first find the right equilibrium between mind and body before they can ever discover the reality of the world. This has always been a hard thing to find, and for Shakyamuni it was even harder than for anyone else, as he was the very first to do so—to find the path of enlightenment and the fundamental rightness of the Four Noble Truths—and to transmit it on to others.

After leaving his palace, Shakyamuni went to practice with Kalama, who taught in the realm of "nothing": not *mu*, but nothing. In fact, when he left Kalama, Shakyamuni told him that his teaching did not lead to detachment or awakening or to the extinction of suffering, but only to the realm of nothing. Naturally Kalama wanted Shakyamuni to stay so that they could work together, but this no longer interested Shakyamuni. He went instead to study with Uddaka, which however was not any more satisfying for him. Uddaka also wanted him to stay and become the master of this school. He offered him his own position, but Shakyamuni was not interested in that either. His quest was to free himself from suffering, not to lead a school. So, he went off alone, into the forest, where he suffered even more, though now rather from solitude and from fear than anything else. Shakyamuni was not a god, he was an ordinary man like anyone else, alone and defenseless, and even the shadows in the forest scared him at night. He said that he felt like a drop of water in the vastness of the ocean; he felt utterly lost. He went without clothes and refused to eat; he did not cut his hair or beard and stood on one leg or crouched on his heels for days at a time. He walked around barefoot in the city and stole in order to eat. He was very young and very idealistic, and even while he practiced his severe austerities, he always showed great compassion and tried to never harm any living creature. He said later that he even felt compassion for a drop of water. At first, he felt as lost as a drop of water, and next he felt compassion towards the drop of water. (When he had satori, however, he never felt lost and alone nor did he feel compassion for the drop of water, for being Buddha he realized, or so it was said, that he himself—as well as this drop of water—spreads throughout the entire ocean).

Here's a Daichi[261] poem called *Buddha's Nirvana*, describing Shakyamuni's trials and tribulations in the forest of death:

Under his crossed legs, every year the grass grows green again.
He became a pitiful creature because he could not yet live his death.
But when his eyes fell on the Great Bear,
In the forest of death, the demons' cries and shrill shrieks were heard no more.

Shakyamuni was indeed a pitiful creature; nevertheless, in the end he did become a normal man again, as he was before when he was a youngster. The demons had returned to darkness, and everything was calmed. He had found the right equilibrium of body and mind. And it's thus we define the expression, "the Middle Way of Awakening."

∽

"Ah," you utter, looking at yourself in the mirror, "I have faith today!" then add as an afterthought, "Didn't have any yesterday..." Now faith is not that, it's not two. At least not Buddhist faith. This faith doesn't suddenly hit you right out of the blue. Because this faith is that mind *forever*. It's the faith without object which each of us possesses, and more often than not without our even knowing it. The faith we all have is that faith we have *even before* we ever heard about God, went to church, met a master or practiced meditation.

Faith in mind is Not-Two.
Not-Two is faith in mind.

---

261 Poem by Daichi Sokei (-1366) and translated by T. Deshimaru (l'Edition Integrale).

"Faith in not-two mind." In short: faith. Faith in mind. Or again, "mind of faith."

> After Dogen had heard Nyojo shout angrily at a monk sleeping in the dojo beside him, "*Shin jin datsu raku!*" "throw down body and mind!" Dogen went directly to Nyojo's room after zazen and repeated the same words: "*Shin jin datsu raku!*" Nyojo, no longer angry, replied to Dogen in a soft voice, "*Datsu raku shin jin*," "body and mind thrown down."

This can be understood to mean: continue exactly as you are doing, without ever stopping. In other words, faith in mind, mind of faith, without ever stopping.

73

Finally, the way of language will be cut off,
And past, present and future will not be limited.

When faith in mind is not-two—*shin jin funi*—then there is no more separation. When there is no more separation, then past, present and future are no longer limited: in other words, they no longer exist. Why is that, one might ask? Because the present exists only in the mind; yes, even the present is an illusion, in that it only exists in relation to the past and future and therefore is non-existent in itself alone.

∽

The last line of this long poem tells us that there is no more past or future in consciousness—in *hishiryo* consciousness, I mean. (*Hi*, "beyond"; *shiryo*, "thinking.") Or again, *mushin*, "no-mind." In this mind, in this *hishiryo*-consciousness, distinctions are abolished. No more time or space (since time and space are pure measurements created by humankind, though granted to better understand the cosmos, it is nevertheless measurement and can therefore point only to measurement and never beyond).

This is not philosophy, but the expression of a fact: the joy of a free person is not-two, which is eternal. No philosophy, no school of thought here, just experience. "Here" refers to the preceding verse—naturally, each verse flows into the next—to the place of *funi* or "not-two." And with this we come to the final verse, where all words, all language, become unnecessary. This is what Master Sosan is telling us at the end of this long poem. Seventy-three verses to finally say that all these words and all these ideas herein expressed are not necessary. Or say, *no longer* necessary. In that place, where the Buddha turns a flower in his fingers and Mahakashyapa smiles, what words could there ever be?

∽

In the 1300s, Master Keizan commented on this last verse of the *Shin-jin Mei.*[262] "When we attain this here-and-now, all of language," says he, "along with its most strange reasons, is completely finished." Then he returns to the verse at hand, the ultimate verse, to remind us that, "Master Sosan in the end abandons words and does not consider any ideas." Keizan goes on to point out that, "In this precise moment [i.e., when beyond ideas and beyond language] we can attain and penetrate the depth of the mind of Buddha and the masters of the transmission. We can completely be done with our personal techniques—the lion's loud roar and the Zen master's *katsu.*"[263] According to Keizan, "we can completely be done with these techniques, and we can go back home and sit in zazen in total intimacy with ourselves." "Go back home," that is return to ourselves.

Here's how Keizan says it in verse:

No one makes it to the top of the highest mountain,
No one understands this mysterious place—no buddha or god,
No saint, no sage can express it by virtue of his eloquence,
Or even through [his] silence.

In other words, forget about it—about making it to the top, about trying to understand, about expounding well-said words and phrases, forget even about silence. This is the answer, *hishiryo* consciousness. Both, neither and beyond.

Finally, the way of language will be cut off…

It's not necessary to have a gift for words, spoken or written. Great masters of the Way were rarely gifted spokesmen and public orators,

---

262 *Shin Jin Mei*, commentary by master Taisen Deshimaru (Cesare Rancilio Editeur, 1981).

263 Keizan is here referring to the Rinzai teaching of loud monosyllabic shouting—the *katsu* or the *kwat!*—in contrast to the Soto way of silent sitting. And as for the masters shout or the lions roar, both are the same.

they weren't even interested in it; what interested them was to teach the root without words, or at least without many words.

Buddha looked at Mahakashyapa and twirled a flower in his fingers. Mahakashyapa smiled and Buddha said to him in front of everyone—this occurred in one of their gatherings on Vulture Peak—"This wonderful mind of nirvana I transmit to Mahakashyapa." Again, Manjusri, at Buddha's request, went to see Vimalakirti to ask him a question about non-duality, *funi*. In Vimalakirti's tiny room Manjusri asked him, "Vimalakirti, what is the nature of *funi*, not-two?"

Vimalkirti's answer has since become famous: silence. It is written in one sutra that this silence echoed more powerfully than a hundred thousand thunderbolts. In another sutra it is described as "Vimalakirti's lion's roar."

In Zen it was the same. Between Bodhidharma and Eka it was *sampai*, bowing down. Eka did *sampai* and Bodhidharma said, "Here and now, you have obtained the marrow of my bones." For Tokusan it was the *kyosaku*: "Whether you speak or not, thirty blows with the stick in the morning, thirty blows with the stick in the evening."

∽

You can't know Zen without knowing the *Shinjinmei*, or at least the title, and if not in Japanese and not in Chinese (i.e., the *Hsin-hsin-ming* in Chinese), then at least in English as *Faith in Mind*, or in French as *La Foi en l'Esprit*. But few people know the last verses because few manage to read it through to the end. Everyone knows the first verse, *Penetrating the Way is not difficult* ... and some of the others, like *Do not run after phenomena... Do not seek the truth...* and, *The substance of the Way is generous...*

Few are familiar with the end of this long poem. This is where we learn that the way of language has been finally broken off, and that at this moment there is no more past, present or future. Here and now, we are in the world of heart and mind. *I shin den shin,* there where it is no longer word to heart or word to mind, but more precisely heart to heart or mind to mind.

Finally, the way of language will be cut off,
And past, present and future will not be limited.

All the masters, ancient or otherwise, use language to explain and express themselves, and do so even more in our own times. Always talking, conferences, lectures, *teishos* in the Buddha Hall, round-table colloquies in the dojos, inter-religious exchanges at the university, talks, *causeries*, discussions, replying to all the irrelevant questions, reacting positively, negatively or with indifference, responding, giving the right answer, having the last word.

Then too, you have all the modern electronic means at the masters' disposal and by which they can express themselves city-wide, state-wide and more. On car-radio speakers, the late-night TV shows, Internet, e-mails, Facebook. There's no end to the talking of the masters, these days. It goes on without stop. Like a record stuck on words forever. And all this through frontal brain activities, which entail everything one can imagine except for the actual practice, *hara* and thalamus.

In the end however, language is not the real question. Language or no language, everything depends on mind. And, that which has to do with sound and tone are not to be taken to heart.

The sounds and intonations of language exist only in order to free us from attachment.[264] Just don't be fooled by them, with their well-turned words and sonorous consonants. This is mind beyond words and reason . . . and that's the teaching. Mind is transmitted, faith is transmitted and that's the *Shinjinmei,* faith in mind.

∽

Here is what Master Deshimaru says: "If you become my disciple, you must understand the satori that cannot be expressed by language." (Nor, I should say, by silence).

---

264 "The thousands of words, the infinity of concepts, only exist to free us from attachment," said Sekito.

So, it's not speaking; nor is it about pitting speech and silence against each other. Because, as Deshimaru continues to say, "If the language or the words come from *ku,* this language, these words are beyond that which is expressed through language"… and again, even beyond that expressed by silence.

By even considering the use of language, of words, of sounds and their silences, we distance ourselves from the true teaching. Satori is the practice of the unknown and the invisible, of *ku* and the *kesa.*

As has already been said by most religious thinkers today, time has neither beginning nor end. This is *ku,* the emptiness from which all things come; and also for Buddhists *ku* is the *kesa,* the transmission of the cloth or robe of the Buddha; this is what is unlimited, this is what exists here and now and yet cannot be explained by language. Nor can it be understood. One doesn't think the *kesa,* one doesn't understand it, one doesn't know it either; but one does realize it, at least when one wears it then one realizes the *kesa.*

This is what we have faith in, not just in a piece of cloth but in the cloth of not-two. Wearing the *kesa* is manifesting our lives, as well as that of the lives of all the monks, nuns and sages of the past, present and future.

Shakyamuni said to Mahakashyapa, "Believe in the *kesa* when I am gone." He didn't say "Believe my words, believe in the sutras."

This doesn't mean, however, that we should not read and study the sutras; it simply means that it is impossible to understand or to express the infinite, the cosmos, with our mind. And so we have the *kesa.* The same one Buddha gave to Mahakashyapa and that Bodhidharma brought with him to Shaolin, in the northern mountains of China.

Finally, the way of language will be cut off,
And past, present and future will not be limited.

Since the first verse, which says, "The great Way is not difficult…," until the last which says, "The Way of language is cut off," Sosan has repeatedly explained the essence of Zen to us. Now his speech is over. Speech is limited, and his own is the perfect example of what it is to be limited. This, I believe, is what he is saying in this last verse. That, in fact, there is more to life than what speech or language can attain.

All this has now passed away. But not mind, not Sosan's in any case.

Indeed, language has passed away. Same with Sosan: he passed away shortly after finishing this great work, the *Shinjinmei*. His body and his personal consciousness were extinguished forever by death. But not his mind. His mind, as we see it and feel it now, comes not from anything personal, but from a consciousness which is cosmic. It was the same with his death. It happened under a tree while he was in *kinhin*.

"His death was very beautiful," master Deshimaru once said, "Standing in *kinhin*, in this magnificent posture, under a pine tree."

APPENDIX

On Gender Bypass

In our times, we find the use of "he and she" everywhere, almost on every page, even in books on the Buddhist teachings. Carry this to its extreme, and one day we'll find we have "he-*and*-she" on every page of the sutras and in the Bible as well. My own way of seeing life, death and conflict, and I should think other Buddhist teachers do as well, is neither "he" nor "she," neither one nor the other. Neuter or non-gender simply means "not this nor that." Its opposite, the other side, is usually referred to as "gender selective" or "gender inclusive." But it could also be referred to as "one and the other" or again "one which differs from the other," male differing from its female equivalent. Though this may seem to be a recommendable approach today, I don't believe it will be applicable in the long run; but if not inapplicable, inapt.

It's through the ego—and this I believe is really what we are talking about, the nature of the ego—that we have "man and woman" in the first place, and by its very nature we also have, and will continue to have, more and more opposition and separation. Not everything however is ego: our fundamental nature is not ego, which also means not separate. It is "one." Anyhow, this is the teaching. And not one *with* the other, as we have in the "he and she" expression of life. In fact, the word "neuter," as a Buddhist practitioner might say, is not even "one." This notion is well depicted in the statues of the Bodhisattva Avalokitesvara. He (or she) is neither one nor the other—that is, the observer can't distinguish the difference; however, at times Avalokitesvara is simply depicted as a man while at other times simply as a woman.

Sometimes it is pointed out, by those activists engaged in the very hard and unending work of changing and ameliorating the abhorrent injustices undergone by women everywhere and since forever, that they at least are doing something about it. While others, who isolate themselves in meditation, what are they doing, but to sit on their posteriors all day long looking at themselves? Of course, if one neglects the invisible world and argues that since it is indeed invisible it simply does not exist, then this is true—the wise and the greats are not helping anyone by their meditations.

However, all the wise and the greats throughout the ages, men and women alike, see it quite differently; even those who do not adhere to any one religious or spiritual belief and practice, all of them recognize the force and the beyond-grasping of the invisible world. The woman Zen master Houn Jiyu-Kennett says, concerning this matter of using the gender selective: "No Zen master thus limits himself. No master distinguishes between the two."[1]

It is perhaps too late to change all this now and return to the neuter gender, but there's a possibility that we can still preserve religious texts from this worse-than-useless dichotomy of words and that we cut out the "and" from the pronoun "he and she." What's more, I believe one can remove the pronoun altogether, the "she" or even the "he," that is one or the other, were the author of these words to prefer it this way. In the larger vision of life that we may have, these two words really mean the same thing.

In order, I suppose, to preserve us from its antithesis, the masters all say the same though expressed differently. Swami Nirmalananda says that one should be "without black or white, emptiness, fullness, darkness, light, man or woman. Unless the universe is empty, nothing can move in it."[2] And Master Deshimaru in his commentary of the *Gakudo Yo Jin Shu*: "To do zazen facing the wall means facing nature and not facing people... We are facing nothing."[3]

Ph. Rei Ryu Coupey
Paris 20/2/2020

---

1 *The Roar of the Tigress, The Oral Teachings of Rev. Master Jiyu-Kennett* (1924-1996), Tuttle Publishing.

2 From his brochure *Zen, a Way of Life*, 1985.

3 Edition Intégrale, Association Zen Internationale, 1986.

GLOSSARY

Amida Buddha (Skt., Amitabha), lit. "Endless Light." Mahayana Buddha embodying wisdom and mercy; venerated by the Pure Land School of Chinese and Japanese Buddhism, in the belief that simply invoking this name can lead to rebirth in paradise. See also *nembutsu.*

Asura. See *samsara.*

Atman. Hindu term for the soul or immortal quality of human beings. The existence of an *atman* is denied in Buddhism, which teaches that all phenomena are empty. See also *skandha.*

Avatamsaka Sutra, lit. "Sutra of the Buddhas' Garland." Mahayana sutra which became very important in China, in the various Ch'an schools as well as the Hua-yen (Jap., Kegon) School. It teaches that the human mind is the cosmos itself, and that Buddha, mind and all beings are one. The sutra exists only in Tibetan and Chinese translations; the oldest Chinese translation dates from the fifth century.

Baso Doitsu (Ch., Ma-tsu Tao-i, 709-788). Disciple of Nangaku and master of Hyakujo, Nansen, Daibai Hojo and layman P'ang; patriarch of Rinzai Zen known for his intense training methods, including shouts, gestures and blows with a stick, designed to jolt disciples out of their everyday thinking and into enlightenment. See also *Sekito Kisen.*

Bodaishin, lit. "mind of awakening." The mind that aspires to the Way, to the highest dimension; the mind that observes *mujo*, impermanence.

Bodhidharma (Jap., Bodaidaruma or Daruma, 470-543?). Disciple of Indian master Prajnadhara (Jap., Hannyatara) and master of Eka; first Chinese Zen patriarch and twenty-eighth after Shakyamuni Buddha in the Indian lineage. The son of a Brahmin king, he spent the last decade of his life in China. When he arrived there, he occupied a cave on the site of the Shorinji Monastery. (Ch., Shao-lin) on Mount Suzan (Ch., Sung-shan), where he sat facing the wall for nine years.

Bodhisattva. Human or celestial being who incarnates the Mahayana ideal. Contrary to the *arhat* in Hinayana Buddhism, who dedicates himself exclusively to his personal salvation, the bodhisattva vows to put aside his own liberation and be reborn until all beings are saved. See *shiguseiganmon.*

Bodhi tree. Fig tree (*ficus religiosa*) under which Shakyamuni Buddha had the experience of awakening after forty-nine days of zazen.

Bonno. Illusion; attachment; a product of personal consciousness. The vow to cut *bonnos* is one of the four great vows of the bodhisattva. See *shiguseiganmon.*

Bovay, Missen Michel (b. 1944). Zen master, close disciple of Master Taisen Deshimaru; former president of the International Zen Association in Europe; currently head of the Zurich Zen Dojo in Switzerland; received Dharma transmission from Okamoto Roshi in 1998.

Budo, lit. "the way of the warrior." Term designating the traditional Japanese martial arts.

Chikuso. See *samsara.*

Daibal Hojo (Ch., Ta-mei Fa-ch'ang, 752-839). Disciple of Baso and master of Koshu Tenryu. After thirty years of Buddhist book-learning, he met Baso, became his disciple and received his transmission. Then he left to practice zazen alone in the moun- tains for thirty years before accepting disciples of his own.

Daichi Sokei (1290-1366). Japanese Zen master famous for his poetry. He became a monk under Kangan Gin (1217-1300), a disciple of Dogen, and later practiced with Keizan for seven years. At age twenty-five he went to China, where he remained for eleven years. When he returned to Japan, he received the transmission from Meiho Sotetsu (1277-1350), a close disciple of Keizan.

Daikaku (posthumous name of Rankei Doryu, Ch., Lan-ch'i Tao-lung, 1213-1278). Chinese master and calligrapher of the Rinzai School; studied with many Chinese masters, most notably Wu-chun Shih-fan (Jap., Bushun Shiban); traveled to Japan in 1246, where he founded the Kenchoji Monastery in Kamakura in 1253.

Danken. Nihilism; theory which propounds the non-existence of any dimension other than the phenomenal world; the belief that existence ends with death. See *joken*.

Deshimaru, Taisen (1914-1982). Disciple of Kodo Sawaki; Japanese master of Soto Zen who spent the last fifteen years of his life teaching in Europe. Received monastic ordination, as well as the robe, bowl and spiritual transmission, from Kodo Sawaki in 1965. Founded more than a hundred dojos in Europe, North Africa and Canada, as well as La Gendronnière Temple in France's Loire Valley. According to temple records, he ordained more than five hundred monks and nuns, and more than twenty thousand people practiced with him at one time or another.

Deva. See *samsara*.

Dharma. 1) the universal truth, teaching and Buddhist doc- trine pronounced by Shakyamuni Buddha; 2) the truth, ultimate reality or universal order; 3) phenomena, or manifestations of reality.

Diamond Sutra (Skt., *Vajrachchedika-parjnaparamita-sutra*). Independent section of the *Prajnaparamita Sutra,* which took on considerable importance, principally in the countries of Southeast Asia; explains that phenomena are not reality, but merely illusions, projections of our own minds.

Do (Ch., Tao or Dao). The Way; in Zen, the Buddha-Dharma.

Dogen Zenji (1200-1253). Disciple of Chinese master Nyojo and master of Ejo; introduced Soto Zen to Japan and founded Eiheiji Temple in the northern mountains of Japan. Born into a noble family, he studied Rinzai Zen and the koan method for several years with masters Eisai and Myozen, then crossed the sea to China where he met Soto master Nyojo. He practiced with Nyojo on Mount Tendo for three years before returning to Japan as the heir of Nyojo's Zen. His masterwork is the *Shobogenzo*, which contains the major part of his teaching. His poems are col- lected in the *Sanshodoei*, with the exception of the *Eiheikoroku* poems, which were reserved for his closest disciples and kept secret for many years.

Dojo. In Zen and the martial arts, a place to practice the Way.

Doshin (Ch., Tao-hsin, 580-651). Fourth Ch'an patriarch, disciple of Sosan and master of Konin; created a community of five hundred disciples on Mount Shuang-feng, where he died in zazen.

Doshu. How each person communicates the Way; expression of the Way through the body, speech, awareness and behavior; expression of the self, of one's awakening and one's understanding of the Dharma.

Eikheikoroku. Ten-volume collection of Master Dogen's sayings and poems; represents Dogen's teaching, as recorded by his direct disciples, from the time of his occupation of Koshoji Temple until his death.

Eisai Zenji (also Myoan Eisai or Senko Kokushi, 1141-1215). Japanese master of the Rinzai lineage, disciple of Hsu-an Huai-ch'ang (Jap., Kian Esho) and Dogen's master before Nyojo; founder of Shofukuji, the first monastery in Japan in which Rinzai Zen was practiced.

Eka (Ch., Hui-k'o, 487-593). Second Zen patriarch, disciple of Bodhidharma and master of Sosan; reported to have cut off his left arm to present to his master as a sign of his earnest desire to study the Dharma. He remained with Bodhidharma for nine years, practicing only *shikantaza.* After receiving the transmission, he went to live in the city, where he worked as a street sweeper and spread the Dharma.

Engaku. Level of buddha-for-self; someone who practices in order to be in good health and become a saint. See *pratyeka buddha.*

Engo Kokugon. (Ch., Yuan-wu K'o-ch'in, 1063-1135). Chinese Rinzai master, disciple of Goso Hoen and master of Gokoku Keigen, Kukyu

Joryu and Daie Soko; editor of the *Pi- yen-lu,* one of the best-known collections of koans.

Eno. (Ch., Hui-neng, 638-713). Disciple of Konin and master of Seigen Gyoshi and Nangaku Ejo; author of *The Platform Sutra.* He arrived at Konin's temple on Mount Obai when he was twenty-four and left after only six months. For fifteen years he lived with fishermen and hunters, then taught the Dharma on Mount Sokei for thirty-six years until his death.

Fukanzazengi, lit. "General Presentation of the Principles of Zazen." Written by Master Dogen in 1227, soon after his return from China. This text, which cites the *Shinjinmei,* emphasizes the fact that zazen, far from constituting "a means to achieve enlightenment," is the fundamental practice of all buddhas.

Fuke (Ch., P'u-hua, d. 860). Chinese Zen master, disciple of Banzan Hoshaku; known for his eccentric behavior; friend of Master Rinzai and his disciples, with whom he played the role of a "holy fool."

Funi, lit. "not-two." The non-dualistic quality of reality.

Fuyodokai (Ch., Fu-jung Tao-kai, 1043-1118). Zen master in the Soto lineage; master of Tanka Shijun; highly respected in Zen for having restored the original purity of the practice while avoid- ing the two major pitfalls of the time: the intellectualism of the Soto School's *go i* (lit. "five degrees of enlightenment") and the theatricality of the Rinzai School's koans.

Gaitan. Corridor at the entrance of a dojo; reserved for kitchen staff who must leave the dojo during zazen, as well as anyone who is sick, tends to move, or might in any way disturb the atmosphere of the dojo.

Gassho. Joining both hands at nose-level, forearms horizontal, and bowing forward from the waist; ancient universal gesture expressing veneration, humility and respect, as well as the unity of body and mind: *funi,* non-duality.

Gendronnière (La). Zen temple located in France's Loire Valley, founded by Master Taisen Deshimaru in 1979; main temple of the sangha of Master Deshimaru's disciples, recognized by the Japanese Soto Zen authorities and regrouping over two hundred Zen dojos and groups worldwide. In 1984, Niwa Zenji came to La Gendronnière to give Dharma transmission to three of Master Deshimaru's disciples. In addition to a two-month summer retreat and intensive sesshin in winter, spring and fall, the temple hosts workshops, symposia, conferences and other activities focusing on Zen Buddhism. Above all, it is a practice center dedicated to sesshin, daily zazen and *samu*.

Genjokoan, lit. "Accomplished Koan" or "Accomplished Law." *Shobogenzo* chapter placed by Dogen at the beginning of the seventy-five-volume edition; undoubtedly the chapter most often translated, cited and commented on, despite its difficulty and density; deals essentially with the relationship between practice and enlightenment; includes the well-known parables of the moon and its reflection, wood and ashes, the bird and the fish, and the famous maxim, "Studying the Way is studying oneself..."

Genmai. Rice soup eaten after morning zazen while chanting the *Gyohatsunenju* (Meal Sutra).

Genpo Merzel (b. 1944). Contemporary American Zen master, disciple of Taizan Maezumi Roshi, from whom he received Dharma transmission in 1980; follower of the Sanbo Kyodan School, a mixed form of Rinzai and Soto Zen developed by Haku'un Yasutani and Daiun Sogaku Harada.

Gozu (Ch., Niu-t'ou, also known as Hoyu, Ch., Fa-jung, 594-657). Disciple of Doshin, co-disciple of Konin; created his own branch of Zen—"Gozu Zen"—which continued to be taught for a century after his death, then died out; author of "The Mind's Chant," a long poem similar to the *Shinjinmei*.

Gutei (Ch., Chu-chih, ninth century). Disciple of Koshu Tenryu, from whom he inherited "raised-thumb Zen," which he taught all his life.

Gyoji, lit. *gyo*, practice, action, behavior; *ji*, to maintain, to keep. Continuous or eternal practice, without beginning or end; the uninterrupted sequence of meditation and activity; title of a *Shobogenzo* chapter in which Dogen uses the history of the patriarchs to teach correct behavior.

Hakuin Ekaku (1689-1769). One of the most important masters in the Rinzai School; reaffirmed the importance of zazen, which this school had neglected in favor of intellectual text study; well versed in the koan system, he created a new presentation of it which is still used in Rinzai; he was also an accomplished painter, calligrapher and writer.

Hannya Shingyo. Abbreviated name of the *Maka Hannyaharamita Shingyo*, or *Heart Sutra*, chanted every morning after zazen in all Zen temples. This short sutra formulates the "heart" or essence of the Mahayana teaching on *ku* (emptiness).

Hannayatara (Skt., Prajnadhara). Twenty-seventh patriarch in the Indian Ch'an lineage; master of Bodhidharma.

Hara (also known as *kikai tanden*). Vital-energy center located just under the navel, which connects human beings to the cosmos. In Zen and the martial arts, energy which is free from tension and personal will is expressed through the *hara*.

Hekiganroku (Ch., Pi-yen-lu), lit. "The Blue-Green Cliff Record." Oldest collection of koans, written in the twelfth century by Ch'an master Yuan-wu K'o-ch'in (Jap., Engo Kokugon). Valued for the important teachings and anecdotes it contains, this text is also considered a masterwork of classical Chinese poetry.

Hinayana (also known as Theravada), lit. "Small Vehicle," as opposed to Mahayana, "Great Vehicle." Ancient Buddhism which developed between the Buddha's death and the end of the first century BCE; presents a doctrine of salvation, the quest for nirvana through retreating from the world, and respect for monas- tic rules; implanted mainly in southern Asia (Ceylon, Thailand, Burma, Cambodia and Laos).

Hishiryo, lit. *hi*, beyond; *shiryo*, thinking. Thinking from the depths of not-thinking, beyond personal consciousness. This term, which in fact contains the secret, inexpressible essence of Zen, appears for the first time in the *Shinjinmei*. It is also found in a famous mondo between Master Yakusan and a monk ("How does one think without thinking?" asks the monk. "*Hishiryo*," replies Yakusan.), and in the teaching of Master Dogen. Along with *shikantaza* and *mushotoku*, *hishiryo* is one of the three pillars of the teaching of masters Kodo Sawaki and Taisen Deshimaru.

Hokyozanmai (Ch., San-mei-k'o), lit. "Samadhi of the Precious Mirror." Poem composed in the ninth century by Tozan Ryokai which celebrates the true nature of all things; recited every day in Japanese Zen temples; considered to be one of the found- ing texts of Soto Zen, along with the *Shinjinmei*, *Shodoka* and *Sandokai*.

Hotei (Ch., Pu-tai, d. 916). Chinese monk whose name means "sack of hemp," as he always carried one on his back. According to legend, his true identity was revealed upon his death: he was an avatar or incognito incarnation of Maitreya, the Buddha of the future. The image which remains of him is that of the Laughing Buddha, as represented in numerous statues in Chinese monasteries.

Hotetsu (Mayoku) (Ch., Ma-ku Pao-che, eighth-ninth centuries). Ch'an master, disciple of Baso Doitsu. Famous for his *mondo* about the fan.

Ikkyu Sojun (1394-1481). Rinzai master, poet and calligrapher, known for his eccentricity and iconoclasm. He called himself "Crazy Cloud" or "Blind Donkey," and claimed to prefer taverns and brothels to monasteries. In 1474 he was appointed abbot of Daitokuji, the temple where he had practiced for ten years in his youth before opting for a life outside of monasteries. He took great care not to name any successors.

Inmo, lit. "this," "that" or "thus." In Buddhism, reality "as it is," "thusness," the evident and indescribable character of things; term often used by Master Dogen, including as a title for one of the chapters of his *Shobogenzo*. In modern times, Professor D. T. Suzuki uses the word "suchness." Master Deshimaru did not use "suchness," and almost never *inmo*. He sometimes used the Japanese term *nyo* ("true freedom"), often repeating it—*nyo nyo*—and translating it as "infinite" or "eternal." But most of the time he simply used the English word "free."

Ippen, (1239-1289). Wandering monk, founder of the Ji-shu School of Pure Land Buddhism. He believed that faith was an act of the mind and therefore subject to corruption. Consequently, he taught complete abandoning of the self, that is, of all mental attitudes, all attempts at understanding, and finally all religious realization: simply reject everything and invoke the *nembutsu*.

Isan Reiyu (Ch., Kuei-shan Ling-yu, 771-853). Disciple of Hyakujo, co-disciple of Obaku. He met his master when he was twenty-two and served as tenzo in his monastery for twenty years before going off to found a temple in the mountains. He built a hut and remained in solitude for seven or eight years until a large number of disciples gathered around him, including Kyogen and Kyosan. The latter founded, with Isan, the Igyo School of Zen. Isan died in zazen posture.

Ishindenshin, lit. "from mind to mind" or "from heart to heart." A fundamental notion in Zen which describes the trans-mission beyond writing and intellectual understanding, the common intuition between master and disciple of reality as it is.

Jayrata (Jap., Shayata, fourth century). Twentieth patriarch in the Indian Zen lineage, disciple of Kumaralata and master of Vasubandhu.

Jinshu (Ch., Shen-hsiu, 605-706). Disciple of Konin and co-disciple of Eno; founder of the Northern School of Ch'an, which advocated a gradual approach to the practice, and which survived for only a few generations after his death.

Jiun Sonja (1718-1804). Japanese master of the Shingon School, Sanskrit specialist and celebrated calligrapher. One day, his mother asked him to stop giving lectures, reproaching him for becoming a connoisseur of Buddhism. She advised him to settle down in a small, isolated temple and to devote his time to meditation.

Joken. Theory which propounds the eternal nature of the world and the self. See also *danken.*

Joshu Jushin (Ch., Chao-chou Ts'ung-shen, 778-897). One of the greatest Ch'an masters, disciple of Nansen, whom he followed for more than forty years. After his master's death, he set out wandering to deepen his Dharma experience with other Ch'an masters, finally settling in a small monastery where he became a master in his own right at the age of eighty. He had thirteen Dharma successors, yet his lineage died out after a few generations.

Joza. Term used in the seventh and eighth centuries when speaking to a co-disciple; equivalent of "monk" or "friend."

Kai. Precept. In Zen, the ten *kai* are the rules of natural morality which the disciple accepts from the master during the bodhisattva and monastic ordinations.

Kakunen musho, lit. "infinite sky, nothing sacred." When the Indian master Bodhidharma arrived in China, the emperor asked, "What is the sacred truth?" "*Kakunen musho*" was his reply.

Kalpa. Cosmic cycle; an infinitely long period of time.

Kan. Great vow made by all buddhas and bodhisattvas; profound aspiration to practice the Way and go beyond oneself.

Kanbun. Hybrid of classical Chinese and Japanese used in formal writings through World War II.

Kanji. Written Japanese alphabet of pictograms representing words or ideas, as opposed to *kana,* which represent syllables.

Karma. Law of cause and effect; the logical sequence of human behavior (thoughts, words and actions) and its good and bad consequences. Karma encourages correct behavior through the awareness of the effects of our comportment on the phenomenal world, rather than by following "commandments" or awaiting reward or retribution in heaven or hell. Both individual and collective karma exist, and both transcend birth and death. Each person's practice influences the karma of humanity as a whole.

Kassan Zen'e (Ch., Chia-shan Shank-hui 805-881). Disciple of ferry-man-master Sensu Tokujo; an exemplary *tenzo* under several different masters; appears in Dogen's *Mountains and Rivers Sutra* and *Eiheikoroku.*

Katagiri Dainin (1928-1990). Zen master, student of Eko Hashimoto in Japan and assistant to Shunryu Suzuki in the United States; founder of the Minnesota Zen Center.

Keizan Jokin (1268-1325). Considered the most important Japanese Soto Zen master after Dogen; practiced under the direction of Ejo and Gikai (two of Master Dogen's closest disciples); founder of Sojiji, one of the two principal Soto temples in Japan, along with Eiheiji; author of the *Denkoroku,* a collection of accounts of the Dharma transmission from Shakyamuni Buddha to Eihei Dogen.

Kendo, lit. "the Way of the sword." The art of Japanese samurai swordsmanship.

Kennett, Jiyu (1924-1996). English-born Soto master; studied Theravada Buddhism and Rinzai Zen before receiving Dharma transmission in 1963 from Keido Chisan Koho at Daihonzan Sojiji. She founded Shasta Abbey in California and several other temples and meditation groups in North America and Europe and was also the founder of the Order of Buddhist Contemplatives.

Kesa. Large garment made of many pieces of cloth carefully stitched together, which monks and nuns wear draped around their shoulders over their *kolomos*. Presented by the master to the disciple during the ordination ceremony, the *kesa* is an object of faith and veneration. It symbolizes the transmission of and adherence to the uninterrupted line of Buddha's disciples, and existence in a dimension which transcends the small ego.

Ketsumyaku. Certificate given by the master to the disciple during ordinations; represents the lineage of masters who connect the newly ordained person to Shakyamuni Buddha.

Ki (Ch., *chi*). Vital energy or activity that animates all creatures; resides in the *hara* and is cosmic in nature; a key concept in Taoism and traditional Chinese medicine.

Kinhin. Slow walking meditation to the rhythm of one's breathing, practiced during the interval between two zazens.

Koan. Originally, in China, a law or judgment handed down from public authorities; in Zen, a universal truth expressed by a phrase from a sutra or a master; a paradox that only intuition can resolve, which steadfastly defies logical analysis; used as part of formal education in Rinzai Zen as a means to push disciples past their limits and into enlightenment. Soto Zen, which places no value on special states and considers satori the normal condition, generally does not use koans in the formal sense in disciple training. Nevertheless, for both Rinzai and Soto, the koan represents the hidden, ungraspable aspect of reality.

Kolomo. Long black robe with large sleeves worn by Zen monks and nuns, usually over a white or grey kimono.

Konin (Ch., Hung-jen, 601-674). Disciple of Doshin and master of Jinshu and Eno, who founded the Northern and Southern schools of Ch'an, respectively. All existing branches of Zen came from the Southern School. Konin met his master when he was fourteen and immediately impressed him with his profound understanding. After Doshin's death, he founded a monastery on Mount Obai.

Koshoji. Kyoto monastery where Dogen lived for ten years before founding Eiheiji. Here he formed his first community of monks according to the model he had experienced with Nyojo in China. It is also where he wrote most of the *Shobogenzo*, and where he met Ejo, who would become his successor.

Ku (Skt., *sunyata*). Often translated as "emptiness" or "void," as opposed to *shiki*, "phenomena." But the term should not be seen as expressing a nihilistic view of the world. It means infinity, the unborn from which all things born and finite come, and to which they return. It is the origin, the common identity without which differences (phenomena) could not exist.

Kusen. Oral teaching given during zazen; an *i shin den shin* teaching which is addressed directly to the listeners' *hishiryo*-consciousness, without passing through the intellect. Kusen appears to be a specificity of the Kodo Sawaki/Taisen Deshimaru lineage: most other lineages prefer lectures (*teisho*).

Kyogen Chikan (Ch., Hsiang-yen Chih-hsien, d. 898). Disciple of Isan Reiyu; an intellectual and great scholar who studied with Hyakujo but did not succeed in intimately under- standing the essence of Zen. When Hyakujo died, Kyogen followed his co-disciple, Isan, with whom he came to full awakening.

Kyosaku, lit. "wake-up stick." Used during zazen to hit the trapezius muscles of practitioners disturbed by drowsiness or mental agitation. The *kyosaku* is not a form of punishment but a way to help restore the normal condition.

Maezumi, Hakuyu Taizan (1931-1995). Soto-Rinzai master certified by Hakujun Kuroda, Koryu Osaka and Hakuun Yasutani, making him a successor in three Zen lineages; founder of the Los Angeles Zen Center, the White Plum Asanga and several temples in the United States and Europe; certified a dozen disciples.

Mahakashyapa (sixth century BCE). One of the principal disciples of Shakyamuni Buddha; known for his self-discipline and moral strictness; assumed leadership of the sangha after Buddha's death; considered the first Zen patriarch.

Mahayana, lit. "Great Vehicle." Branch of Buddhism which includes Zen, popular primarily in Tibet, China, Korea and Japan. Its ideal—to save all beings rather than seeking individual salvation—is incarnated by the bodhisattva.

Mantra. In Hinduism and yoga, a sacred phrase given by the guru to the disciple, which encompasses the very essence of the divinity to which the teacher is dedicated; in Buddhism, a short invocation, usually taken from a sutra, whose sound, charged with energy (*ki*), carries a spiritual virtue or protective power. Mantras play an especially important role in Amidism (*nembutsu*) and Tibetan Buddhism.

Marpa (1012-1097). Celebrated yogi of Tibet, also called "the Translator"; disciple of Naropa and master of Milarepa; studied with Naropa in India for sixteen years before returning to his homeland to translate the sacred texts into Tibetan.

Menzan Zuiho (1683-1769). Zen master and celebrated Soto scholar; author of more than fifty works, including biographies of Master Dogen and commentaries on his teaching; sought to return the Soto temples of his time to the more orthodox ways of Dogen, an influence which continues in Japan to this day.

Milarepa (1025-1135). Considered the greatest saint of Tibet; disciple of the yogi Marpa, from whom he learned the *mahamudra*—freedom from emptiness and *samsara*.

Mondo, lit. "question/answer." Any form of exchange whose purpose is an attempt to understand the Dharma. When conducted in a dojo, *mondos* provide an opportunity for matters germane to existence and the practice to be clarified, not in the intimacy of private master-disciple interviews (*dokusan*), but for the benefit of the entire sangha. Many *mondos* have become part of Zen history for the edification of generations of disciples.

Morimoto, Kazuo (b.?). Disciple of Taisen Deshimaru; translator and professor at the Institute of Oriental Culture, Tokyo University; author of *From Derrida to Dogen: Deconstruction and the Cancellation of Body and Mind* (Fukuatke Books, 1989).

Mu. Particle meaning "nothing," "nothingness," or "no." Connotes absence rather than negation; found in Japanese expressions such as *mushotoku* ("non-profit"), *mushin* ("no-mind") and *muga* ("non-ego");

figures in the first koan in the *Mumonkan* (a monk asks Master Joshu, "Does a dog have Buddha-nature?" "*Mu*," replies Joshu).

Mujo (Skt., *anitya*). Impermanence; one of the three characteristics of existence, which gives rise to the other two: suffering (*duhkha*) and impersonality (*anatman*); the fundamental condition of all life. The study of *mujo* is an essential part of practicing the Way. Master Daichi wrote, "*Mujo* always lies in wait, at every moment, and when it strikes, it strikes with such speed and brutality that you are thunderstruck before you know what hit you."

Mumon Ekai (Ch., Wu-men Hui-k'ai, 1183-1260). Rinzai master, disciple of Gatsurin Shikan and master of Shinchi Kakushin; best known for his koan compilation, the *Mumonkan*.

Mumonkan (Ch., *Wu-men-kuan*), lit. "The Gateless Gate." Volume of forty-eight koans collected and commented on by Mumon Ekai in 1229.

Mushin, lit. "no-mind." No personal mind; no-thought; freedom from dualistic thinking.

Mushotoku, lit. "non-profit." No merit; nothing to obtain; refers to practicing without object or goal; giving freely. Master Deshimaru said it was the fundamental Zen teaching that brought him to the practice.

Nagarjuna (second-third centuries). Indian Buddhist philosopher, founder of the Madhyamika School (also known as "The Middle Path") and fourteenth patriarch after Buddha; known for his teachings on the doctrine of *ku* (Skt., *sunyata*, "emptiness"), which earned him the name "Father of Mahayana." His principal works are the *Madhyamaka-karika* and the *Mahaprajnaparamita Shastra*. Shortly before the end of his life, he burned all his books and sutras and consecrated himself exclusively to the study of the *kesa*.

Nansen Fugan (Ch., Nan-ch'uan P'u-yuan, 748-835). Disciple of Baso Doitsu and master of Joshu Jushin, among others. Seven years after his master's death, he went into isolation on Mount Nansen, where he practiced zazen for thirty years. Then he spent the last ten years of his life in a monastery, surrounded by more than a hundred disciples.

Naraka. See *samsara.*

Nembutsu. Recitation of the name of Amida Buddha. In Amidism, the fervent recitation of the phrase *Namu amida Butsu* ("praised be Amida Buddha") is believed to lead to rebirth in the heaven of the Pure Land. See also *Shin School.*

Nirvana. 1) definitive freedom from *samsara* (rebirth); 2) extinction of all desires and attachments; 3) the deepest *samadhi* in which consciousness is no longer tempted by illusions. In Zen, nirvana and *samsara* are identical in the eyes of someone who has penetrated the true nature of things, which is *ku* (emptiness).

Nirvana School. Lineage of Chinese Buddhism which appeared in the fifth century; devoted to the *Mahaparinirvana Sutra*; holds that all beings have Buddha-nature and that anyone can access Buddhahood through sudden enlightenment.

Noumenon (Skt., *svabhava*), lit. "self-nature." Lasting substance; independent existence.

Nyojo (Tendo) (Ch., T'ien-t'ung Ju-ching, 1163-1228). Ch'an master of the Soto School, disciple of Shingetsu Shoryo and master of Dogen Zenji; traveled from dojo to dojo, coming into contact with all types of Zen existing in his time: some mixed zazen with Taoism, Confucianism and the recitation of the *nembutsu*, others with koan study. Rejecting them all, he became abbot of Tendo Monastery in Southern China and taught only zazen.

Nyorai (Skt., *Tathagata*). 1) being who has arrived at supreme enlightenment; 2) the cosmic principle, the essence of the universe, the absolute.

Obaku Kiun (Ch., Huang-po Hsi-yun, d. 850). Ch'an master, disciple of Hyakujo Ekai and master of Rinzai Gigen and twelve others; known as a stately man of pure and simple character. The prime minister P'ei

Hsiu became his disciple and had a monastery constructed where Obaku accepted to live.

Pratyeka Buddha. A buddha-for-self; someone who practices to escape *samsara*, who has attained enlightenment by and for himself. See also *engaku.*

Preta. See *samsara.*

Rakusu. Small *kesa* worn around the neck, in the dojo and in daily life. As opposed to the *kesa*, the *rakusu* is not reserved for monks and nuns—everyone who has received the bodhisattva (lay) ordination receives and wears it.

Reikai Vendetti (d. 2001). Zen monk, disciple of Master Taisen Deshimaru; director of the Toulouse Dojo in France, he also led retreats in Corsica and Reunion Island; an accomplished painter whose work includes portraits of Buddhist masters (*Pilgrimage to Eminent Masters*, Editions Sully, 1999).

Reiun Shigon (Ch., Ling-yun Chih-ch'in, ninth century). Disciple of Isan Reiyu; author of "For thirty years I sought a master swordsman," this poem describing his satori: *How many times did the leaves fall and the branches burst into bud? But from the moment I saw the peach blossoms in flower, From that time, I have had no doubts.*

Rensaku. A series of blows administered by the master or an assistant with the *kyosaku* on the muscles situated between the shoulder and the neck; used when an error has been committed, to awaken the mind of the disciple, and also to awaken the concentration of the whole sangha.

Rinzai School. Lineage founded by Master Rinzai Gigen (d. 866), whose origin dates back to seventh-century master Nangaku Ejo, a disciple of Eno, as was Seigen Gyoshi, source of the Soto lineage; one of the two great branches of Zen still alive today, along with Soto; emphasizes obtaining satori and using koans as a meditation tool.

Ryutan (or Ryotan) Soshin (Ch., Lung-t'an Ch'ung-hsin, ninth century). Disciple of Tenno Dogo and master of Tokusan Senkan. He met his master in his childhood and regularly brought him rice cakes.

Samadhi (Jap., *zanmai*). State of meditation and open awareness during zazen; pure, unconscious concentration without object. Master Dogen said, "The *samadhi* of the buddhas and the patriarchs is frost and hail, wind and lightning."

Sampai. Three consecutive prostrations, with forehead touching the ground and hands raised to receive the Buddha's feet.

Samsara. The cycle of existences (birth, death, rebirth) conditioned by attachment; opposite of nirvana; composed of six possible modes of existence: *shomon* (human), *asura* (warrior), *deva* (god), *chikuso* (animal), *preta* (hungry ghost), *naraka* (hell being).

Samu. Activities of monks and practitioners for the benefit of the temple or sangha: gardening, construction, cleaning, publishing work, etc.; sometimes called "work practice"; differs from a job in the sense that, rather than aiming to accomplish a task, it is the complement of zazen: the continuity of stillness and inner silence within activity.

Sandokai, lit. "Fusion of Difference and Sameness." Poem written by Sekito Kisen in the eighth century; one of the founding texts of Zen, recited daily in Japanese Soto monasteries; cited and commented on by many masters. It is because the many proceed from the One that differences exist. The *Sandokai* ends with this famous line: "You who seek the Way, please, do not waste the present moment."

Sangha. Assembly of monks; community of disciples; one of the "Triple Treasures" of Buddhism, along with Buddha and Dharma.

Sanshodoei, lit. "Poems on the Sansho Path." Volume of sixty-three *waka* (Japanese-style poems with five lines and thirty-one syllables: 5-7-5-7-7) composed by Master Dogen and published for the first time in 1472, over two hundred years after his death. *Sansho*, lit. "umbrella pine," is another name for Dogen's great temple, Eiheiji.

Satori. Enlightening or awakening produced by the fundamental cosmic power rather than by the ego; the actualization of *mushotoku*; not a special state of consciousness, but a return to the normal condition. In the Rinzai School, satori is the result of a successful practice and the object of a vehement quest; in the Soto School, practice itself is satori, in other words, fusion with the natural order of things.

Sawaki, Kodo (1880-1965). Great Japanese Soto master of the twentieth century and master of Taisen Deshimaru; ordained by Master Koho Shonyu in Kyushu when he was eighteen; studied with Master Shokoku Zenko; for most of his life he eschewed temple life and traveled around Japan teaching Zen, which earned him the nickname "Homeless Kodo."

Sekito Kisen (Ch., Shih-t'ou Hsi-ch'ien, 700-790), lit. "Stonehead." Disciple of Seigen Gyoshi and master of Yakusan Igen; considered the first link in the Soto Zen lineage; author of the *Sandokai*, one of the founding texts of Soto Zen. When he died in zazen at the age of ninety, his body became mummified, and can still be seen in Japan's Sojiji Temple. A poem says, "West of the river lived Baso; south of the lake, Sekito. Men went from one to the other; whoever did not meet them lived in ignorance."

Sensei. Common Japanese term used by students to address their teachers; in Zen and the martial arts, connotes the respect and love which characterize the disciple's relationship with the master.

Seppo Gison (Ch., Hsueh-feng I-ts'un, 822-908). Ch'an master, disciple of Tokusan Senkan and master of Gensha Shibi and Unmon Bunen; entered his first monastery at the age of twelve, and lived in many during his lifetime, often assuming the role of tenzo. When he was fifty he founded his own temple on Mount Seppo, where more than fifteen-hundred monks lived.

Sesshin, lit. "to touch the mind." Period (usually between two and ten days) when the sangha comes together for intense practice focusing on zazen and *samu*.

Shankara (Skt., Shankaracharya, 788-820). Indian saint, poet and philosopher; reformist Hindu renowned for his knowledge and wisdom; founded many monasteries during his brief life.

Sheng-Yen (b. 1931). Contemporary Chinese Zen master, who received transmission in both the Soto and Rinzai lineages from masters Dong Chu and Ling Yuan, respectively; teaches in Taiwan and New York, where he is abbot of Dharma Drum Mountain Monastery and founder of the Ch'an Meditation Center.

Shiguseiganmon. The four vows of the bodhisattva:
However innumerable sentient beings, I vow to save them all.
However inexhaustible the passions, I vow to extinguish them all.
However immeasurable the dharmas, I vow to master them all.
However incomparable the Buddha's truth, I vow to attain it.

Shiho. Transmission conferred by the master to the disciple, who is then authenticated as one of the successors of Buddha in that lineage.

Shikantaza, lit. "just sitting." The seated posture that encompasses the whole universe; does not use techniques such as breath-counting or koans.

Shiki. Phenomena; form; opposite of *ku* (emptiness), the source of *shiki.*

Shin School (Jodo-shin-shu, lit. "Authentic School of the Pure Land"). Founded by Shonin Shinran (1173-1262), for whom salvation came, not from personal effort (*jiriki*) but from "the strength of the other" (*tariki*). Shinran, who was married, was opposed to all forms of monastic life. The Shin sect, which experienced a great expansion in the thirteenth century, is still very popular in Japan. Taisen Deshimaru and Kodo Sawaki appreciated its characteristic gentleness and fervor.

Shinjindatsuraku, lit. "throwing down body and mind." Phrase pronounced by Master Nyojo during zazen and frequently repeated by Master Dogen. It perfectly describes what zazen practice is.

Shobogenzo, lit. "The Treasury of the Eye of the True Law." Master Dogen's main work, compiled in part by his disciple Ejo; the first great Buddhist text in Japanese; a dense work of inexhaustible wealth, which recounts and develops all the teachings received in China by the founder of Japanese Soto Zen. Not content to "follow the traces of ancient masters," Dogen improvises on traditional subjects with great freedom and impressive virtuosity.

Shodoka (Ch., Cheng-tao-ko), lit. "Song of Awakening." Second most important poem in Ch'an, after the *Shinjinmei*; collection of sixty-eight verses written by Master Yoka Daishi which contain the basic tenets of Ch'an.

Shomon. See *samsara.*

Shukke, lit. "one who has left home." A Zen monk or nun who is no longer a prisoner of duality and leaves behind their attachment to family, ownership and social position.

Shusso. Master's assistant during zazen or during sesshin; responsible for the proper atmosphere and order in the dojo.

Skandha. The five aggregates that form the personality: physicality, perception, awareness, concept (or action) and knowledge. Doomed to impermanence, decrepitude and death, the *skandha* are causally conditioned elements which make up the personality and are a source of suffering as long as we are not aware of their emptiness (*ku*).

Sosan (Ch., Seng-Ts'an, d. 606). Disciple of Eka and master of Doshin; third Zen patriarch; author of the *Shinjinmei*, the first Zen text.

Sotoba (Ch., Su Tung-p'o, 1036-1101). Chinese poet, essayist, painter, calligrapher, and ordained bodhisattva.

Soto School. Zen school founded in ninth-century China by Master Tozan Ryokai (Ch., Tung-shan Liang-chieh) and his student Sozan Honjaku (Ch., Ts'ao-shan Pen-chi); also called "Silent-Enlightenment Zen" as opposed to "Contemplating-Words Zen" (Rinzai); stresses *shikantaza* rather than the koan practice essential to Rinzai. Soto was introduced to Japan by Dogen in 1227 upon his return from China. Three generations later, the school developed two branches, headquartered at

Eiheiji and Sojiji, and today the superiors of these two temples take turns leading the school. Master Deshimaru and his successors are part of the Soto lineage.

Sutra. Sermon given by Buddha, reconstructed from memory by his disciple Ananda, according to tradition, during the first Buddhist Council which met in 480 BCE, just after Shakyamuni's death. The sutras usually begin with the words, "Thus have I heard." While the Hinayana sutras (*tripitaka*) came to us in their Pali or Sanskrit versions, the Mahayana sutras are mostly known to us in their Tibetan or Chinese translations.

Suzuki, D.T. (1870-1966). Buddhist scholar, translator and propagator of Zen in the West; adept of the koan method; studied Zen with Shaku Soen and his descendant, Sokatsu Shaku, who asked him to translate Zen texts into English for the scholarly readership.

Swami Prabhavanda (1893-1976). Contemporary Hindu monk; member of the Ramakrishna Order of India; author of numerous works on the spiritual traditions of India; founder of the Vedanta Society of Southern California.

Tanden. See *hara*.

Tanka Tennen (Ch., Tan-hsia T'ien-jan, 739-824). Disciple of Sekito Kisen, then of Baso; friend of layman P'ang. At the age of eighty, after a life marked by anti-conformist behavior, he founded a monastery on Mount Tanka, where he had a following of three hundred monks.

Tenno Dogo (Ch., T'ien-huang Tao-wu, 738-807). Ch'an master, disciple of Sekito Kisen and master of Ryutan Soshin.

Tenzo, lit. "kitchen master." Cook in a temple or monastery; a very important person in Zen; hero of many stories and anecdotes. Great masters such as Isan, Tozan and Seppo served as *tenzo*. The *tenzo's* role was the subject of a text by Master Dogen entitled *Tenzo Kyokun* ("Instructions for the Tenzo").

Tokujo (Sensu) (eighth-ninth centuries). Disciple of Yakusan Igen and master of Kassan Zen'e.

Tokusan Senkan (Ch., Te-shan Hsuan-chien, 781-867). Disciple of Ryutan Soshin and master of Seppo Gison; scholar renowned for his knowledge of the *Diamond Sutra* who burned all his books to follow the Way and dedicate himself to the practice of zazen; famous for his educational method christened *bokatsu* (from *bo*, "stick," and *katsu*, "shout").

Tozan Ryokai (Ch., Tung-shan Liang-chieh, 807-869). Disciple of Ungan Donjo and master of Ungo Doyo, among others; founder, with Sozan Honjaku, of the Soto School; author of the *Hokyozanmai*, one of the founding Zen texts, still recited in Japanese monasteries.

Ungan Donjo (Ch., Yun-yen T'an-sheng, 781-841). Disciple of Yakusan Igen and master of Tozan Ryokai. After the death of his first teacher, Hyakujo Ekai, Ungan studied with Yakusan and eventually became his successor. He then went to live on Mount Ungan, "Cloud Cliff."

Ungo Dyo (Ch., Yun-chu Tao-ying, d. 902). Disciple of Tozan Ryokai, he continued the Soto lineage founded by his master.

Vasubandhu (fourth--fifth centuries). Twenty-first patriarch of the Indian Zen lineage; scholar and author of commentaries on Mahayana texts such as the *Diamond Sutra* and *Lotus Sutra.*

Wanshi Shogaku (Ch., Hung-chih Cheng-chueh, 1091-1157). Disciple of Tanka Shijun; reputed Chinese Soto master greatly admired by Dogen; known for his pointed debates with Rinzai master Daie Soko (Ch., Ta-hui Tsung-kao) on the advantages of Soto's "*mokusho* Zen" ("silent sitting Zen"), as compared to Rinzai's "*kanna* Zen" ("spoken Zen," or "koan Zen"); author of the first *Zazenshin*, which would later be adapted by Dogen.

Yoka Daishi (or Genkaku, Ch., Yung-chia Hsuan-chueh, 665-713). Disciple of Eno, the sixth patriarch; nicknamed "One-Night Satori" in reference to his brief encounter with Eno, after which the latter confirmed his awakening; author of the *Shodoka*, one of the four oldest Zen texts.

Zafu. Round cushion filled with kapok used for sitting zazen; modeled on the grass cushion on which Shakyamuni had his satori.

Zazen. Zen meditation practice; sitting with legs crossed and back straight on a zafu, facing the wall in the Soto tradition and facing the center of the dojo in the Rinzai tradition. Breathing is slow and deep, the mind observes thoughts without following or rejecting them. See also *hishiryo*, *mushotoku*, *shikantaza* and *shin jin datsu raku.*

Zazenshin, lit. "Needle of Zazen." Poem on the meaning of zazen, the essence of the Dharma, written by Wanshi Shogaku in the twelfth century and later commented on and reworked by Master Dogen in the *Shobogenzo.*

Zeisler, Etienne Mokushu (French 1943-1990). One of Deshimaru's closest disciples as well as his personal translator and interpreter. After Deshimaru's death, Etienne became head of the Paris dojo and ran the entire sangha until his own untimely death, eight years later.

INDEX

T

Z

INDEX OF ZEN STORIES

ABOUT THE AUTHOR

Rei Ryu Philippe Coupey, born and raised in New York City, is a Soto Zen teacher in the lineage of Kodo Sawaki. He met his Master, Deshimaru, in 1972 and followed him as a close disciple until the master's death. Today, after fifty years of Zen practice, Coupey directs a large community of practitioners in Europe. The practice is *shikantaza*: simply sitting, without goal or profit-seeking mind. Coupey is the primary author of several books, and others done in collaboration with Deshimaru. He also publishes Zen-fiction writing under the pseudonym of MC Dalley. He is a member and officer of the International Zen Association (AZI).

ABOUT HOHM PRESS

Hohm Press (along with our affiliate Kalindi Press) is committed to publishing books that provide readers with alternatives to the materialistic values of the current culture, and promote self-awareness, the recognition of interdependence, and compassion. Our subject areas include parenting, transpersonal psychology, religious studies, women's studies, the arts and poetry.

Contact Information: Hohm Press, PO Box 4410, Chino Valley, AZ, 86323, USA; 800-381-2700, or 928-636-3331; email: publisher@hohmpress.com

Visit our websites:

www.hohmpress.com www.kalindipress.com